CISCO® PACKETIZED VOICE AND DATA INTEGRATION

McGRAW-HILL TECHNICAL EXPERT SERIES

To order or receive additional information on these or any other McGraw-Hill titles, in the United States please call 1-800-722-4726, or visit us at www.computing.mcgraw-hill.com. In other countries, contact your McGraw-Hill representative.

Cisco® Packetized Voice and Data Integration

Robert Caputo

CCIE™ #13312

McGraw-Hill

New York San Francisco Washington, D.C.
Auckland Bogotá Caracas Lisbon London
Madrid Mexico City Milan Montreal New Delhi
San Juan Singapore Sydney Tokyo Toronto

McGraw-Hill

A Division of The McGraw·Hill Companies

1 2 3 4 5 6 7 8 9 0   AGM/AGM   9 0 4 3 2 1 0 9

0-07-134777-1

*The sponsoring editor for this book was Steven Elliot, the managing editor was
Jennifer Perillo, the editing supervisor was Ruth W. Mannino, and the production supervisor was Claire Stanley. It was set in New Century Schoolbook by
Victoria Khavkina of McGraw-Hill's desktop composition unit in cooperation
with Spring Point Publishing Services.*

Printed and bound by Quebecor/Martinsburg.

This book is dedicated to my loving wife, Karma.

Contents at a Glance

CONTENTS

Contents

Contents

LIST OF FIGURES

FOREWORD

What's new about voice these days? Well, just about everything—from advanced applications integrating call centers with the World Wide Web, to the arrival of new products, carriers, and network service providers—all of which promise to change the way we live, work, learn, and play. At the core of these next-generation networks—where data, voice, and video converge—are the latest Cisco Systems routing and switching technologies—sending multimedia streams over IP, ATM, and Frame Relay.

The advent of voice over packet technology challenges the telecommunications industry in ways not seen since human voices first replaced electrical dots and dashes on the telegraph wires. The technical challenges are significant. Congestion, delay, packet loss, bandwidth scarcity, and echo are only a few of the obstructions users face in obtaining the quality and reliability they're accustomed to in traditional telephone networks.

Planning is key to success, and this book discusses pertinent issues when planning a packetized voice network. Network-wide quality of service (QoS), telephony device integration, IP and dial numbering schemes, PSTN integration, capacity planning, scalability, and fault tolerance are all represented. Case studies bring concrete examples of these concepts. Knowledge gained from the author's years of design and troubleshooting of complex internetworks helps planners resolve difficulties in areas such as voice encoding and compression algorithms, voice activity detection, echo cancellation, latency, jitter, and packetization.

Cisco's networking innovations, extended to support voice/data integration—including physical layer telephony connections, telephony, and IP network signaling plus the mapping of multiple logical addressing schemes to physical endpoints—are reviewed. Specific Cisco products, and their capabilities, are identified. Samples of voice networking scenarios are presented and their implementation details provided and analyzed. Plus there are tips for integrating packetized voice into existing data network environments.

This book will bring success for network managers and engineers tasked with bringing the packetized voice network from plans to operation. Readers will realize the benefits of these new technologies without having to get their hands dirty or break a sweat—REALTECH has already done all that. Here you have a quiver of proven solutions. Read the book, draw your bow, and hit the bull's-eye of market-driven voice over packet solutions—the first time.

—Raymond M. La Chance
President & CEO
REALTECH Systems Corporation

ACKNOWLEDGMENTS

This book would not be possible without the tremendous support and assistance I received from McGraw-Hill's Editorial and Production staff: Steven Elliot, the executive editor first brought me this opportunity and is largely responsible for this book; Jennifer Perillo, the managing editor, took on the difficult job of making sure I turned in my final submissions; Franchesca Maddalena ably assisted Steve and me throughout the process; and Ruth Mannino, the editing supervisor, championed the copy editing, composition, and proofreading of the book.

Special thanks go to the entire staff of REALTECH Systems. These individuals continue to demonstrate the technical excellence and professionalism that has built this company and further set the stage for more explosive growth and leadership in the telecommunications industry.

I would also like to thank several co-workers and friends for their contributions and support of this project: Ken Yanneck and Ray LaChance, the co-founders of REALTECH, whose sustained interest and support of my work enabled me to write this book; Stephen Conway, an intern who worked with me to edit and review the final text and diagrams; Cuong Vu, a CCIE who provided unfailing technical support; Steve Ziganto, a CCIE who shared his hands-on case study work; John Grady, an experienced technical writer who offered publishing and editing advice; Frank Sicilia, a client who facilitated field experience and testing; Kevin Foo Siam who assisted me; Damon Yuhasz, a CCIE who was always available for help; Mark Abolafia, who first brought the idea of this book to me and then supplied managerial support; Jacqueline Kim, whose technical expertise and generous help was invaluable; and Selcuk Benter, who provided me with logistical as well as technical assistance.

My thanks also go to Chuck Scheifele and Walter Jabs at Cisco Systems, who opened doors to a world of knowledge and experience at Cisco, while also giving me their own technical support.

—Rob Caputo

CISCO® PACKETIZED VOICE AND DATA INTEGRATION

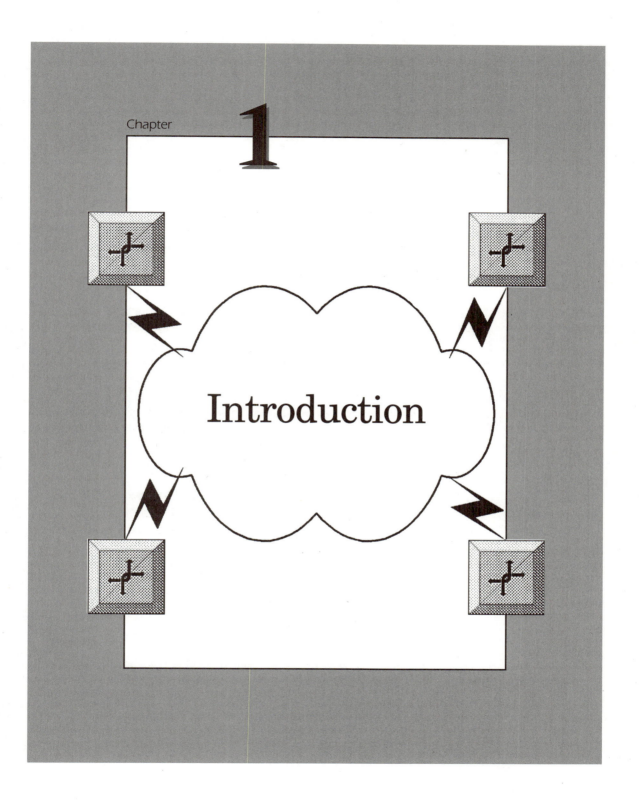

Chapter

1

Introduction

This chapter will cover the following:

- Topics covered
- Who should read this book?
- Level of detail

The convergence of voice and data to a common transmission facility is at the forefront of development and marketing at all leading data networking and telecommunications equipment providers, as well as carriers and value-added service providers. Support for this trend is demonstrated by the recent wave of partnerships and mergers among leading data and telecommunications corporations, such as Cisco/Stratacom, Nortel/Bay Networks, Lucent/Ascend, along with carrier announcements such as Sprint's ION, MCI WorldCom's OnNet, and AT&T's INC and new carriers such as Level 3 Communications and Quest. Cisco's early investments in this arena are beginning to pay off as its voice-enabled product line grows and matures. This book is intended to help network managers and engineers to understand and integrate this technology into their Cisco-based infrastructures.

The excitement over packet-based voice implementations is fueled by several factors, including new voice processing technology, the promise of computer telephony integration, reduced operating costs, increased network bandwidth, the ubiquity of the Internet and IP capable networks, and, of course, marketing hype.

Cisco was quick to forecast this trend and began acquiring technology and expertise early on with acquisitions such as Stratacom, Ardent, and many others. True to its tradition of technological agnosticism, Cisco made investments in voice technology for ATM, Frame Relay, and IP networks. Even today, Cisco continues to invest in each technology and is making tremendous strides toward enabling interoperability among the technologies and platforms that support them. Examples are the limited interoperability between the MC 3810 series products and the 2600/3600 series using the Frame Relay Forum's FRF.11 and FRF.12 standards, as well as planned integrated voice over X capabilities for the MGX 8850 and Cisco 7200 series routers.

In particular, Cisco's 2600, 3600, and AS5300 series routers and access servers have enjoyed tremendous success within the voice over IP (VoIP) marketplace. These products give Cisco market leadership in both the number of ports shipped and in total revenue. The voice enabled router market segment is also the largest and most lucrative segment of the market to date. The modularity of the 2600 and 3600 series provides customers flexibility in terms of network and voice interfaces, as well as a build-as-you-grow paradigm which fits many customers' budgetary constraints.

The full-functioning router capability and wide variety of interfaces make the Cisco 2600 and 3600 routers ideal for remote and branch offices where they can serve as the office's LAN router, WAN access, and voice trunking device. By integrating voice capabilities with the existing voice-enabled Internetwork Operating System (IOS) services into a single chassis, these effectively replicate the functionality once provided by T1 multiplexors at small sites. This is an initial step toward replacing TDM with packet-based technology.

The Cisco AS5300, when equipped with the voice/fax feature card, becomes a highly competent voice-packet gateway. It offers digital voice interfaces for PBX systems interconnections and integration with the PSTN using digital PRI or channelized T1 interfaces. Distributed processing of voice calls using specialized Digital Signal Processors (DSPs) enables a single AS5300 to support up to 96 concurrent calls in a T1 configuration. This makes the AS5300 ideal for enterprise environments supporting digital PBX interfaces and requiring integration with other Cisco voice-enabled products.

As always, the foundation of Cisco's offering lies in the intelligence embedded in the IOS. The efficiency of the IOS enables rapid packet processing and data transfer within the system, thus reducing latency and ensuring high voice quality. Quality of service (QoS) enhancements within Cisco's IOS prioritize voice traffic and ensure that it receives sufficient bandwidth and low network latency and jitter throughout the network. Cisco's extensive QoS features provide a level of end-to-end QoS, regardless of the underlying transport, that is unmatched in the industry today. Cisco's voice products leverage the IOS's flexibility, adaptability, installed base, and breadth of features to provide a solid platform for achieving superior voice connectivity and integration.

TOPICS COVERED

The book begins by presenting the prevailing motivators behind voice over IP deployment within enterprise networks. The discussion highlights some of the key benefits to the technology and lists some of the applications being deployed.

This is followed by an overview of voice technology and then packet-based QoS techniques. The book then focuses on Cisco's voice networking concepts and configuration methods. Finally, these concepts and techniques are integrated to provide comprehensive voice networking configurations for common implementations. Case studies are included to reinforce the concepts presented.

Telephony Basics

Basic telephony concepts are presented to help gain a better understanding of voice traffic's characteristics and the background for existing voice networks and products. This begins with a discussion on the components of an analog telephone and the roles each performs, followed by how phones are connected, or networked, including topics such as call setup, signaling, pulse and tone dialing, and phone switching components.

After analog telephony, the case for digital telephony is made and the associated concepts are introduced. The digital telephony section begins with a discussion on how voice signals, which are inherently analog, can be digitally encoded. The next step is to discuss the transmission facilities for digital voice and its requisite signaling techniques.

Once these basics are introduced, the concepts associated with the transmission of voice over packet networks are discussed. The key topics in this area are voice encoding and compression algorithms, voice activity detection, echo cancellation, latency, jitter, and packetization. These topics lay the groundwork for understanding packetized voice networking implementations and challenges.

Quality of Service

One of the major issues in data networking today is quality of service. QoS is an especially important topic for packetized voice networking, which demands priority service from the network and is intolerant of the transient delays and variable throughput rates experienced on most packet networks. Given frame relay's popularity in enterprise networks, an entire chapter is dedicated to the discussion of frame-relay-specific QoS issues. Specific QoS topics include traffic classification, queuing, scheduling techniques, signaling techniques, traffic shaping, and rate enforcement. Included in the discussion of each topic are basic examples for implementation and notes on implementation details.

Cisco Voice Concepts

Cisco's unique approach to networking is extended to support voice/data integration. As with other networking applications, Cisco logically isolates voice networking concepts and applies them to configuration constructs in an efficient, scalable manner. A review of these concepts is included so that they can be better understood and therefore more effectively applied in the real world. These sections cover physical layer telephony connections, telephony and IP network signaling, and the mapping of multiple logical-addressing schemes to physical endpoints.

Network Planning

Planning is essential to the success of any network implementation. The book introduces the topics and issues to consider when planning a packetized voice network. These issues include network-wide QoS, telephony device integration, IP- and dial-numbering schemes, PSTN integration, capacity planning, scalability, and fault tolerance.

Network Implementation

Network implementation details which help bring the packetized voice network from the planning stage to operation are presented. Samples of voice networking scenarios are presented, and their implementation details provided and analyzed. In addition to basic configuration and analysis, tips are provided for integrating packetized voice into existing data network environments.

Products

The specific Cisco products addressed within the text are the Cisco 2600, Cisco 3600, and Cisco AS5300 routers and access server. Details on their architecture and configuration subtleties are provided to help plan a smooth implementation and integration within enterprise networks. These products have been chosen because they are ideally suited for most enterprise environments.

WHO SHOULD READ THIS BOOK?

Network managers and network engineers who are looking to gain insight into Cisco's packetized voice networking products should find value in this book. Concepts are presented in a generic format that does not require extensive knowledge of Cisco's hardware and software. Configuration sections assume a fundamental understanding of Cisco's IOS and its familiar command line interface. For example, QoS and voice configuration steps are presented in detail, but basic IP addressing and system configuration are not.

LEVEL OF DETAIL

Concepts and technology are presented in sufficient detail to gain an understanding of how they work and interact with other related processes. The level of detail is similar to that of a vendor white paper. The information provided is meant to stimulate an interest in the technology through understanding its basic operation, as well as its role within voice and data networks. Detailed algorithm analysis, state models, and engineering diagrams are beyond the scope of this text.

SUMMARY

Cisco has made bold strides toward integrating voice technology into enterprise data networks. This book serves as a guide for understanding the concepts of voice networking and for implementing integrated voice and data networks utilizing Cisco's voice-enabled router products.

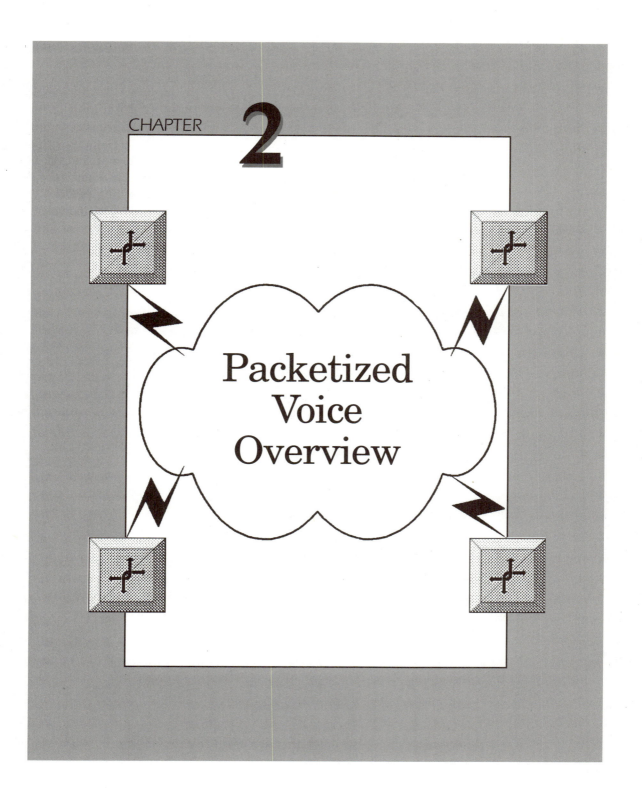

Packetized
Voice
Overview

This chapter will cover the following:

- Business drivers
- Basic transport of voice over an IP network
- Voice over IP basics
- Enabling technologies
- Management issues
- Cisco voice-enabled routers

Introduction

The economics of voice and data integration coupled with advancements in voice/packet technology have ushered in a new networking environment. This new environment promises cost savings, flexibility, and enhanced applications for improved productivity and efficiency. Recent enhancements and developments in hardware, software, and networking protocol design fuel this new converged infrastructure. These technologies have yielded a new breed of networking products and with them new management and operational challenges. This chapter discusses these issues and demonstrates their impact on the voice over IP networking environment.

Business Drivers

Voice over IP promises many benefits for enterprise, service provider, and carrier networks. The motivation to consolidate voice and data services to a single packet switched network is driven by the following advantages.

- Increased efficiency through statistical multiplexing
- Increased efficiency through enhanced features such as voice compression and voice activity detection (silence suppression)
- Long distance savings by diverting calls over the private data network
- Lower administration costs by consolidating infrastructure components
- Possibility of new applications leveraging computer telephony integration

- Voice connectivity over data applications
- Efficient use of new broadband WAN technologies

The increased efficiency of packet networks and the ability to statistically multiplex voice traffic with data packets allows corporations to maximize their return on data network infrastructure investments. Offloading voice traffic to the data network then allows for a reduction in the number of costly dedicated circuits servicing voice applications.

Implementation of newer technologies such as Gigabit Ethernet, Dense Wave Division Multiplexing (DWDM), and Packet over Synchronous Optical Network (SONET) within LAN, MAN, and WAN environments provides increased bandwidth for data networks at lower price points. Once again, these technologies offer significantly better price/performance when compared with standard TDM connectivity.

New applications and services such as "click to talk" and desktop video conferencing improve productivity and offer new opportunities for service differentiation. Real-time fax over IP and Internet faxing applications also reduce long distance toll charges for geographically dispersed organizations.

Basic Transport of Voice over an IP Network

To transport voice signals over an IP network, several elements and functions are required. In its simplest form, the network would consist of two or more voice over IP capable devices linked by an IP network. Looking at the simple network in Figure 2-1, we can tell that somehow the VoIP devices convert voice signals into IP data streams and forward them to IP destinations which, in turn, convert them back to voice signals. The network in-between must support IP traffic and can be any combination of IP routers and network links.

Voice-to-Data Conversion

Voice signals are inherently analog waveforms. To transmit them over a digital data network, they must first be converted to some type of digital format. This is done using various voice-encoding schemes. The source and destination voice encoders and decoders must implement the same

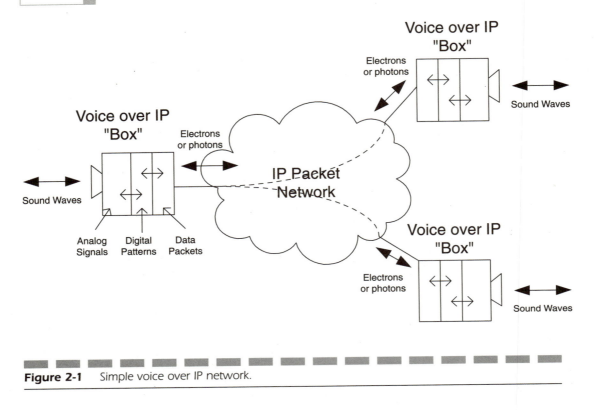

Figure 2-1   Simple voice over IP network.

scheme so that the destination device can successfully reproduce the analog signal that the source device encoded in a digital format.

Raw Data to IP Conversion

Once a voice signal is digitally encoded it becomes just another form of data for the network to transport. Voice networks simply setup physical connections between communicating end points (a circuit) and transmit the encoded signals between endpoints. IP networks don't form connections in the same way that circuit switched networks do. IP networks require that data be placed in variable length datagrams or packets. Addressing and control information is then attached to each datagram and is sent through the network and forwarded, hop-by-hop toward its destination. To support the transport of digital voice data over this type of network, the voice over IP device must take the voice data, encapsulate them into IP datagrams (packets), attach addressing information, and forward them into the network.

Transport

Intermediate nodes within the network inspect the addressing information attached to each of the IP datagrams and use that information to forward the datagram to the next hop along the path to its destination. The network links can be any topology or access method that supports IP traffic.

IP-to-Data Conversion

The destination voice over IP device receives the IP datagram and processes it. In processing the datagram, the addressing and control information is removed so that the original raw data remain. The raw data are then presented to the voice decoding process.

Conversion from Data Back to Voice

The voice decoding process interprets the raw data generated by the source station and runs them through the decoding function. The output from the decoding function is an analog signal resembling the original voice signal received by the source station line feed.

In summary, the transport of voice traffic over an IP network requires a conversion of the signal from analog to digital, packetization of the digital voice data, transport of the packetized information through the network, de-packetization of the voice data, and conversion of the digital voice data back to an analog signal. This process is depicted in Figure 2-2.

Voice over IP Basics

The previous example only dealt with the base functionality required to transport a voice signal across a simple data network. It lacked several

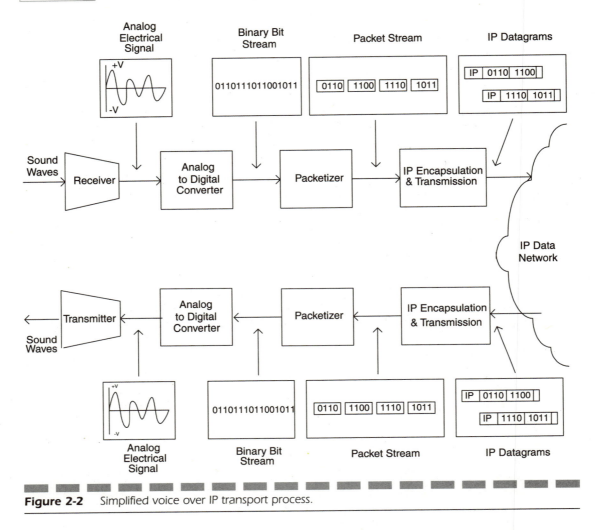

Figure 2-2 Simplified voice over IP transport process.

functions that are required to build a simple voice over IP network. The most basic are voice compression, phone number mapping, call-leg identification (peer establishment), and a protocol for the transport of voice data.

Voice Compression

In order to offset the overhead introduced by converting an analog signal to digital and transporting it over a packet switched network, compression algorithms can be used to reduce the amount of voice data that is transmitted over the packet switched network. Voice compression algorithms operate on the digital signal created by the initial analog to digital conversion and reduce the amount of bandwidth consumed by the voice signal by a factor of up to 8:1 or more. This reduction helps compensate for the addressing information applied (IP, UDP, and RTP headers) to the individual packets and allows for more voice calls to transit links with limited bandwidth.

Phone Number Mapping

The simple VoIP example above assumed that each voice over IP device would only transmit and receive calls from a single node. In more realistic environments, VoIP devices are required to dynamically form connections with multiple devices. In the voice world, destinations are selected using a dial string or phone number. In the IP world, destinations are selected using IP addresses. To allow a VoIP router to communicate with an array of other VoIP routers, a method of mapping the phone numbers dialed by the telephone user to the IP addresses used by the routers is required. This mapping can be performed statically within each router, or dynamically using Domain Naming System (DNS). The planning of connections and their associated phone numbers is called a *dial plan.*

Call Leg Identification

In order to properly identify, process, and forward voice calls, the router divides calls into discrete segments, referred to as call legs. Once identified, the router can apply services specific to each call leg, including terminating sessions.

Session Protocol

The Real Time Protocol (RTP) is a standardized way to transport voice and video traffic over IP networks. RTP adapts connectionless IP traffic to support real-time traffic through providing timing, sequencing, and other control functions. RTP is defined by an Internet Engineering Task Force (IETF) standard to ensure interoperability in multivendor environments.

Enabling Technologies

Widespread deployment of voice over IP is fast becoming a reality due to many innovations in hardware, software, protocols, and standards. Advancement in each of these areas contributes to the creation of a more efficient, capable, and interoperable voice over packet network. The primary innovations are briefly listed in Table 2-1.

Hardware Advances

Hardware advances in the areas mentioned in Table 2-1 are providing both the additional computational power and the additional bandwidth, thus helping to make VoIP a reality.

Digital Signal Processors

Advanced *digital signal processors,* or DSPs, perform computationally intensive tasks required for voice and data integration. As their name professes, DSPs process digital signals and then perform complex functions which might otherwise have to be performed by a general purpose

TABLE 2-1

Key Advancements Enabling VoIP Deployment

Protocols and Standards	Software	Hardware
H.323	Weighted fair queuing	DSPs
MPLS, Tag switching	Weighted random early detection	Advanced ASICs
RTP, RTCP	Dual leaky bucket—generic cell rate algorithm	DWDM
RSVP	Committed access rate	SONET
Diffserv, CAR	Cisco express forwarding	CPU processing power
G.729, G.729a: CS-ACELP	Extended access lists	ADSL, RADSL, SDSL
FRF.11 / FRF.12	Token-bucket algorithms	
Multilink PPP	Frame-relay traffic shaping	
SIP	Precedence-based CoS	
Packet over SONET	IP and ATM QoS/CoS integration	

CPU. Their specialized processing capabilities combined with their low cost make DSPs well suited to carry out signal processing functions in VoIP systems. The computational overhead for G.729 voice compression on a single voice stream is tremendous, requiring up to 20 MIPS. This makes it unreasonable for a single processor system to effectively process multiple voice streams and still perform routing and system management functions. The use of multiple DSPs offloads this function from the central CPU and allows the system to process additional calls based upon DSP availability. DSPs are also well suited for functions such as voice-activity detection and echo cancellation because they process voice traffic in real time and have quick access to onboard memory.

Advanced Application-Specific Integrated Circuits

Application-specific integrated circuit (ASIC) development has yielded faster, more complex, and therefore more capable ASICs. As their name suggests, ASICs are chips that perform a single application, or small set of functionally similar applications. Given their narrow focus, they are highly optimized for their specific functions and generally perform their tasks one or more orders of magnitude faster than a general purpose processor would. Just as reduced instruction set computer (RISC) chips focus on performing a limited number of operations quickly, ASICs are preprogrammed to perform an even more limited number of functions even more quickly. Once developed, ASICs are inexpensive to produce and are used in networking devices including routers and switches to perform such processes as route lookups, packet forwarding, packet classification and inspection, and queuing functions (WFQ, WRR, FIFO, etc.). Their use in these devices results in higher performance and lower cost. They benefit the emerging VoIP market in that they provide increased bandwidth and better QoS support within networks. Examples of ASICs are the silicon queuing engine within the 12000 GSR or the switching elements within a Catalyst 5500 (SAINT, EARL2, etc.).

Dense Wave Division Multiplexing

Dense wave division multiplexing, or DWDM, is breathing new life into older fiber networks and providing astronomical bandwidth in the fiber backbones deployed by newer carriers. DWDM technology leverages the capabilities of fiber optics and advanced optical transmission equipment. Wave division multiplexing derives its name from the fact that it transmits multiple wavelengths of light (LASERs) over a single strand of fiber. Current systems are capable of transmitting and discerning 16 different wavelengths, while future systems promise to support anywhere from 40 to 96 different wavelengths. This is significant because for every wavelength added, another information stream is provided. The result is that an OC-48 (2.4-Gbps) network can be upgraded to support 16 times that without having to lay new fiber in the ground. Most newer fiber-optic networks are provisioned to run at OC-192 speeds (9.6 Gbps), which, when combined with DWDM, results in a capacity of over 150 Gbps on a single pair of fiber-optic strands. The immense bandwidth provided by DWDM is providing ISPs and carriers higher powered backbones and making bandwidth cheaper and more accessible. This helps support the increased bandwidth demands of VoIP solutions and actually reduces QoS demands on the network since bandwidth is more plentiful. The increased transmission rates not only provide fatter pipes with less opportunity for congestion, but also introduce significantly less latency.

Synchronous Optical Network

Synchronous Optical Network (SONET) has been the backbone for carrier fiber optic networks for some time now. SONET continues to be deployed in both long distance and local markets due to its proven track record and excellent reliability with near lossless failover characteristics. Products from Cisco Systems and other vendors leverage SONET's flexibility and reliability through increased integration with SONET and internetworking equipment. Advances in SONET technology have yielded higher transmission rates and have lowered costs for bandwidth. Widespread deployment within local markets is also helping to provide a cost-effective platform for VoIP networks to run over.

Digital Subscriber Line

The various flavors of digital subscriber line technology (xDSL) are helping to solve the local loop bandwidth problem which plagues Metropolitan and Wide Area Networks today. Symmetric DSL provides the ability to transmit and receive at up to T1 speeds over common POTS twisted-pair wiring. Asymmetric DSL (ADSL) and Rate Adaptive DSL (RADSL) offer asymmetric transmission rates where the user-side download speeds may be as great as 8 Mbps and the user-side upload speeds may be up to 1 Mbps. These and the other DSL variants are helping to provide the necessary bandwidth to business and residential users and to significantly reduce costs. With lower cost DSL local loops, companies now access the Internet and service provider-based VPNs at significantly increased speeds enabling higher call volumes for VoIP calls.

Central Processing Unit Technology

Central processing units (CPUs) have continued to increase in functionality, power, and speed. This has enabled widespread deployment of multimedia PCs and improved the performance of system functions bound by CPU power. The PC's ability to process streaming audio and video has created an expectation within the user community that making voice calls over the data network is a logical next step. This computing power enables both advanced multimedia desktop applications and advanced functionality in the network elements supporting voice applications.

Software

Compressed Real-Time Protocol

Compressed Real-Time Protocol, or CRTP, is a mechanism that operates on the RTP headers used to encapsulate digitized voice segments. CRTP draws heavily from Van Jacobson's TCP header compression algorithm and manages to reduce the standard IP/UDP/RTP header from 40 bytes to a mere 2–5 bytes. This is significant, as it reduces both bandwidth consumption and the time required for a voice packet to traverse a low-speed network link. The efficiencies gained by CRTP help offset some of the overhead associated with packetized voice traffic. Tables 2-2 through 2-5 demonstrate both packetization overhead and the efficiency gains achieved using CRTP as well as some of the efficiency losses incurred by packetizing voice traffic. A 6-byte data-link header is assumed as this size

TABLE 2-2

Bandwidth Requirements for Packetized Voice

Voice Compression Algorithm	Algorithm Bandwidth Requirements, kbps*	Packetized Bandwidth Requirements before CRTP, kbps	Packetized Bandwidth Requirements after CRTP, kbps
G.711 PCM	64	80	68
G.726 ADPCM	32	48	35
G.729 CS-ACELP	8	24	11

*Per channel.

TABLE 2-3

Packetization
Overhead and
Bandwidth
Consumption with-
out CRTP

Voice Compression Algorithm	Payload Size, bytes*	Packet Size w/o CRTP, bytes†	Packetization Overhead, %	Total Bandwidth Requirements, kbps
G.723.1 MP-MLQ	30	76	153	20.3
G.729 CS-ACELP	20	66	230	26.4
G.726 ADPCM	80	126	57.5	50.4
G.711 PCM	160	206	28.8	82.4

*Per packet.
†Including G-byte data-link header.

TABLE 2-4

Packetization
Overhead and
Bandwidth
Consumption with
CRTP

Voice Compression Algorithm	Payload Size, bytes*	Packet Size with CRTP, bytes†	Packetization overhead, %	Total Bandwidth Requirements, kbps
G.723.1 MP-MLQ	30	38	27	10.1
G.729 CS-ACELP	20	28	40	11.2
G.726 ADPCM	80	88	10	35.2
G.711 PCM	160	168	5	67.2

*Per packet.
†Excluding data-link header.

TABLE 2-5

CRTP Efficiency
Gains

Voice Compression Algorithm	CRTP Efficiency Gain, %
G.723.1 MP-MLQ	101
G.729 CS-ACELP	135
G.726 ADPCM	43
G.711 PCM	23

is consistent with frame relay, PPP, and HDLC header sizes. Low-bit-rate encoders, such as MP-MLQ and CS-ACELP, benefit the most from CRTP because of their smaller payload relative to the IP/UDP/RTP header size. Their gains are significant when considering the transmission of multiple voice calls over low-speed links. Without CRTP, only two MP-MLQ or CS-ACELP calls could be supported on a 56-kbps link; with CRTP, four calls could be supported over the same link. Further, lower end-to-end delays will be incurred for each call since the serialization delay for each packet will be 100 to 135 percent lower.

Weighted Fair Queuing

Weighted fair queuing, or WFQ, was first introduced in IOS v11.0 and has since become the default queuing mechanism for WAN interfaces running at less than 2 Mbps. WFQ classifies traffic streams, queues them individually, and ensures fair access to the exit interface by intelligently scheduling queue transmissions using a weighted algorithm. Traffic is classified by network and transport-layer information as well as traffic rates and frame sizes. Low-bandwidth sessions are given higher priority to prevent them from being starved by the higher bandwidth sessions. This behavior results in more consistent and predictable transmission delays for both high-bandwidth sessions such as file transfers and low-bandwidth interactive sessions such as Telnet or chat. Weighted fair queuing's greatest virtues are that it operates automatically without requiring the user to configure complex queue structures and that it seamlessly supports all protocols. WFQ is important in voice environments because it automatically prioritizes voice traffic, especially when QoS parameters are set, and provides a consistent queuing delay through the network.

Weighted Random Early Detection

Weighted random early detection, or WRED, is a lightweight congestion avoidance technique that enables higher overall link utilization and goodput. Random early detection monitors link congestion and traffic flows and randomly drops packets from individual traffic flows, allowing their upper-layer protocols to adapt to the congestion condition. This technique optimizes the transmission rates of the individual flows and prevents both congestion collapse and synchronization issues. Weighted Random Early Detection provides a means for supporting multiple priority levels, each with different discard thresholds. WRED helps voice over IP networks by providing preferential service to voice traffic while intelligently controlling nonvoice traffic and optimizing link efficiency.

Generic Cell Rate Algorithm

Generic cell rate algorithm, or GCRA, was originally known as the dual leaky-bucket algorithm. As the newer name implies, GCRA provides a means for controlling the rate at which traffic flows into the network. The dual leaky-bucket algorithm uses common traffic control parameters such as minimum cell rate and burst size along with a complicated queuing and scheduling algorithm to police and shape traffic flows through the network. GCRA is directly applicable to ATM traffic, but variants of the leaky-bucket algorithm are applicable to variable-length packet networks as well. GCRA can be used in voice over IP networks to guarantee minimum bandwidth levels to voice traffic and to shape nonvoice traffic and prevent it from introducing undue delay to voice traffic.

Committed Access Rate

Committed access rate, or CAR, is a value-added feature from Cisco that runs on the 7x00 class routers. CAR provides a means of controlling the bandwidth received or transmitted through an interface to a set of destinations. The set of destinations can be a discrete number of sites, specific TCP or UDP ports, or simply all traffic through the interface. CAR measures traffic flow using a token-bucket algorithm and can tag, drop, or simply forward traffic based upon decision criteria for meeting or exceeding traffic rates. CAR is helpful in engineering networks to support differentiated service levels as multiple CAR policies can be applied to a single interface to control access to network bandwidth. It is useful in voice environments to help ensure that voice traffic receives the appropriate amount of bandwidth across the backbone.

Token Bucket—Generic Traffic Shaping

Cisco's generic traffic shaping uses a token bucket algorithm to monitor and shape traffic flow through a given interface. A token bucket algorithm differs from a leaky-bucket algorithm in two important ways. First, it transmits traffic at media rate instead of a specified rate, and, second, it provides greater adaptability for bursty traffic. Generic traffic shaping allows for excess traffic to be transmitted, but does so at a lower priority. The interface's queuing mechanism then filters out noncompliant traffic. Generic traffic shaping is of value in voice over IP networks because it provides a lower cost (processing-wise) way of controlling traffic flows and allows for both voice over IP traffic to be prioritized and nonvoice over IP traffic's effects to be limited.

Frame-Relay Traffic Shaping

Cisco's implementation of frame-relay traffic shaping uses a single leaky-bucket algorithm to solve some of the QoS problems associated with frame-relay interaction. Frame-relay traffic shaping provides a means for limiting output rates on an individual PVC basis. The strict output rates enforced by the leaky-bucket algorithm prevent the router from transmitting traffic in excess of the individual committed rates for each PVC. This overcomes a common problem where "hub" sites with high-speed access lines overwhelm "spoke" sites with lower-speed access lines. Traffic shaping minimizes packet loss and helps ensure that critical traffic gets through, which is of significant importance to voice traffic.

IP Precedence

The IP precedence bits are special bits reserved within the headers of IP datagrams. The developers of the Internet Protocol envisioned that they would one day be used to prioritize traffic, but until recently, they have been ignored by most systems. Cisco uses the IP precedence bits to provide network-wide classes of service by integrating precedence bits into queuing and classification algorithms. CAR, WRED, and WFQ all utilize the IP precedence bits to help prioritize traffic. In voice environments, IP precedence bits are important as they are frequently used to ensure that voice traffic receives high priority when transiting the network.

IP to ATM Class of Service

Cisco has introduced a method for providing differentiated classes of service for IP traffic transiting an ATM network. Within the scheme, traffic is queued on a per-ATM virtual circuit basis and IP QoS mechanisms are performed on the individual queues. This feature relies on ATM's ability to guarantee cell delivery rates. IP to ATM class of service (CoS) is in its infancy, but will grow to support complex methods of forwarding IP traffic over ATM networks, including flexible selection of output VCs based upon traffic priority. Thus, in the future, the router will be able to transmit delay sensitive voice traffic over a CBR or rt-VBR circuit, while transmitting normal data traffic over an ABR circuit. This feature is of significant value to voice over IP networks with ATM backbones in that it helps to marry the QoS mechanisms from both technologies to form a more cohesive network that can provide consistent voice quality.

Protocols

Real-Time Protocol/Real-Time Control Protocol

The Real-Time Protocol (RTP) and *Real-Time Control Protocol (RTCP)* were created to transport real-time traffic, such as video and audio, over the Internet and/or Internet Protocol-based networks. RTP is a session-layer protocol that usually runs on top of UDP/IP and is defined in RFCs 1889 and 1890. UDP is the favored transport-layer protocol because its connectionless nature enables its use in broadcast and multicast environments. RTP addresses some of the elements required for real-time traffic which are missing from UDP, including sequence numbering and time stamping. Sequence numbering enables the receiver to verify that datagrams have been received in order and that intermediate datagrams were not lost. Time stamping helps ensure proper playback rates regardless of datagram arrival times. Additionally, a payload-type field helps the receiving station identify which application or process to hand off the data to. Given this functionality Cisco and most of the VoIP community have chosen to use RTP for the transport of packetized voice in IP networks.

RTCP carries out the control functions for RTP streams. RTCP performs four discrete functions:

1. Communication of information and statistics about the RTP stream to the application
2. Identification of the RTP source
3. Limiting of control traffic
4. Secondary transport for small amounts of information

This protocol is important in voice environments for its ability to identify RTP sources and for the statistical information it provides applications.

Resource Reservation Protocol

Resource Reservation Protocol, or RSVP, is a protocol developed to allow applications to dynamically request specific levels of service from the network. RSVP's application-based approach enables it to be customized based on specific application requirements. RSVP-enabled applications communicate their bandwidth and network latency requirements to receiving applications. The receivers then issue RSVP requests to the network elements along the return path to the source station for these resources. Once a network element agrees to support a request, it is expected to honor that request for the duration of the reservation. In voice over IP environments, a voice-enabled router can issue RSVP reservations for each individual voice call and rely on the intermediate network elements to dynamically allocate the appropriate resources for the call.

In addition to standard RSVP requests over packet networks, Cisco offers a means to map RSVP reservations to ATM SVCs called RSVP-ATM QoS interworking. This feature is supported by the 7500 series and enables the router to dynamically set up an ATM SVC with the appropriate QoS parameters to support the RSVP request. In hybrid packet and cell environments, RSVP-ATM QoS interworking provides enhanced QoS integration and leverages ATM's intrinsic QoS capabilities to support packet-based requests.

Diffserv/Committed Access Rate

Cisco's committed access rate (CAR) and the goals of the IETF's differentiated services (diffserv) working group are similar. The diffserv group is developing a standards-based approach to classifying IP traffic, setting bits within the IP header to identify a specific QoS, providing preferential service based on QoS levels, and supporting the QoS levels throughout the network. Cisco's committed access rate is an early implementation that provides rate control for IP traffic, interpretation and setting of IP precedence bits, and differentiated service throughout the network based upon IP precedence bits. This feature is significant in voice environments as it helps provide network-wide classes of service for IP traffic.

H.323

H.323 is an International Telecommunications Union (ITU) standard which was created in 1996 and updated in 1998. It provides a foundation for audio, video, and data communications across a packet-based network infrastructure. H.323 provides standards for voice-encoding, simple bandwidth management, admission control, address translation, call control and management, and links to external networks. The voice over IP community has adopted H.323 standards in an effort to foster the interoperability of equipment from multiple vendors. H.323 provides a solid foundation for building multimedia networks and has become critical for developing large-scale VoIP networks.

G.729/G.729a

G.729 and G.729a are standard for voice-encoding algorithms. These algorithms analyze standard PCM voice segments and use a complex algorithm to encode them. Once encoded, a lookup pointer for the audio pattern's location in a shared code dictionary is forwarded to the receiving node. Since the actual audio signal is not sent over the network (just the code), this algorithm results in significant bandwidth savings. G.729 and G.729a are particularly significant in the voice over IP arena because their low-bandwidth requirements (8 kbps) help to offset the overhead introduced by encapsulating voice traffic in data packets.

Session Initial Protocol

The *Session Initiation Protocol,* or SIP, is the IETF initiative for providing audio and/or video transport over the Internet. It is an application-layer control (signaling) protocol for creating, modifying, and terminating sessions with one or more participants. These sessions include Internet multimedia conferences, Internet telephone calls, and multimedia distribution. Members in a session can communicate via multicast tree or a mesh of unicast relations. SIP is defined by RFC 2543 and is being considered by a number of vendors and service providers.

Packet over SONET

Packet over SONET provides higher speed, more efficient transmission of IP traffic across service provider backbones. Given that most of the high-speed links deployed are point-to-point links between routers, the signaling overhead and cell tax associated with ATM is an unnecessary inefficiency. Packet over SONET maps PPP or HDLC frames directly into SONET frames avoiding the segmentation and reassembly processes associated with ATM. This improves efficiency significantly by increasing the effective throughput over an OC-3c link from approximately 135 Mbps to over 155 Mbps. Both the performance gains and ease of implementation have made Packet over SONET a popular choice for large-scale IP networks. Packet over SONET is significant in voice environments in that it provides a more efficient way to transfer IP packets across network backbones.

FRF.11/FRF.12

The Frame-Relay Forum's FRF.11 specifies an implementation of voice over frame relay, while FRF.12 specifies a method for segmentation and reassembly of frame-relay frames at the data-link (frame) level. FRF.12 is somewhat analogous to ATM's cell structure in that it provides a maximum frame size for transmission through the network to help control delay and variability in frame arrival rates. It differs from ATM in that frame size is not fixed and varies with the link speeds involved. FRF.11

support is important because it provides interoperability not only between Cisco's MC3810 and Cisco 2600/3600 products, but between these products and products from other vendors which are FRF.11 compliant. FRF.12 is significant in both voice over frame relay and voice over IP environments as it specifies a means for limiting the delay and variability introduced by variable-length frames.

Multilink PPP

A subset of the Multilink PPP specification includes *link fragmenting and interleaving,* or LFI. LFI allows a single frame to split up and simultaneously transmit over multiple links in the multilink bundle yielding improved utilization across all links and reducing transmission delays. The far-end router receives the frame segments, reassembles them, and routes the complete frame as appropriate. This function is also used to help reduce latency and prioritize voice traffic in voice over IP networks. In voice networks, LFI helps bound the transmission delay by splitting large frames into smaller segments with a well-defined transmission delay. To ensure that voice traffic is serviced appropriately, a separate queue is created for voice traffic and given priority access to the network link. Delay is bounded by injecting voice frames in-between the segments of larger frames. Multilink PPP's LFI feature can be enabled over single PPP links, as well as multilink bundles.

Management Issues

Although voice over IP networking brings many advantages, it is also introduces several management challenges for network administrators. Effective management of any service is essential to its success; however, packetized voice networks require a higher level of management because of the stability of the existing voice networks. Transient network delays and errors, which may have been acceptable for simple data traffic, are often unacceptable when the network is supporting voice traffic. Also, for any migration to be successful the new implementation must replicate the services available in the existing environment. For VoIP networks, this means that they must successfully replicate not only the high standards for availability, but also the full functionality of existing voice systems including call logging and auditing, monitoring and diagnostic techniques, and security. These issues are discussed in the following sections.

Availability and Uptime

Most voice networks today offer rock-solid availability. Very few people question whether their phone will work when they arrive at the office in the morning nor do they question whether or not a call to a given destination will go through. These services are simply expected to be present all the time. Failures within most phone systems are extremely rare, and failures with the PSTN are even more rare. These services are always expected to function.

Data network outages, however, are more commonplace. Server- and network-related issues still plague enterprise networks, and the Internet has instilled in users an acceptance of a best-effort service where individual sites and/or ISPs are expected to experience temporary outages from time to time. While users may not expect to have any problems reaching a company via the phone, they are tolerant of slow access to a web site or even a message indicating that the site is temporarily unavailable. This represents one of the larger challenges of integrating voice and data networks. Simply put, the data network must be engineered to provide consistent performance with reliability expectations similar to those of existing voice networks.

Managing network availability and uptime is crucial for VoIP deployments. Existing management tools must be modified to support a VoIP-centric view of application network availability

Configuration

Configuration management is not really a new concern for either data or voice networking environments; however, the specific requirements have changed. The actual configuration of VoIP networking equipment requires attention to details from both environments. Voice-specific concepts and implementation details must be thoroughly understood as should the advanced data networking concepts, such as IP QoS.

Configuring voice over IP routers requires data network administrators to learn basic telephony. Dial plans and physical interface specifications all become of issue when interfacing with voice networks. These configuration details require a significant understanding of not only the voice concepts, but also Cisco's implementation of these concepts. Configuration details for such things as voice ports, dial peers, and number expansions are all new concepts for data engineers.

Most packet networks today are best-effort environments where bandwidth is often applied as a cure-all for network QoS issues. Until recently, very few QoS techniques were available for IP networks. Engineers familiar with basic IP routing may not be familiar with VoIP's QoS requirements or how to configure the IP networking equipment to meet them. Queuing and signaling techniques such as WRED and RSVP are new concepts to most network administrators, and must be understood for successful deployment and maintenance of voice over IP networks. Managing these services poses a challenge for network administrators, as well as existing network management applications which do not address these issues.

Dial Plans

Managing a dial plan is another new concept for data engineers. While data engineers are familiar with concepts like IP addressing and phone numbers, the creation and maintenance of a dial plan require new skills that most data engineers do not possess. For instance, mapping out call flows and determining trunking requirements is roughly analogous to network capacity planning, but both the terms and operational impact are different and must be understood before a successful plan may be devised.

Call Detail Recording

The ability to track voice calls is essential in voice networks for auditing, billing, traffic profiling, capacity planning, and network design. Collecting this information, storing it, and subsequently accessing it is a tremendous task. Per-call statistical information must be aggregated from all voice-enabled routers on the network. This requires a robust management platform to poll the devices, a database function to store the information, and a database client application to query the database and produce useful reports. The information then needs to be formatted appropriately and archived for future reference.

Monitoring and Diagnostics

Monitoring voice activity and diagnosing problems in a voice over IP environment requires a diverse set of skills. Three categories of monitoring and diagnostic skills are required: basic telephony connectivity, IP and data network connectivity, and voice over IP specific connectivity. Management applications, tools, and procedures need to be developed and deployed to cover all of these areas.

Performance Management

As mentioned earlier, network performance is an important element in supporting voice calls over a data infrastructure. Oversubscribed circuits and congested WAN and LAN links lead to network delay and inconsistencies which will result in poor voice quality and/or missed calls. Proactive network performance monitoring must be performed in order to keep a handle on network conditions and engineers must continually design around potential trouble spots. In addition to network performance monitoring, voice call performance must also be monitored. Statistics such as call-completion rates and voice-quality parameters must be collected, stored, and regularly reviewed to ensure that the voice network is receiving proper service levels from the data network.

Cisco Voice-Enabled Routers

Cisco's voice-enabled router product line includes several access routers and servers. These products are targeted at both enterprise and service provider markets and include support for a full suite of voice services. The MC3810 supports voice over ATM and interworking with Cisco IGX 8400 series ATM switches, but not voice over IP (yet). The remaining products all support both voice over IP and voice over frame relay. Table 2-6 is a brief chart representing some of the functionality and port density differences between the products.

This book is dedicated to the Cisco 2600, Cisco 3600, and Cisco AS5300 products. The MC3810 is not covered because of its lack of voice over IP support. The AS5800 is also not covered as its scope and capacity is well beyond that of an enterprise system.

The following sections provide an overview of the Cisco 2600, Cisco 3600, and AS5300. A fourth section describes the voice/fax functionality of the network module for the Cisco 2600/3600 and a fifth section describes the voice/fax functionality of the AS5300 voice/fax card.

TABLE 2-6

Cisco
Voice-Enabled
Router Comparison

Voice Router Summary	VoIP	VoFR	VoATM	No. of Analog Interfaces	No. of Digital Interfaces
Cisco 2600	Yes	Yes	No	4	N/A
Cisco 3600	Yes	Yes	No	12	N/A
Cisco AS5300	Yes	Yes	No	N/A	(4) T1/E1
Cisco MC3810	No	Yes	Yes	6	(1) T1/E1
Cisco AS5800	Yes	Yes	No	N/A	(2) T3/E3

Cisco 2600

The Cisco 2600 is a high-performance multiprotocol router targeted at branch offices. The 2600 utilizes a RISC processor for added processing power and supports the following base configurations: 1-2 Ethernet or Fast Ethernet ports, a single token ring port, or a single Ethernet port/single token ring port. In addition to the built-in LAN ports, the 2600 provides two WAN interface slots, a single network module slot, and an advanced integration module slot. The Cisco 2600 runs Cisco's IOS and supports a full complement of IOS features and services. Voice is supported through a 1- or 2-port network module.

Cisco 3600

The Cisco 3600 comes in three sizes, a 2-slot 3620, a 4-slot 3640, and a 6-slot 3660. Each system utilizes a high-performance RISC processor and accepts a wide array of WAN and LAN interfaces from low-speed async ports through OC-3c ATM. The products target an enterprise's remote and branch offices. The 3600 series supports the full suite of IOS features and services, including QoS, and voice functionality. Voice support is achieved through the same voice network module used in the 2600 series.

Cisco AS5300

The AS5300 access server is a high-performance access device suited for POTS/ISDN dialup access and digital-voice connectivity. It features a 64-bit RISC processor and field replaceable 4- or 8-port T1/E1 cards, digital modem cards, and voice fax cards. A fully configured AS5300 can support up to four T1/E1 digital voice interfaces. Abundant processing power provides full support Cisco IOS-based QoS and scalability services. Voice support is provided via the 48/60 port T1/E1 voice/fax card.

Cisco 2600/3600 Voice/Fax Network Module

The voice/fax network module comes in a 1- and 2-slot version. Each slot accepts a 2-port analog voice interface configured as FXS, FXO, or E&M. The network module provides dedicated DSPs for low-latency voice encoding and packetization, offloading these processor intensive tasks from the router's main CPU. This provides flawless voice packetization without impairing the performance of the router. Voice activity detection conserves bandwidth by not transmitting frames during idle periods, and echo cancellation ensures compatibility in a wide array of environments. FRF.11 and FRF.12 provide connectivity to MC3810-based voice over frame-relay networks. H.323 compliant voice over IP support ensures compatibility with third-party VoIP products and Cisco gatekeepers.

Cisco AS5300 Voice/Fax Carrier Card

The AS5300's voice/fax carrier card supports up to 48 or 60 VoIP connections. A dedicated RISC processor and multiple DSPs offload processor-intensive voice packetization and compression functions from the AS5300's main CPU. The voice/fax card works in conjunction with Cisco's IOS-based QoS mechanisms to ensure high-quality voice connections end-to-end. PSTN integration, RADIUS authentication and billing, and support for interactive voice response scripts round out the functionality to provide a complete solution for enterprise packetized voice connectivity.

SUMMARY

Voice over IP represents a tremendous market opportunity and offers enterprise network administrators an opportunity to reduce costs through implementing a common network infrastructure. Packetized voice solutions are being enabled by a new generation of hardware, software, and collaborative networking protocols. The promises of packetized voice also bring the attendant challenges of network integration, QoS, and management.

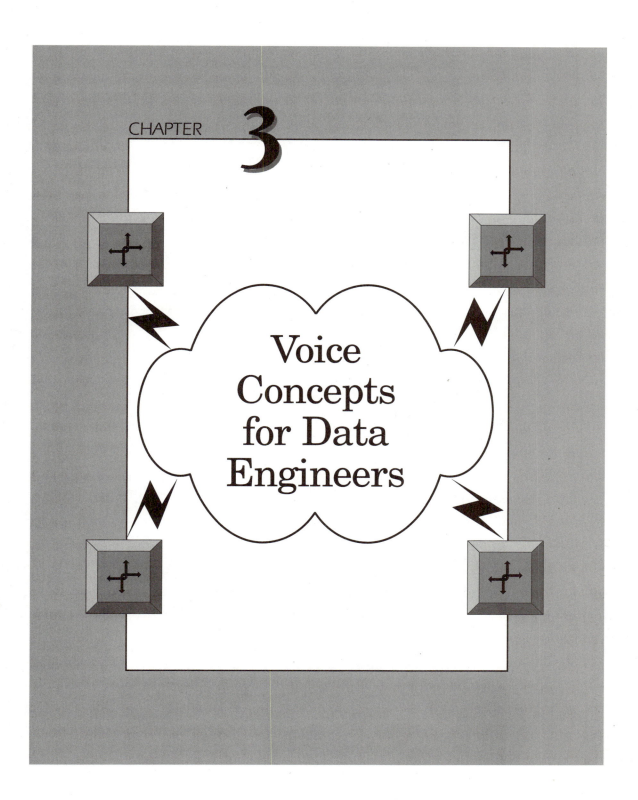

CHAPTER 3

Voice
Concepts
for Data
Engineers

This chapter will cover the following:

- Analog telephony
- Digital voice
- Voice compression
- Factors that affect voice quality

Introduction

Telephony was created more than 100 years ago. The basic analog telephone and the supporting network have slowly evolved into large PBX systems and digital networks utilizing fiber transmission facilities. This chapter discusses the basics of both analog and digital telephony to better understand how next generation VoIP networks will integrate with these systems.

Analog Telephony

Basic Telephone Technology

When talking about the basics, it makes sense to start at the beginning. The standard analog phone has been around for more than 100 years. It is the first piece of telephony most people come into contact with, and is certainly the most ubiquitous telephony device. To successfully interconnect telephony devices, it is necessary to understand the basics of how they operate. This section provides an overview of the basic analog phone operation and connectivity. The subsequent sections present more detail for analog telephony and discuss digital voice concepts.

Basic Cabling and Connectors

Standard network cabling is a single pair of twisted-pair copper wiring. The network termination point is an RJ-11 jack, usually mounted on a wall for home applications. The 2-wire connection has two pins—tip and ring—whose names are derived from the earlier systems where plugs were used to manually connect calls from one circuit to another. A sam-

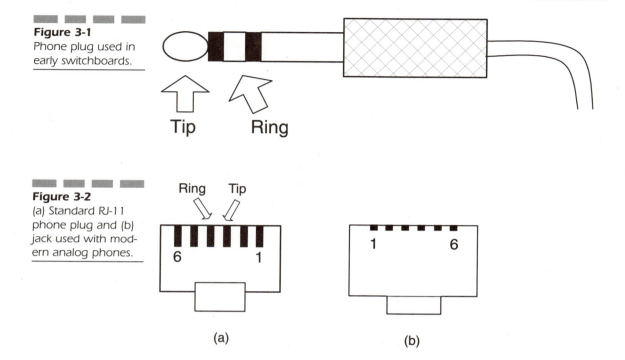

Figure 3-1
Phone plug used in
early switchboards.

Figure 3-2
(a) Standard RJ-11
phone plug and (b)
jack used with mod-
ern analog phones.

ple phone plug is drawn in Figure 3-1, where the black bands are insula-
tors and prevent current flow between the tip section and the ring section.

Originally, these plugs were at each end of patch cords which were
used to manually connect calls through a switchboard at a central office.
Today, calls are automatically switched at the central office (CO), thus
eliminating the phone plugs, but the concepts of tip and ring live on.
Standard phone connections are made with RJ-11 modular jacks and
plugs, simple connectors which use metal pins within the jack to connect
to metal rails within the plug. The metal rails in the plug connect to the
wire leads from the twisted-pair cabling. The RJ-11 modular jack and
plug are depicted in Figure 3-2. The two leads utilized by the phone are
referred to as tip and ring. This can be confusing for data-centric engineers who are familiar with transmit/receive pairs and positive/negative
leads. However, tip and ring are still used to define the leads. For reference, the tip lead runs at 0 V dc and the ring lead supplies −48 V dc in
the United States. Analog phones utilize this voltage to power the phone
and for signaling.

Voice Signal

Voice travels over the 2-wire circuit as an analog signal. The signal is generated by a microphone within the phone handset. The microphone generates the voice signal by responding to the audio waves and generating a current. In simplified form, the audio waves hit the microphone diaphram moving a magnet within a coil. This movement induces a current. The current generated by the microphone is groomed and transmitted over the copper wire between phones.

Similarly, the signal is reproduced by the far-end phone by passing the current through the transmitter. Within the transmitter is a speaker, which is essentially the opposite of a microphone. When current is passed through the coil, it induces an electromotive force on the speaker's magnet, which in turn, causes the speaker diaphram to move. The motion of the diaphram re-creates the audio signal.

The audio signal has two important characteristics, *frequency* and *amplitude*. The frequency is the rate at which the audio wave fluctuates and is directly related to the pitch of the sound. Low-pitched bass sounds have low frequencies, and high-pitched treble sounds have high frequencies. Microphones vibrate in synch with the frequency of the audio wave and generate an electrical signal with the same frequency. The amplitude of the audio wave is directly related to the volume of the sound. Loud sounds have larger amplitudes than quiet sounds. Larger amplitude sound waves move the microphone magnet further and create electrical signals with larger amplitude.

Signaling

Signaling allows the phone to communicate with the network and other phone systems. Off-hook notification, dialtone, ringing, number dialing, and busy signals are all examples of signaling used in analog telephony.

Off Hook

The first hurdle in building a telephone network is knowing when a phone is taken off-hook. Once the phone switch identifies that the phone is off hook, it can provide dial tone and listen for dialed digits. Given the 2-wire connection between the phone company and the installed phone, a method of in-band signaling is required to indicate the off-hook condition. Loop start is the most common method of alerting the CO switch and seizing

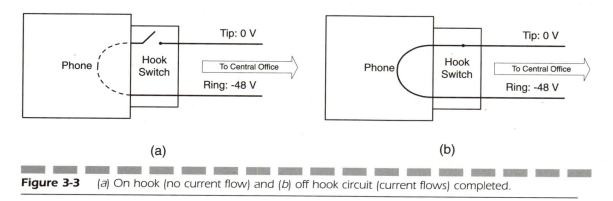

Figure 3-3   (a) On hook (no current flow) and (b) off hook circuit (current flows) completed.

the phone line. When a phone is taken off hook, it closes the off-hook switch which completes the circuit by connecting tip and ring through the phone's circuitry. Once the circuit is completed, dc current flows from the phone switch through the phone powering the phone's electronics and indicating to the phone switch that the phone is off hook. In response, the phone switch provides dialtone over the circuit. The completing of the circuit forms a contiguous wire loop between the phone switch and the end phone. This is sometimes referred to as the local loop. A logical view of both on-hook and off-hook conditions is presented in Figure 3-3.

Ringing

While on hook, the circuit between the phone switch and the phone is open. When the phone switch needs to connect a call, it has no means of completing the circuit between the switch and the phone. Without the dc current generated by closing the off-hook switch, the phone does not have the power to make any noise. To overcome this, the phone network places the phone's ringing device between the off-hook switch in the phone and the phone switch. As such, the ringer in an analog phone is placed in parallel with the incoming tip and ring lines. To activate the ringer, the phone switch generates a ring tone by sending an ac signal at 20–47 Hz on the circuit. It is usually a 90-V signal at 20 Hz. The ring tone crosses the ringer's leads and activates a bell or, more commonly today, an electronic circuit which generates a ring tone. The ac nature of the signal causes the bell to ring without requiring the hook switch to be closed. The basic phone layout is depicted in Figure 3-4.

Upon answering the phone, the dc circuit is completed and the switch, recognizing this, disables the ring tone. While the switch is ringing the

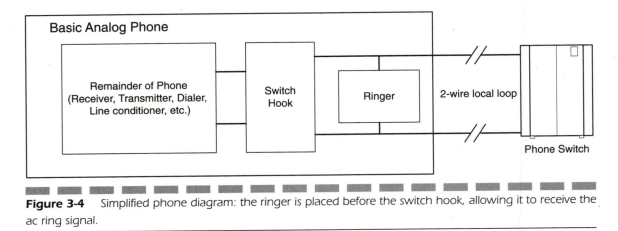

Figure 3-4   Simplified phone diagram: the ringer is placed before the switch hook, allowing it to receive the ac ring signal.

call destination, it also generates a ringing tone in band, back to the call initiator.

Dialing

Dialing from an analog phone can be performed in one of two ways: pulse or tone. Pulse is the simpler of the two and consists of transmitting sequences of pulses that indicate the numbers being dialed. The pulses are generated by opening and closing the local loop in short bursts. A digit is represented by the number of on/off bursts made in succession. There is a direct relationship between pulses and dialed digits, so the number 4 requires four pulses. The phone switch acknowledges a pulse if the circuit is closed, for 40 ms. The period of the pulse waves is 100 ms, so the expected time for the circuit to be open is 60 ms. The circuit-open time between pulses is called the *break time*, and the time the circuit is closed during the pulsing is called the *make time*. The time between pulses should be 700 ms. All phone switches should support pulse dialing and most phones provide the option of using pulse dialing. Figure 3-5 displays the line voltage over the local loop when dialing the digit 3. Note the time intervals for each pulse.

Tone dialing or touch-tone dialing uses a process called *dual tone multifrequency*, or DTMF. DTMF breaks up the keyboard into columns and rows. For each row, the keypad generates a unique frequency. Thus, when any of the buttons in that row are pressed, the keypad will generate the same frequency. Similarly, for each column the keypad generates a unique frequency. By pressing a single key, two frequencies are actu-

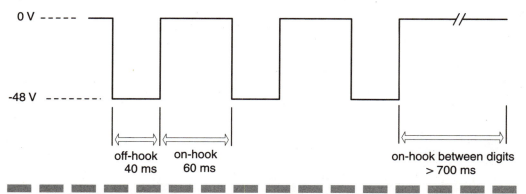

Figure 3-5   Pulse dialing—line voltage during the three successive off-hook/on-hook intervals required to dial the number 3.

Figure 3-6
DTMF frequencies: identifies the frequencies associated with each row and column of the keypad.

	1209 Hz	1336 Hz	1477 Hz	1633 Hz
697 Hz	1	2	3	A
770 Hz	4	5	6	B
852 Hz	7	8	9	C
941 Hz	*	0	#	D

ally generated, one for the row and one for the column. The switch recognizes the frequencies sent over the line and can identify the digit pressed by using simple logic circuits and its knowledge of the keypad matrix and frequencies. Figure 3-6 represents the keypad and the frequencies associated with each row and column.

For example, pressing the number 4 would generate a 1209-Hz tone and a 770-Hz tone. Whether pulse or tone, the dialing digits are sent in band and interpreted by the phone switch for call routing.

Network Call Progress Tones

The switched network indicates various network conditions by sending network call progress tones to the appropriate phone set. These tones include dialtone, busy signals, congestion (fast-busy), a receiver off-hook notifier, and other special messages. The frequencies and on/off times for these signals are provided in Table 3-1.

TABLE 3-1

Call Progress Tones

Tone	Frequency, Hz	On Time, s	Off Time, s
Dial tone	350 + 440	continuous	n/a
Ring back	440 + 480	2	4
Busy	480 + 620	0.5	0.5
Congestion	480 + 620	0.2	0.3
Off-hook notifier	1400 + 2060 + 2450 + 2600	0.1	0.1
No such number	200 to 400	continuous	n/a

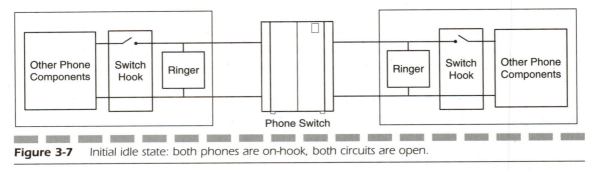

Figure 3-7   Initial idle state: both phones are on-hook, both circuits are open.

Basic Call Processing Sequence

In order to review the concepts discussed above, a step-by-step walk-through of a call setup is provided.

In the initial state (see Figure 3-7), both phones are on hook and both circuits are open.

Step 1.   The user lifts the handset of the phone. This activates the off-hook switch, completes the dc circuit, and triggers the phone switch, which generates the dialtone of the link. (See Figure 3-8.)

Step 2.   The user acknowledges the dialtone and dials the digits for the phone number associated with the destination. The digits are sent in band and received by the phone switch. (See Figure 3-9.)

Step 3.   The phone switch interprets the digits, looks up the destination in its routing table, and identifies the outbound path for the call. (See Figure 3-10.)

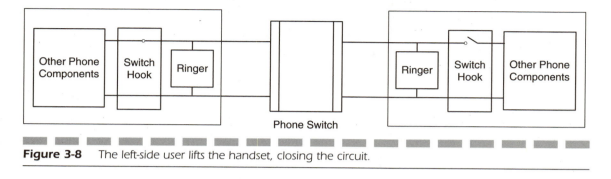

Figure 3-8   The left-side user lifts the handset, closing the circuit.

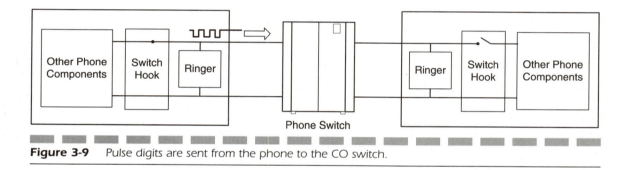

Figure 3-9   Pulse digits are sent from the phone to the CO switch.

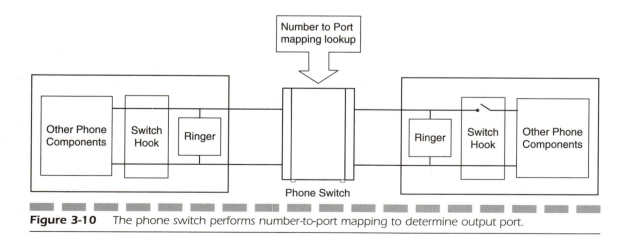

Figure 3-10   The phone switch performs number-to-port mapping to determine output port.

Step 4. The phone switch generates a ring signal on the destination phone by sending the 90-V, 20-Hz ac signal down the output port. The switch also generates the ringing sound back to the call initiator. (See Figure 3-11.)

Step 5. The remote phone rings, and the user picks up the phone, completing the dc circuit. (See Figure 3-12.)

Step 6. The switch senses the completed circuit, disables the ringing and ring back, and connects the call.

This is a simplified description of call processing for a call which is placed in and out of two ports on the same phone switch. Calls which span multiple switches require more complicated call processing. These techniques are discussed later in the chapter.

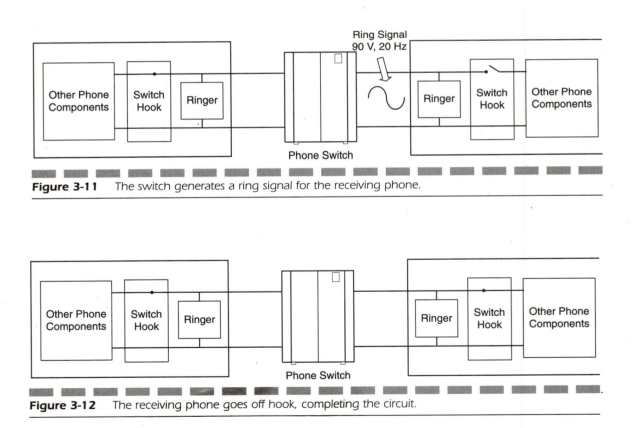

Figure 3-11   The switch generates a ring signal for the receiving phone.

Figure 3-12   The receiving phone goes off hook, completing the circuit.

Other Analog Devices

The only phone discussed up until this point has been the standard analog phone. Other phones and phone systems also access the PSTN through analog local loops; these include Key Systems and PBXs. These systems are common within branch or remote offices containing more than just a few users, as they allow the user community to share a pool of trunk lines to the PSTN.

Key Systems

Key systems are small phone switches which allow multiple phone sets to share a common pool of external phone lines. A key system connects to standard phone lines from the local central office and essentially mimics the operation of a standard phone. The individual phone sets connect to the key system as well and have a button or key for each external phone line. By pressing the associated button, a user connects his/her phone set to that external phone line. Incoming calls are sent to all phones which have a button for that external line. Since a key system interfaces with the phone company over standard telephone lines, no special configuration is required at the central office switch.

Key systems often include additional features such as hold, transfer, paging, and speed dial. These functions are performed by the key system's controller. Also, since regular phone lines are used to connect to the central office, each line has a unique phone number that can be dialed individually from the outside. It is often desirable to have the phone company link all of the lines into a hunt group so that a single phone number can be used for external access.

PBX

PBX is an acronym for Private Branch eXchange. It is a phone switch located on the customer's premises, which is capable of switching (connecting) phone sets to each other and to the PSTN. PBXs are common in larger organizations requiring more than 15 or 20 phones. Unlike key systems, each phone set connected to the PBX has a unique extension number. This enables intraswitch phone calls to be made without requiring an external phone line. Incoming calls can be sent to an operator who can connect them to the appropriate extension or they can be automatically routed using dialed number information provided by the central office switch. PBXs often provide the ability to link with other PBXs over dedicated links called *trunk lines*. PBXs also incorporate special types of interfaces both between PBXs and between the PBX and the central office switch.

Interface Types and Signaling Methods

The example earlier in the chapter described the operation of a common telephone which uses the loop start technique for indicating off-hook conditions. Key systems and PBX systems supporting large user communities over shared public phone lines created a need for improved signaling techniques. Specifically, these systems required quicker, more accurate methods for seizing the phone line (going off-hook) and more reliable methods for communicating dialed digits. The use of these systems also created a need for additional interface types to handle their increased signaling and trunking requirements. The interface types and signaling methods which overcome some of the limitations of loop start in larger-scale configurations are described below.

Types of Voice Interface for Routers

FXS FXS stands for Foreign eXchange Station. It is the standard analog telephone interface with which most people are familiar. FXS interfaces are used to connect to basic telephone devices such as phones, modems, faxes, key systems, and analog PBXs. FXS interfaces use a standard RJ-11 2-wire jack and, in effect, mimic the PSTN.

FXO FXO stands for Foreign eXchange Office. The port on a standard phone is an FXO port since it communicates with central office switching. Voice-enabled routers use FXO ports to interface with the PSTN. An FXO port acts as if it is a standard telephone requiring dialtone to place calls. The standard RJ-11 modular jack is used.

E&M E&M signaling is commonly called "ear and mouth." However, its origin actually comes from the terms *earth* and *magnet*. Earth represented electrical ground and magnet represented the electromagnet used to generate tone. E&M signaling provides on-hook/off-hook signaling and minimizes glare. It is commonly used for PBX trunks or tie-lines. Several types of E&M exist, each specifying different ways of signaling the off-hook condition between PBX and CO switch. E&M signaling is supported over 2- and 4-wire implementations. Cisco supports E&M types I, II, III, and V in its VoIP products.

E&M uses 6 to 8 of the pins on an RJ-48 modular jack, depending on the type of E&M used. Off-hook and incoming calls are signaled using one of the five types of E&M signaling. Since E&M interfaces don't provide dialtone, they use one of three signaling techniques to initiate dialing. They are immediate start, wink start, and delay start.

FXO/FXS Signaling Techniques

LOOP START Loop start is described in detail earlier in the chapter, but is presented here for completeness. Upon lifting the phone set and taking the phone off hook, loop-start phones complete the local loop circuit between the phone and the central office switch by connecting tip to ring through the phone set. The central office switch recognizes this, determines that phone is off hook, and responds by providing dialtone on the line. By placing the phone set back on hook, the circuit is broken and current no longer flows through the local loop. The central office switch then recognizes this and disconnects the call.

GROUND START PBXs often use ground start for signaling off-hook conditions. Ground start minimizes the risk of both sides of the link (PBX and phone switch) going off hook at the same time. Loop-start circuits run this risk because the 4-s wait in-between ring cycles provides up to 4 s where an incoming call can be on the line; however, the end station does not know it because a ring tone has not yet been generated. During that time the user may pick up to the phone to dial, not knowing that an incoming call was waiting. The collision of outbound and inbound calls is called glare. Ground start avoids this by allowing either side of the link to provide instantaneous off-hook signaling. Using ground start, the PBX momentarily grounds the ring lead indicating to the phone switch that it would like service. The phone switch interprets the signal and begins listening for dialed digits. The phone switch indicates incoming calls by grounding the tip lead toward the PBX. This virtually eliminates the possibility of glare.

Signaling Techniques

E&M signaling is not restricted to the 2-wire implementations discussed with FXO and FXS configurations. The 2- and 4-wire implementations describe the number of wires used to transmit the audio signals to and from the telephony devices. The 2-wire implementation is similar to a standard phone in that full-duplex audio signals are transmit-

TABLE 3-2

E&M Signaling
Pinout and
Descriptions

Name	Pin	Description	Types Used
E = ear or earth	7	Signal from trunking side to signaling side (router or CO to PBX)	I, II, III, IV, V
M = mouth or magnet	2	Signal from signaling side to trunking side (PBX to router or CO)	I, II, III, IV, V
SB = signal battery	1	Connects to 48-V dc battery (sometimes ground)	II, III, IV
SG = signal ground	8	Connects to electrical ground	II, III, IV
T = tip	6	Audio path from signaling side to trunking side on 4-wire circuits	I, II, III, IV, V
R = ring	3	Not used on 2-wire implementations	I, II, III, IV, V
T1 = tip-1	5	Audio path from signaling side to trunking side on 4-wire circuits	I, II, III, IV, V
R1 = ring-1	4	Full-duplex audio path on 2-wire implementations	I, II, III, IV, V

ted over a single pair. The 4-wire implementations provide separate paths for receiving and sending audio signals. Table 3-2 describes the different leads, their functions, along with their associated pins on the trunking side.

E&M signaling defines a signaling side and a trunking side for each connection. The PBX is the signaling side, while the trunking side is the telco, channel bank, or voice-enabled router. The signaling side sends its on-hook/off-hook indicators over the M lead and the trunking side sends its on-hook/off-hook indicators over the E lead. This provides each side of the link with a dedicated signaling path.

Five different types of E&M signaling exist, each with a slightly different method for signaling. All five types are presented below.

1. E&M type I signaling is popular in the United States. During inactivity, the E lead should be open and the M lead should be connected to ground. A PBX indicates an off-hook condition by connecting the M lead to the battery. The router or CO side indicates an off-hook condition by connecting the E lead to ground.

2. E&M type II signaling is also used in the United States. During inactivity, both the E and M leads should be open. A PBX indicates an off-hook condition by connecting the M lead to the signal battery (SB) lead which is connected to the battery at the CO side. The router or CO side indicates an off-hook condition by connecting the E lead to signal ground (SG), which is connected to ground at the PBX side. Type II signaling is symmetrical and allows for signaling nodes to be connected back to back using a crossover cable.

3. E&M type III signaling is not commonly used in modern systems. During inactivity, the E lead is open and the M lead is set to ground by connecting it to the SG lead from the CO. A PBX indicates an off-hook condition by disconnecting the M lead from the SG lead and connecting it to the SB lead from the CO. The router or CO side indicates an off-hook condition by connecting the E lead to ground.

4. E&M type IV signaling is not currently supported by Cisco's VoIP router interfaces.

5. E&M type V signaling is used in the United States and is common in Europe. During inactivity, both the E and M leads should be open. A PBX indicates an off-hook condition by connecting the M lead to ground. The router or CO side indicates an off-hook condition by connecting the E lead to ground. Type V signaling is symmetrical and allows for back-to-back connections using a crossover cable.

Table 3-3 summarizes the E&M types and the conditions they use to indicate on- and off-hook conditions.

TECHNIQUES FOR SEIZING THE LINE The various E&M signaling types identify on-hook/off-hook conditions, but they do not include a method of identifying when it is safe to send dial strings. Several techniques which perform this task been developed to work with E&M ports. They are immediate start, wink start, and delay start.

1. *Immediate start* is the most basic technique of the three. It operates under the assumption that the device on the other side of the link will listen for dialed digits immediately after recognizing the off-hook

TABLE 3-3

Lead States by E&M Type and Hook Condition

| E&M Type | Off-Hook | | On-Hook | | Symmetric |
	E Lead	M Lead	E Lead	M Lead	
I	Ground	Battery	Open	Ground	No
II	Ground	Battery	Open	Open	Yes
III	Ground	Loop current	Open	Ground	No
IV	Ground	Ground	Open	Open	No
V	Ground	Ground	Open	Open	Yes

condition. Immediate start simply indicates the off-hook condition by using one of the E&M techniques above, waits a small time period, and then sends the desired digits.

2. *Wink start* is the most commonly used protocol for identifying when it is safe to send digits. The idea is for the originating station to wait for an acknowledgment from the receiving station before transmitting the digits. After the originating station goes off hook, it waits to hear a momentary off-hook signal (wink) from the receiving station. Upon hearing the wink, the originating station sends its dialed digits over the line. If the originating station detects a continuous off-hook message from the receiving station, it assumes that both stations tried to grab the link at the same time and then performs error recovery.

3. *Delay dial* provides a means for the CO switch to delay the originating PBX's transmission of dial digits until the switch is ready to process them. After initiating an off-hook signal, the PBX waits 200 ms. In that same time interval the CO switch senses the off-hook condition and returns a constant off-hook signal to the PBX. After waiting the allotted 200 ms, the PBX checks the E lead (from CO to PBX). If it is on hook, then the PBX dials. If it is off hook, then the PBX waits until it goes on hook before dialing. This allows the CO switch to delay the sending of digits merely by holding the line off hook until it is ready to receive the digits.

Digital Voice

Transporting Voice

When transporting analog voice long distances, problems with signal loss are often encountered. To counteract this, amplifiers can be used to boost the signal along the path. However, amplifiers amplify both the voice signal and any ambient line noise which may have been picked up on the long circuit. So as the voice signal degrades in magnitude, the ratio of line noise to voice signal increases and the output becomes unacceptable. This problem limits the effectiveness and reach of analog-based long distance connections.

Digital transmissions do not suffer from these limitations. Since the only values transmitted are 0s and 1s, it is easy to differentiate the signal from line noise. Similarly, it is easy to regenerate the signal properly and eliminate any incurred line noise at the regeneration point. This allows digital transmissions to span greater distances while maintaining acceptable signal loss and signal-to-noise levels throughout the network. Given the advantages of digital transmission, a method of converting voice signals, which are inherently analog in nature, to a digital format was required.

Pulse code modulation, or PCM, was the solution developed. The concept behind PCM is to sample the audio wavelength at regular intervals and to encode an integer value for its amplitude at each interval. After conversion, the integer values are transmitted over a digital circuit as binary 0s and 1s. The receiving station then uses these integers to reconstruct the waveform and produce an analog signal equivalent to the original analog signal.

One of the factors that affects the quality of PCM voice is the number of wavelength samples taken every second. The more frequent the samples, the more accurately they will portray the shape of the wavelength. Figure 3-13 demonstrates the differences between two sampling rates. The samples are represented by the bars in each graph. Figure 3-13*b* uses a sampling rate which is twice that of Figure 3-13*a*. Noticeably, the samples in Figure 3-13*b* do a better job of approximating the actual curve than do the bars in *a*, which miss entire inflections in the waveform. Determining the optimum sampling rate for voice traffic has thus become an important area of research.

Nyquist's theorem states that in order to effectively reconstruct an analog signal, the waveform must be sampled at twice the maximum analog frequency of interest. In other words, to effectively reconstruct signals of up to 1000 Hz, the waveform must be sampled at 2000 Hz and digitally encoded creating 2000 digital values of the waveform per second. If the values were one byte in magnitude, they would require 16,000 bps (2000 samples / second * 8 bits/byte) to characterize the signal. Normal voice signals generally fall within the frequency range of 300 and 3400 Hz. In order to transport this frequency range, an upper limit of 4000 Hz was selected. Using Nyquist's theorem, the minimum required sample rate is 8000 Hz. PCM voice therefore samples analog voice at a rate of 8000 times per second. Figure 3-14 shows how a higher sampling frequency will approximate the waveform more effectively.

The second challenge is to encode the waveform at each sample interval. In order to map the amplitude of an analog waveform to digital values, a consistent method of transforming analog values to digital values is required. The greater the range of permitted values, the more accurate a representation can be made. However, using a large range of values requires additional bits. For example, using an 8-bit data field provides 256 different values while a 16-bit data field provides 65,536 different

Figure 3-13
Waveform approximation, showing (*a*) extremely low sample frequency and (*b*) twice the frequency of samples in *a*.

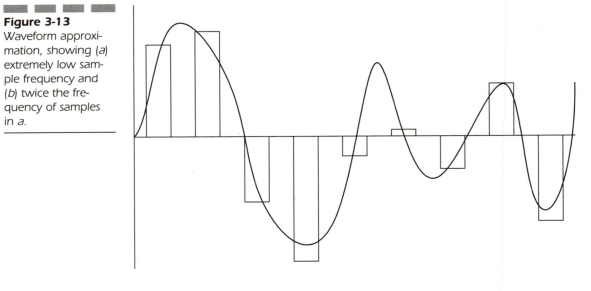

(a)

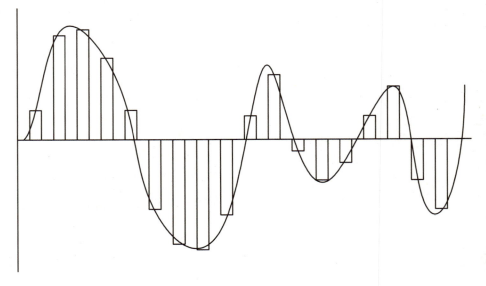

(b)

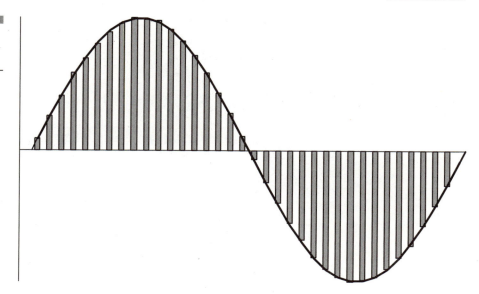

Figure 3-14
More granular wave-
form sampling.

values for amplitude quantization, but requires twice as much bandwidth to transmit. To limit the amount of data required to store the amplitude, an 8-bit representation was agreed upon by the industry. However, to support a large range of amplitudes without overshadowing lower levels, a logarithmic scale is used to encode amplitude values in the 8-bit field. This allows the 8-bit field to represent amplitude values of 12 to 13 bits in size by effectively compressing the value using the logarithmic scale. The benefit is that the logarithmic scale provides for more granular quantization of low-amplitude signals and coarser quantization of larger amplitude signals. This operation of compressing the amplitude value on encoding and expanding it upon decoding is called *com-pand*ing. The logarithmic parameter used for the encoding is sometimes called a *compander*.

Not surprisingly, two different companders are in use today, resulting in two different coding schemes called *mu law* and *a law*. The mu law coding scheme uses a compander which provides slightly better signal-to-noise ratios for low-amplitude signals, while a law uses a compander which provides lower idle channel noise. Mu law is used in the United States and Japan, while a law is used in European networks. The selection of a coding mechanism is usually a country-wide standard. The mu-law device is responsible for performing any mu-law to a-law conversions when crossing borders.

The above information establishes that PCM uses an 8000-Hz sample rate and that 8-bit amplitude values are generated every interval. This

translates to a 64-kbps bandwidth requirement (8000 samples / second *
8 bits / sample = 64,000 bps). Both a-law and mu-law PCM encoding is
described in the ITU-T G.711 recommendation.

Digital Voice Signaling

Converting analog voice signals to digital signals was only half of the
battle. The second half is communicating standard telephony conditions
and call routing within the network. This communication is accomplished through a standard set of signaling techniques. Signaling in digital networks can occur either in band or out of band. In-band signaling
"steals" bits from the data stream to carry signals while out-of-band signaling allocates a separate dedicated channel for signaling.

In-Band Signaling

In-band signaling is performed using a technique called *channel associated signaling* (CAS) or *robbed-bit signaling*. The term *channel associated
signaling* is derived from the fact that bits within each DS-0 (channel) are
used to indicate the status of that DS-0. The term *robbed-bit* comes from
the fact that the bits used to perform the signaling are taken from the
data stream. A single bit from every 6th frame is used for signaling. CAS
defines A bits as bits from frames which are even multiples of 6 and B bits
as bits from frames which are odd multiples of 6. Using this scheme, A
bits are taken from the 12th, 24th, 36th,… frames and B bits are taken
from the 6th, 18th, 30th,… frames. If extended superframe (ESF) framing is used, C and D bits are available. In this case, the 24-frame ESF is
the delimiter for identifying bits. The A bit is taken from the 6th frame,
the B bit is taken from the 12th frame, the C bit is taken from the 18th
frame, and the D bit is taken from the 24th frame.

The bits from CAS are used to communicate on-hook/off-hook conditions, as well as DNIS and ANI information. *Dialed number identification
service*, or DNIS, provides the phone number which the source dialed. It is
used for intelligent call routing and for accounting purposes. *Automatic
number identification*, or ANI, provides the phone number of the source
stations (caller ID) and is used for authentication and accounting.

On-Hook/Off-Hook Signaling

Just as with analog circuits, the endpoints on digital circuits need to
inform each other when they want to use the circuit for call origination

or termination. Similarly, there are several techniques for performing this signaling. They are the familiar E&M, loop start, and ground start and are described below.

E&M   E&M signaling is used with PBXs and provides a means for direct-inward-dialing (DID) and two-way dialing. It is broken into three different types, each with a different mechanism for initiating dialing. All three types set the A and B bits to 0 for on-hook and to 1 for off-hook.

1. *E&M Immediate Start*

    Much like the immediate start algorithm from the analog world, immediate start simply indicates its off-hook condition and then transmits it dial digits. The receiving switch will go off-hook after receiving the digits.

2. *E&M Feature Group B*

    E&M Feature Group B mirrors the wink-start algorithm from the analog world only it communicates with the binary A and B bits. The transmitting side goes off-hook to indicate that a call is coming. At this point the terminating side responds with an off-hook wink lasting approximately 200 ms. After the wink, the terminating side goes back on-hook and listens for the dial digits. After the digits are received and the call is established, the terminating side goes off hook for the duration of the call.

3. *E&M Feature Group D*

    E&M Feature Group D adds a second layer of acknowledgment to confirm the reception of dialed digits. It functions in the same manner as E&M Feature Group B until the reception of digits from the source. At this point, the terminating side sends a second 200-ms wink to the source signal that it has received the digits. After the wink, the terminating side remains on hook until the call is answered, at which point it remains off hook for the duration of the call.

FXS LOOP START AND GROUND START   Since a T1 circuit is always active, the act of closing the local loop or grounding is not actually performed; rather it is simulated using the A and B bits of CAS.

FXS Loop Start   For loop start, the following convention is used: Only the CPE device sets the A bit. It uses 0 for on hook and 1 for off hook. The network can only set the B bit and sets B = 0 for no ring and B = 1 for ring. For outgoing calls, the CPE device simply sets the A bit to 1 and then sends its dial digits. For incoming calls, the network toggles the B bit to between 1 and 0 in the familiar 2-s ring, 4-s wait pattern. Once the CPE answers and sets the A bit to 1, the network resets the B bit to 0 for the duration of the call.

FXS Ground Start   For ground start, the CPE device uses only the A bit, and sets A = 0 for on hook and A = 1 for off hook. The network uses both the A and B bits. The A bit indicates circuit open (A = 0) and circuit closed (A = 1). The B bit is used for ring indication with the inverse values from loop start. In ground start, B = 0 for ring and B = 1 for no ring. Operation is similar to loop start, except the network now indicates off-hook status using the A bit.

Out-of-Band Signaling

Common channel signaling uses one signaling element for all channels. Primary rate ISDN does this by allocating a single D channel to handle signaling for the remaining 23 B channels. Call setup, call supervision, call tear down, and supplementary services are provided by the ISDN Q.930/931 signaling specifications. ISDN's Q.920/921 specification maintains the connection between the ISDN end device and the telco switch. It provides a transport for the Q.931 messages that include fields for addressing, control, and CRC.

Q.931 SIGNALING   Q.931 signaling provides call establishment, information, and clearing, and additional status notification. The messages available for these functions are presented in Table 3-4. Call establishment and termination in ISDN-based digital networks is handled using these features. As the table suggests, ISDN provides a significantly more robust feature set than the simple loop start, ground start, and E&M protocols.

Voice Compression

Voice compression reduces the payload of voice information required to transport a voice signal over the network. As we have already seen, standard PCM voice digitization samples the analog waveform 8000 times per second, generating an 8-bit value each sample interval and resulting in a 64-kbps bit stream. Since the digitized voice is simply a stream of 0s and 1s, various compression algorithms can be run against it to produce smaller quantities of data resulting in bandwidth savings.

TABLE 3-4

ISDN Q.931
Message Types

Call Establishment	Call Information	Call Clearing	Miscellaneous
Alerting	Hold	Disconnect	Congestion
Call proceeding	Hold ack	Release	Control
Connect	Hold reject	Release	Facility
Connect ack	Resume	Complete	Information
Progress	Resume ack	Restart	Notify
Setup	Resume reject	Restart ack	Register
Setup ack	Retrieve		Status
	Retrieve ack		Status inquiry
	Retrieve reject		
	Suspend		
	Suspend ack		
	Suspend reject		
	User		
	Information		

Compression Algorithms

Adaptive Differential Pulse Code Modulation

Adaptive differential pulse code modulation, or ADPCM, is a variation on the waveform-based encoding. ADPCM calculates the difference in the waveform from sample to sample as well as the rate of change of the amplitude. ADPCM can generate 2, 3, 4, or 5 bits of data every sample interval, resulting in bandwidth requirements of 16, 24, 32, and 40 kbps, respectively. ADPCM is often used at the 32-kbps level, and provides adequate voice quality and a 2:1 bandwidth savings over PCM. Lower bit rates provide noticeably worse voice quality. The ITU-T describes ADPCM in its G.726 recommendation.

Code Excited Linear Predictor

LD-CELP stands for low-delay code excited linear predictor (CELP). It listens to a stream of 16-bit linear PCM data and produces a 10-bit codebook pointer from every five PCM samples. In other words, LD-CELP listens to five samples from the PCM stream, interprets the waveform type, and assigns a single 10-bit codebook pointer to that segment of voice. LD-CELP then groups four consecutive 10-bit pointers into a subframe and bundles two subframes together for transmission as a single frame. Since LD-CELP generates 10 bits of data every 625 µs (five PCM samples), it transmits at a rate of 16 kbps. The following equation demonstrates this:

$$1600 \text{ samples/s} * 10 \text{ bits} = 16 \text{ kbps}$$

LD-CELP is described by the ITU-T's G.728 recommendation.

CS-ACELP (conjugate structure algebraic code excited linear predictor) is a successor to LD-CELP, and is commonly used in voice over IP networks. Like LD-CELP, CS-ACELP interprets 16-bit PCM data and produces a mathematical approximation of the waveform for transmission. CS-ACELP listens to 80 PCM frames (10 ms) and maps them to ten 8-bit codewords from the codebook. Cisco's implementation bundles two 10-ms samples into a single frame. Additionally, CS-ACELP performs noise reduction and pitch synthesis to enhance the voice quality. The ten 8-bit codewords result in 80 bits of data every 10 ms, or 8 kb every second. CS-ACELP provides an 8:1 reduction in bandwidth compared with standard PCM. The ITU-T's G.729 describes CS-ACELP. G.729 Annex A or G.729a describes a less computationally taxing version of 8-kbps CS-ACELP.

Cisco's voice-enabled routers contain specialized CODECs (coder/decoders) to perform the encoding of voice traffic. This offloads the computationally intensive process of voice interpretation and compression from the router CPU and provides consistent performance.

Comparing the Voice Encoding Techniques

Voice quality is a subjective measurement. Different people react differently to each compression technique. To help quantify the quality of a given technique, the mean opinion score (MOS) scale was developed. To develop the MOS numbers, test listeners rated various speech patterns sent through each compression technique for quality of sound on a scale of 1 to 5, with 5 being the best. The results are then averaged to produce the mean opinion score.

Table 3-5 includes the various compression techniques as well as each technique's bit rate, MOS, coding delay, and the processing power required for compression.

TABLE 3-5

Comparison of
Compression
Techniques

Coding	ITU-T Standard	Bit Rate, kbps	MOS	Processing Power, MIPS	Frame Size, ms	Coding Delay, ms
PCM	G.711	64	4.1	0.34	0.125	0.75
ADPCM	G.726	32	3.85	14	0.125	1
LD-CELP	G.728	16	3.61	33	0.625	3-5
CS-ACELP	G.729	8	3.92	20	10	10
CS-ACELP	G.729a	8	3.7	10.5	10	10
MP-MLQ	G.723.1	6.3	3.9	16	30	30
ACELP	G.723.1	5.3	3.65	16	30	30

Cisco's voice-enabled routers currently support G.711, G.729, and G.729a coding schemes. G.723.1 support is planned.

Looking at Table 3-5, the trade-offs between the coding schemes become apparent. PCM uses the most bandwidth, yet receives the best MOS rating, uses the least amount of processing power, and introduces the least amount of latency. This has made PCM inexpensive to deploy and highly effective in transporting voice traffic over long distances. By contrast, CS-ACELP provides significant bandwidth savings at the expense of increased processing requirements, increased latency, and a slightly lower MOS rating.

Factors That Affect Voice Quality

Compression

The compression algorithms each have an effect on voice quality. Eliminating all other causes of degradation, voice quality will be only as good as the compression algorithm's ability to accurately reconstruct the voice signal at the receiving station. The MOS ratings give an idea as to how well each algorithm performs these tasks. Selecting the right algorithm to meet the demands of the user community is important. In some cases, this may mean using standard 64-kbps PCM.

Voice Activity Detection

Voice activity detection, or VAD, is a technique employed by digital signal processors which reduces the volume of voice traffic transmitted by automatically detecting silent periods in conversations and suspending traffic generation during those periods. Approximately 50–60 percent of most conversations is silence. This is due to the fact that while one party is speaking the other party is usually listening silently. With VAD enabled, the bandwidth that normally would have been consumed with silent voice data can be saved and allocated to other traffic types, like data.

VAD works by monitoring the power of the voice signal, changes in power, the frequency of the incoming voice signal, and changes in that frequency. VAD's challenge is in correctly identifying when speech stops, and also when it starts again. VAD waits approximately 200 ms after it perceives that speech has stopped before disengaging the packetization process. This pause helps prevent VAD from clipping the trailing portion of speech or engaging in the middle of a small break in the speech pattern. Similarly, a delay of 5 ms is introduced by the CODEC to "hold on" to voice information in the event that speech is detected. This means that when VAD determines that a voice signal is once again present, the previous 5 ms of voice are transmitted along with the current voice signals. This delay reduces, but does not eliminate, front-end clipping where the beginning of speech is clipped.

Echo

Echo is caused by electrical reflections in the voice network. These reflections are usually the result of an impedance differential between the 4-wire switch connection and the 2-wire local loop. A little bit of echo is always present, and it is actually comforting to the speaker to hear his or her voice echoed back through the handset. However, an echo which is delayed more than 25 ms is distracting and disconcerting for the speaker. Since echo is usually caused at the remote end of the circuit, an increase in network delay beyond 25 ms will require some means of counteracting the echo.

The PSTN handles echo in two ways. One is to lower the power of the signal, thus minimizing the magnitude of the echo. The second is through the use of echo cancellers. Echo cancellers are placed in between the CO switch and the 4-wire-to-2-wire converter connected to the local loop. In packet networks, they are often integrated into the DSP used for packetization.

Echo cancellers operate by combining the echo signal with its exact opposite. Since the echo canceller is in line between the signal origin and the point at which it is reflected, its job is to simply remember the voice patterns that flow through it, wait for them to return as echo, and then apply the inverse of the original voice pattern to the returning echo. Figures 3-15 through 3-19 illustrate this process.

The DSPs in packet networks now offer integrated echo cancellation. To accomplish this, the DSP reserves memory space to record processed signals and store them while waiting for return echo. The time during which the DSP can wait for the return echo is limited by the size of the memory allocation on the DSP.

Echo cancellation enables networks with larger delays to be built since echo is removed close to its source.

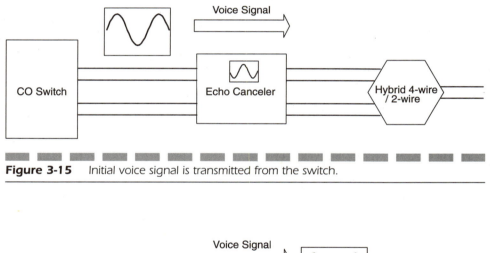

Figure 3-15   Initial voice signal is transmitted from the switch.

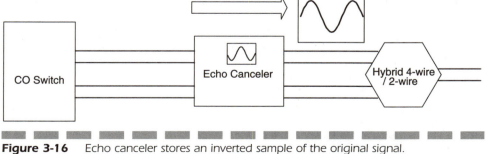

Figure 3-16   Echo canceler stores an inverted sample of the original signal.

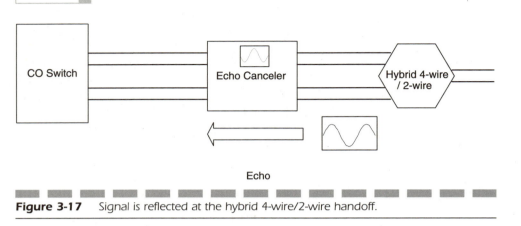

Figure 3-17 Signal is reflected at the hybrid 4-wire/2-wire handoff.

Figure 3-18
Echo canceler combines echo with inverted sample in memory.

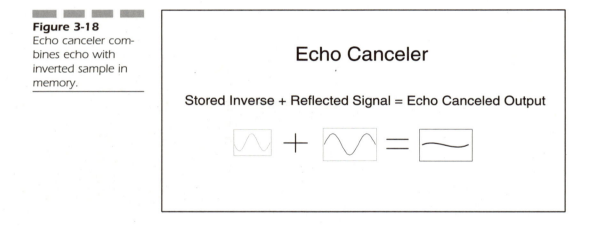

Echo Canceler

Stored Inverse + Reflected Signal = Echo Canceled Output

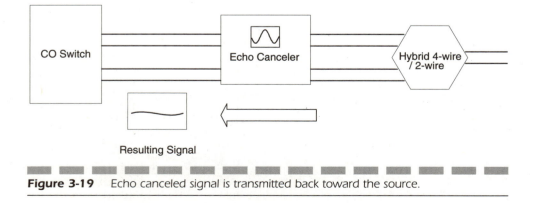

Figure 3-19 Echo canceled signal is transmitted back toward the source.

Delay

Delay is important because it directly affects the perceived quality of the phone call. Increased delay leads to talker overlap and echo. Calls with excessive delays are difficult on the participants because they lengthen the amount of time between conversational responses, making it hard to keep a conversation in synch. This creates a situation somewhat analogous to congestion conditions in data networks. The sender's patience in waiting for a response may run out causing him or her to re-ask the question (retransmit) even though the response may already be on the way back.

Troublesome echo is caused when the end-to-end delay in the network is above 25–35 ms. At this point, echo distracts the speaker and begins to degrade the quality of the call. Echo cancellation as described above is an effective means of limiting this problem.

Delay can be divided into two components, *propagation delay* and *handling delay*.

1. Propagation delay refers to the speed at which the electrons flow through the copper wire network to deliver the transmitted message. This is very low since electrons travel at 100,000 miles per second in copper. This translates to approximately 30 ms for a cross-country copper path of 3000 miles. Propagation delay should not be confused with serialization delay. Serialization delay is the time required to transmit data on link and is based upon the operating frequency of the link. The serialization delay of a 100-mile 64-kbps link is 24 times that of a 100 mile T1, yet the propagation delay is the same for both. In summary, propagation delay is based upon the transmission medium (copper/fiber) and the distance while serialization delay is based upon the signaling rate of the circuit.

2. Handling delay is introduced by all the components which handle the voice traffic during its transmission. In a voice over IP network the following items add to the one-way delay of an end-to-end voice transmission:
   - Digitization of analog voice signal
   - Compression of digital voice signal
   - Packetization of voice traffic
   - Queuing of packetized voice
   - Transmission and serialization delay over the initial network link
   - Queuing and serialization delays over all intermediate network elements (routers, LAN switches, WAN switches, LAN/WAN links)
   - Reception and queuing of packet at destination

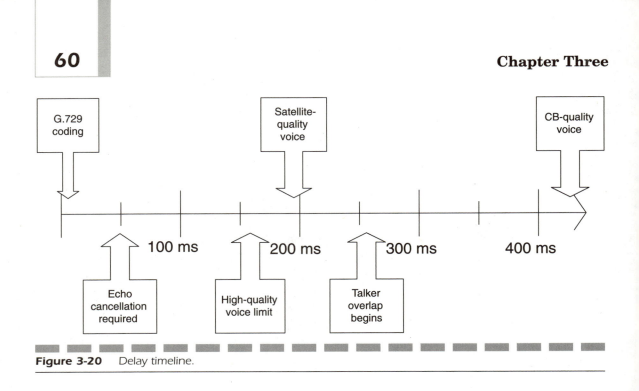

Figure 3-20   Delay timeline.

- Depacketization of voice traffic
- Decoding of digital voice signal
- Translation of digital signal to analog voice signal

Of these elements, the queuing and serialization delays are the most significant in WAN configurations. Two subsequent chapters on quality of service are dedicated to the discussion of these issues. The time line in Figure 3-20 helps identify important delay measurements.

Jitter

Jitter refers to the changing arrival rate of packets from the network due to variations in the transit delay. IP networks do not offer consistent performance and often introduce large variances in the packet arrival rates. This is due to several factors, including queuing delays, variable packet sizes, and the relative load on the intermediary links and routers. To compensate for jitter, voice devices incorporate a playout buffer on the receiving device. The buffer holds on to packets long enough for the slowest packet to arrive in time to be processed in sequence.

The idea of buffering packets before processing them is diametrically opposed to the goal of minimizing delay. Unfortunately, it is a necessary evil. The quality of service techniques discussed in Chapter 3 and 4 can be employed to reduce jitter throughout the IP network. Since jitter cannot be eliminated, the jitter buffer must be carefully tuned to provide an optimal packet-delivery rate while minimizing delay. The process which maintains the playout buffer begins with a minimum and maximum buffer size (measured in ms). During operation, it constantly monitors the arrival rate of packets and dynamically adjusts the playout-buffer size to support the changing network conditions. In low-delay environments, the playout buffer is reduced to the minimum. In environments with highly variable delay, the playout buffer adapts slowly to reduced-delay situations and quickly to increased-delay situations. This ensures that packet loss is minimized by maintaining an adequate buffer size and absolute delay is controlled by maintaining a maximum-queuing delay.

Lost Packets

Not surprisingly, packet loss will also have an adverse effect on voice quality. This can be troublesome when voice traffic is transiting a data network which has been engineered to use packet loss as a means of congestion management. With data, the end stations simply retransmit the lost data and slow down their communication rate. With voice, there is no time for retransmission, and therefore the voice software must adapt. Beyond packet loss due to the intermediate network elements, packet loss in voice networks may also be due to delivery delays which exceed the jitter buffer's tolerance. In the event that a packet is lost, the CODEC can guess at what the missing signal would have been by referencing the previous packet or packets. This technique helps hide the loss of a single packet, but does not work for multiple lost packets. In the event of multiple consecutive lost packets, the CODEC simply inserts silent periods. The invocation of these techniques is recorded statistically, and can be measured to help quantify the effects of the network on voice quality.

Tandem Switching

Some network designs call for voice traffic to be forwarded to a centralized phone switch which is capable of forwarding traffic to the appropriate destination. This is somewhat analogous to a hub-and-spoke IP network where the hub router is responsible for forwarding traffic among the spokes. This type of configuration can have adverse effects on voice quality for two main reasons: recompression and delay.

In order for the voice-enabled router to forward the traffic to the phone switch, it must process the VoIP packets and decode them. Since the compression algorithms are not lossless they do not reproduce an exact replica of the original signal. The phone switch then receives the slightly degraded signal and switches it to the output port. The voice-enabled router then performs compression and packetization of the slightly degraded signal. The result is that at the output voice-enabled router, the quality of the signal is reduced even more. G.729's MOS rating is 3.92 for a single compression cycle. When compressed twice, the MOS is reduced to a marginally acceptable 3.27. If, for some reason, a third compression/decompression cycle were invoked, the MOS rating would become a relatively unacceptable 2.68.

Delay is also increased as a result of the additional processing required. The packetization, queuing, and encoding delays are doubled as are the serialization and network-related delays. The sum of these delays can often exceed the 250–300 ms total delay budget for voice calls.

The degradation of the voice signal can be reduced by using standard PCM encoding, which also decreases the encoding delays in the voice-enabled routers. However, this increases the bandwidth requirements significantly which may make the solution unworkable. The use of tandem switching must be carefully planned and, in general, should be avoided. Attempts should be made to route packets directly to their destinations, even if the routing is through a hub site. Eliminating the intermediary compression and decompression cycles will yield significantly better voice quality and reduced delays.

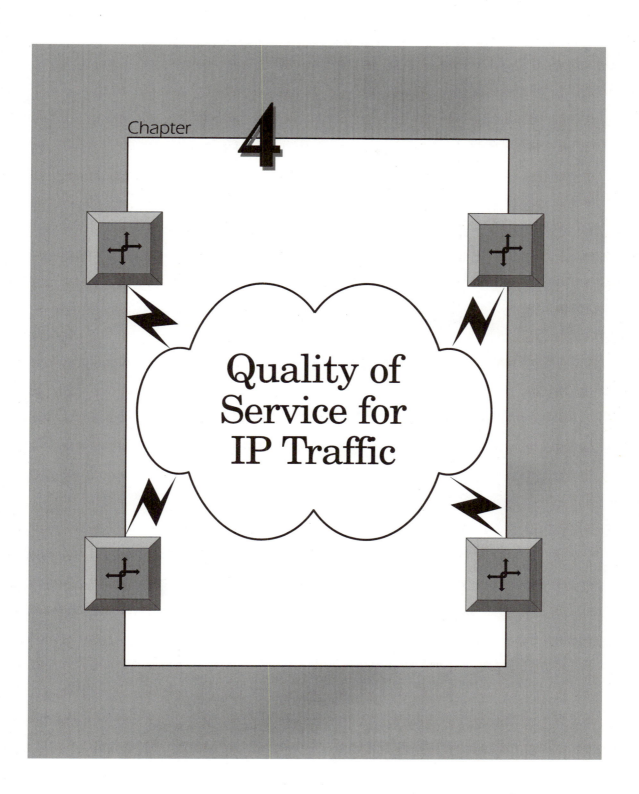

Chapter

4

Quality of
Service for
IP Traffic

Overview

This chapter will cover the following:

- Compressed real-time transfer protocol
- Queuing
- PPP enhancements
- Traffic shaping
- Resource Reservation Protocol
- IP precedence
- Policy-based routing
- Weighted fair queuing
- Weighted random early detection

Quality of service for IP traffic is a difficult topic to characterize in today's networking environment. There is no single standard for implementing end-to-end QoS in IP internets, so many vendors and standards organizations are busy creating new protocols to fill the void. Not surprisingly, Cisco is at the forefront of IP QoS development, and is continually introducing new techniques to address the issue. Protocols and techniques such as RSVP, diff serv, tag switching, multiprotocol label switching, and committed access rate are all attempts to provide quality or class of service to IP traffic. This chapter provides a brief overview of Cisco's IP quality of service features which can be applied on voice-enabled products to deliver toll-quality voice connectivity. Topics covered are limited to those which would be supported by the voice-enabled products.

(Compressed) Real-Time Transfer Protocol

One of the simplest techniques for reducing delay is to simply send less data. The basic principle is that less data require less time to send. Voice over IP traffic uses the Real-Time Transport Protocol (RTP) as defined by RFC 1890. RTP is a session-layer protocol which rides on top of UDP and provides hooks for real-time streaming applications such as voice and video. The RTP header is 8 bytes and when combined with an 8-byte UDP header and a 20-byte IP header, RTP traffic consumes 40 bytes before the payload is even added. This is significant when compared to the average voice payload of 20 bytes. The 40 bytes of overhead is not significant over LANs, but adds significant delay when transmitted over low-speed serial links. To address this problem, an algorithm for compressing RTP was developed using techniques introduced in RFC 1144—TCP/IP header compression. CRTP takes advantage of the following RTP characteristics:

1. RTP header fields change at a constant rate

2. The IP source and destination address are constant for an RTP session

3. The UDP source and destination ports are constant for an RTP session

4. The RTP synchronization source (SSRC) is constant for an RTP session

Based on the first characteristic, the first-order derivative for the field is a constant, which means the second-order derivative is zero. Using this knowledge, routers can set up shortcuts to eliminate the transmission of certain fields. The receiving router needs to store the original header and the first-order differential for each field. As long as there are no changes to the rate of change of the field (first-order derivative), the receiving router can simply add the stored constant for each in subsequent packets. The sending router also must store both the original header and the first-order differential and continuously calculate the second-order differential on successive packets. As long as the second-order differential remains zero, there is no need to signal the receiving router.

Based on characteristics 2, 3, and 4 there is no need to continually send the same data. These values can be stored in a lookup table and referenced using a hashing function. The hashing function will produce a small integer which can be used in place of the full IP/UDP/RTP headers. The sending router computes this integer and transmits it in place of the normal IP/UDP/RTP header. Upon receipt of a CRTP packet, the router simply runs the integer through the hashing function, which references the associated IP/UDP/RTP header for the session and attaches the full header to the packet for forwarding.

The combination of these functions allows the 40-byte IP/UDP/RTP header to be reduced significantly. The compressed header will be 2 bytes unless UDP checksums are used, in which case it will be 4 bytes. The details of CRTP can be found at

ftp://www.ietf.org/internet-drafts/draft-ietf-avt-crtp-05.txt

It is important to remember that CRTP operates on a link-by-link basis only and that both ends must have CRTP enabled to function properly. Cisco allows for the configuration of a passive mode in which the router will compress outgoing packets only after receiving a compressed packet on that interface. Cisco does not recommend using CRTP on serial links running at greater than 2 Mbps. Also, CRTP is restricted to HDLC, PPP, frame relay, and ISDN interfaces.

Configuring CRTP

To configure CRTP on a PPP or HDLC interface, the following interface command is used:

```
ip rtp header-compression[passive]
```

where the optional `passive` keyword configures the router to only compress RTP packets if it has received compressed RTP on that interface.

The maximum number of CRTP sessions is limited to 16 by default. Since there is a 1:1 relationship between CRTP sessions and voice calls, this number may need to be increased. The command to adjust this parameter is

```
ip rtp compression connections n
```

with n representing the maximum number of connections.

EXAMPLE   The following PPP compressed RTP example demonstrates the use of CRTP in a single environment. (See Figure 4-1.)

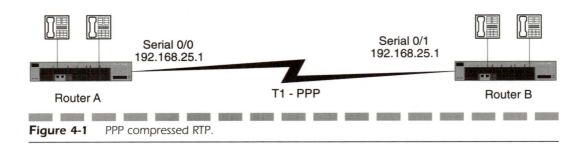

Figure 4-1   PPP compressed RTP.

Router A

```
 !
interface serial 0/0
 ip address 192.168.25.1 255.255.255.0
 encapsulation ppp
 ip rtp header-compression
 !
```

Router B

```
 !
interface serial 0/1
 ip address 192.168.25.2 255.255.255.0
 encapsulation ppp
 ip rtp header-compression
 !
```

Frame-Relay Considerations

The multiaccess nature of frame-relay interfaces necessitates that header compression be handled slightly differently. Since CRTP must be performed on a per-link basis, frame-relay interfaces handle it on a per-PVC basis. Point-to-point subinterfaces are configured the same way as PPP or HDLC interfaces. Point-to-multipoint subinterfaces and basic multipoint interfaces require that CRTP be enabled in the protocol mapping. This is done by using the RTP header-compression keywords in the frame-relay map statements. The syntax for configuring CRTP on frame-relay interfaces follows.

To enable RTP header compression for the entire interface—including all subinterfaces and/or maps—the following interface command is used.

```
frame-relay ip rtp header-compression [passive]
```

Its operation is similar to that of a PPP interface. The `passive` keyword is optional and only compresses packets after receiving compressed packets from the remote end. For CRTP to work, it must be enabled at both endpoints of the PVC.

To enable CRTP on a per-subinterface basis, the above command should not be applied to the main interface. Instead, the following command should be applied to the appropriate subinterface(s).

```
rtp header-compression [active | passive]
```

The `active` keyword indicates that the map should compress all RTP headers and the `passive` keyword specifies that the router should only compress headers after receiving compressed RTP headers.

For multipoint (sub-)interfaces, there is yet another command. To enable CRTP on a per-map basis, the following syntax should be applied:

```
frame-relay map ip address dlci [broadcast] rtp header-compression
   active
```

where *address* is the IP address and *dlci* refers to the dlci defined for the PVC.

EXAMPLE

The following frame-relay compressed RTP example helps demonstrate the use of CRTP in a frame-relay environment. Router A has a single frame-relay interface to voice routers B and C, as well as the nonvoice router, router D. A point-to-point subinterface is used for the connection between routers A and B. Routers A, C, and D are part of the multipoint frame-relay network and use the traditional frame-relay map statements. Since router D is data only, it will not use RTP compression. (See Figure 4-2.)

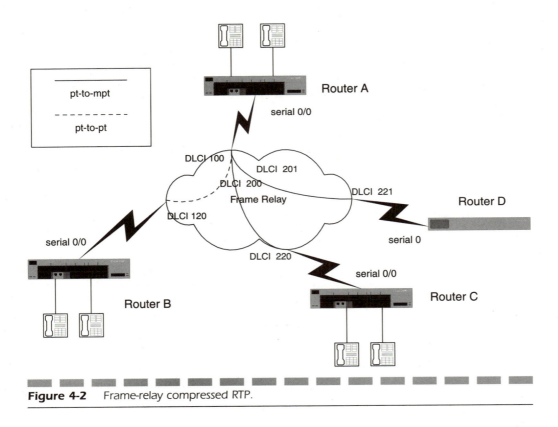

Figure 4-2   Frame-relay compressed RTP.

Router A

```
interface serial0/0
 encapsulation frame-relay
 no ip address
 frame-relay lmi-type ansi
 bandwidth 512
!
interface serial0/0.1 point-to-point
 ip address 192.168.1.1 255.255.255.0
 frame-relay ip rtp header-compression
 bandwidth 128
 frame-relay interface-dlci 100
!
interface serial0/0.10 multipoint
 ip address 192.168.2.1 255.255.255.0
 frame-relay map ip 192.168.2.2 200 broadcast rtp header-compression
  active
 frame-relay map ip 192.168.2.3 201 broadcast
!
```

Router B

```
interface serial0/0
 encapsulation frame-relay
 no ip address
 frame-relay lmi-type ansi
 bandwidth 256
!
interface serial0/0.1 point-to-point
 ip address 192.168.1.2 255.255.255.0
 frame-relay ip rtp header-compression
 bandwidth 128
 frame-relay dlci 120
!
```

Router C

```
interface serial0/0
 encapsulation frame-relay
 frame-relay lmi-type ansi
 ip address 192.168.2.2 255.255.255.0
 frame-relay map ip 192.168.2.1 220 broadcast rtp header-compression
  active
 bandwidth 128
!
```

Router D

```
interface serial0
 encapsulation frame-relay
 frame-relay lmi-type ansi
 ip address 192.168.2.3 255.255.255.0
 frame-relay map ip 192.168.2.1 220 broadcast
 bandwidth 56
!
```

Queuing

Queuing of network traffic is essential for the efficient flow of traffic through the network. Queuing enables routers and switches to handle bursts of traffic, measure network congestion, prioritize traffic, and allocate bandwidth. Cisco routers offer four basic output queuing schemes for the handling of network traffic. They are *first-in, first-out* (FIFO), *priority queuing*, *custom queuing*, and *weighted fair queuing*.

FIFO Queuing

FIFO is the most straightforward form of queuing, and accordingly the simplest to implement and the least resource intensive on the routers. first-in, first-out means simply that. Packets are forwarded out the output interface in the order in which they arrived. Its low processing overhead makes FIFO the method of choice for high-speed LAN interfaces. However, its inability to prioritize traffic or to prevent a given application or user from unfairly overutilizing network bandwidth makes FIFO a poor choice for low-speed links. FIFO queuing is the default queuing mechanism on interfaces running at greater than 2 Mbps.

Priority Queuing

Priority queuing is perhaps the oldest queuing mechanism in Cisco routers after FIFO. Priority queuing allows administrators to classify traffic by protocol or by using standard or extended access lists. Once classified, the traffic can then be queued in one of four queues. These queues, in descending order of priority, are high, medium, normal, and low. Any traffic that does not match the classification scheme is placed in the normal queue by default. Priority queuing allocates bandwidth by emptying all of the higher-priority queues before servicing the next lower queue. This action ensures that any traffic in the high queue has immediate access to the interface. Accordingly, any traffic in the low queue must wait for all of the traffic in the high, medium, and normal queues to empty. As a result, high-priority traffic receives near immediate access to the interface at the expense of potentially starving lower-priority traffic. In the past, enabling priority queuing forced the router to process switch all traffic destined for the interface on which it was enabled, resulting in lower system performance. Recent enhancements to the IOS have changed this slightly. As of IOS release 11.1, the router will fast

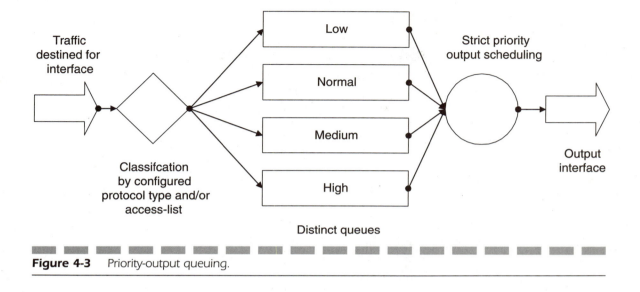

Figure 4-3 *Priority-output queuing.*

switch all traffic for the outbound interface until congestion is experienced. This increases performance because process switching is only invoked when it is required. Figure 4-3 demonstrates the operation of priority-output queuing.

Configuring Priority Queuing for Voice Traffic

Configuration of priority queuing involves defining the traffic types to be queued, assigning priority to each queue, and applying the priority scheme to the interface.

Priority queuing classifies traffic using network protocol type or, for more detailed classification, using access lists. The following access list classifies voice over IP traffic by identifying the TCP and UDP port numbers used by voice over IP.

```
access-list 150 permit udp any any range 16384 16484
access-list 150 permit tcp any any eq 1720
```

The next command assigns this traffic to the high-priority queue.

```
priority-list 1 protocol ip high list 150
```

Once this is done, the only remaining item is to apply the list to the appropriate interface by using the priority-group command.

A sample configuration for including these commands follows.

```
!
interface Serial0/0
 description link to headquarters
 ip address 192.168.121.17 255.255.255.248
 priority-group 1
!
...
!
access-list 150 permit udp any any range 16384 16484
access-list 150 permit tcp any any eq 1720
priority-list 1 protocol ip high list 150
 !
```

All of the traffic which does not match the access list is placed in the normal queue.

If another application requires preferential treatment over the normal traffic, it can be placed in the medium queue, for example if response times for Telnet sessions to a remote host are important. The following additional commands would give Telnet traffic priority over unclassified traffic, but not over voice traffic.

```
access-list 151 permit tcp any any eq 23
priority-list 1 protocol ip medium list 151
 !
```

Details for priority queuing and its applicability to other protocols and applications can be found in Cisco's on-line documentation.

Custom Queuing

Custom queuing was created to address some of the shortcomings of priority queuing. Specifically, it introduced a way to prevent starvation of lower-priority queues and to allocate bandwidth by limiting the amount of traffic transmitted by any single queue. Custom queuing allows for the creation of 16 queues, and for specific byte-count limits, for both transmission and queue depth, to be applied to each queue. By manipulating these byte-count limits, bandwidth can be coarsely allocated to individual traffic flows. Like priority queuing, custom queuing is configured on an individual interface basis and requires a significant amount of manual configuration and tuning to implement. Figure 4-4 demonstrates the operation of custom queuing.

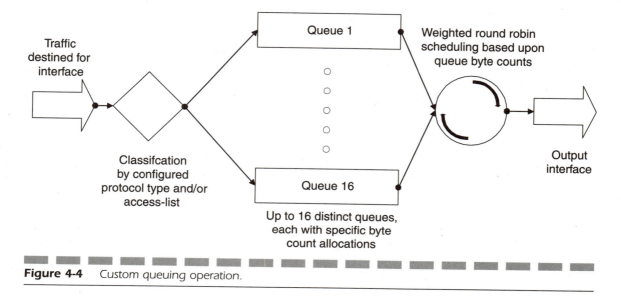

Figure 4-4   *Custom queuing operation.*

Configuring Custom Queuing for Voice Traffic

Like priority queuing, custom queuing requires a significant amount of manual configuration. The steps are similar as well. First the traffic must be classified and queued, then each queue's output rate must be specified, and finally, the queuing technique must be applied to the output interface.

Classification is performed by protocol or access list as in priority queuing. For the voice over IP example, the following access list applies.

```
access-list 150 permit udp any any range 16384 16484
access-list 150 permit tcp any any eq 1720
```

To assign the classified traffic to a queue, the queue-list command is used. For the example, the following is appropriate:

```
queue-list 1 protocol ip 1 list 150
```

With custom queuing, the nonclassified traffic must assigned to a queue using the following command.

```
queue-list 1 default 2
```

Once the queues are defined, they should be assigned byte counts to specify how much from each queue may be transmitted before processing the next queue. This is done with the byte-count option of the queue-list command. The following configuration text applies to the example.

```
queue-list 1 queue 1 byte-count 8000
queue-list 1 queue 2 byte-count 2000
```

Note that the byte-count command does not specify a bit rate; it simply defines how many bytes to process before servicing the next queue. The approximate percentage of bandwidth allocated to each queue can be computed by dividing the queue's byte count by the sum of the byte counts for all of the queues in the queue list. Also, remember that the number represents the number of bytes, not bits.

The configuration for custom queuing described above follows:

```
interface serial 0/0
 ip address 172.16.1.1 255.255.255.0
 custom-queue-list 1
!
queue-list 1 protocol ip 1 list 150
queue-list 1 default 2
queue-list 1 queue 1 byte-count 8000
queue-list 1 queue 2 byte-count 2000
!
access-list 150 permit udp any any range 16380 16480
access-list 150 permit tcp any any eq 1720
!
```

Weighted Fair Queuing

Weighted fair queuing (WFQ) is an automated way to achieve a level of fairness in bandwidth allocation. WFQ queues all traffic, monitors its throughput, and assigns weights based upon the volume of information being sent. WFQ then attempts to allocate bandwidth to the individual conversations fairly, ensuring that low-bandwidth conversations receive equal access to the interface without being overrun by high-bandwidth applications. Thus WFQ improves the response times for low-bandwidth applications such as Telnet when they are sharing a link with a high-bandwidth application such as FTP. Without WFQ, a train of seven 1500-byte FTP frames could precede a single 64-byte Telnet frame in the interface's FIFO queue. These frames would be transmitted, in order, forcing the Telnet frame to wait for their transmission and leaving the Telnet user wondering when that single character would be echoed back.

With WFQ enabled, the Telnet frame would be identified by the queuing mechanism and scheduled for transmission in between the FTP session's frames. This improves the response time for the Telnet application without significantly impacting the FTP session's performance. Another benefit is that applications experience a more predictable response time which enables TCP to optimize its transmission rates. One of the best features of WFQ is that it requires no configuration other than enabling it. Its dynamic queuing and scheduling enables it to work well with mixed or ambiguous traffic patterns. WFQ's effectiveness has led to its inclusion as the default queuing mechanism on serial interfaces running at less than 2 Mbps. Figure 4-5 depicts how WFQ handles routed traffic.

Configuring Weighted Fair Queuing

Weighted fair queuing is the easiest of the queuing techniques to configure. By default it is enabled on serial interfaces rated 2 Mbps or less. To enable fair queuing, simply enter the interface command:

```
fair-queue
```

WFQ's default settings are adequate for most situations, but Cisco allows customization in order to meet a wider array of requirements. The

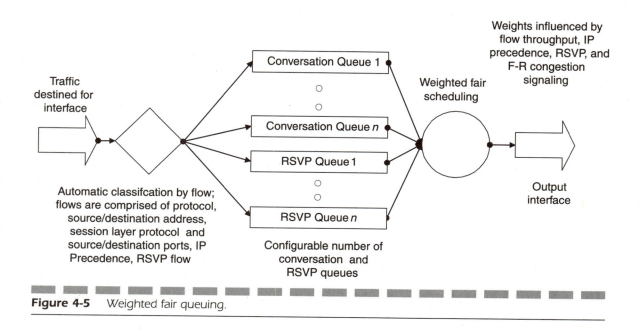

Figure 4-5   *Weighted fair queuing.*

configurable elements are congestive discard threshold, the number of conversation or flow queues available, and the number of queues which may be reserved by RSVP.

The congestive discard threshold specifies how many packets may be queued in each flow's queue. The default is 64 and is usually adequate. Acceptable values are powers of 2 from 2 through 4096 (i.e., 2, 4, 8, 16,…).

The number of conversation queues available controls how many different conversations the router will monitor. The default is 256. Again, this default is usually sufficient. You can monitor the maximum number of queues utilized using the command:

```
show queue interface number
```

Sample output follows with the maximum number of simultaneous active queues experienced by the interface shown in boldface type.

```
sh queue s0/0
Input queue: 0/75/0 (size/max/drops); Total output drops: 426
Queueing strategy: weighted fair
Output queue: 0/64/414 (size/threshold/drops)
 Conversations 0/11 (active/max active)
 Reserved Conversations 0/0 (allocated/max allocated)
```

The number of queues available for RSVP places a limit on how many reservations the WFQ engine will support. Since RSVP links its reservations with WFQ's scheduling engine, it is important to keep reservation queues available. The default value for WFQ is 0. However, enabling RSVP automatically configures WFQ to reserve 1000 queues for RSVP. This capacity is more than sufficient for almost all applications. The value may be set to any integer between 0 and 1000.

To modify WFQ's default configuration, these parameters may be specified after the fair-queue statement. The syntax follows:

```
fair-queue [congestive-discard-threshold [dynamic-queues
    [reservable-queues]]]
```

where

congestive-discard-threshold = depth, in packets, of each queue
dynamic-queues = maximum number of queues (256 is the default)
reservable-queues = number of queues which RSVP may reserve

PPP Enhancements

The link fragmenting and interleaving feature of Multilink Point-to-Point Protocol offers several enhancements which benefit delay sensitive traffic, such as voice. The original intention of link fragmenting and interleaving (LFI) was to improve efficiency when transmitting large packets over multiple parallel links. Rather than sending an entire packet down one link in a multilink bundle, LFI fragments the packet and spreads out the transmission of the fragments over the parallel links. Thus LFI reduces latency since more of the packet is actually in transit at any given time, and increases link utilization since traffic is more evenly split amongst the multiple paths. LFI is roughly analogous to the difference between the serial and parallel ports on a PC. When presented with a byte to transmit, the serial port must send each bit, one by one, down the link, while the parallel port can send the entire byte at once, by breaking it into 8 bits and sending 1 bit over eight different paths concurrently.

LFI's application for voice-carrying IP networks is somewhat different. As we know, one of the bigger challenges for voice and data integration is controlling end-to-end delay, especially when working with low-speed links. Since IP uses variable-length datagrams, it is extremely difficult to predict delay. In the bursty, best-effort datacentric world, large datagrams are preferred because they improve efficiency. However, the serialization delay (the time required to place the actual bits on the physical wire) associated with large frames make large datagrams the enemy of delay-sensitive traffic. A single 1500-byte frame intermixed into a stream of 80-byte voice frames can introduce an unacceptable amount of delay, because the voice packets will be queued behind the large frame and will have to wait for the larger packet's transmission before gaining access to the link.

Consider the serialization delays associated with the link rates and datagram sizes in Table 4-1. Remembering the 250-ms delay budget, it's easy to see how a single 1500-byte FTP datagram sent over a 56-kbps link could ruin the delay budget.

LFI overcomes the problem of variable-length frames by fragmenting frames into smaller fixed-size chunks. The fragmentation is performed after the standard queuing is applied; all frames are susceptible to being fragmented. The size of the fragments is configurable in time measurements of milliseconds. The default is 30 ms, but voice applications require 20 ms to reduce jitter. Referencing Table 4-1, we can see that frames larger that 128 bytes would require fragmentation when using a 56-kbps link since their serialization delay would exceed 20 ms. We can

TABLE 4-1

Serialization Delay*

Packet Size, bytes	Link Rate Access, bps						
	56	128	256	512	640	768	1536
40	5.71	2.50	1.25	0.63	0.50	0.42	0.21
64	9.14	4.00	2.00	1.00	0.80	0.67	0.33
80	11.43	5.00	2.50	1.25	1.00	0.83	0.42
128	18.29	8.00	4.00	2.00	1.60	1.33	0.67
256	36.57	16.00	8.00	4.00	3.20	2.67	1.33
512	73.14	32.00	16.00	8.00	6.40	5.33	2.67
1500	214.29	93.75	46.88	23.44	18.75	15.63	7.81

*Time in ms.

also see that it is not necessary to fragment frames on links of 640 kbps or greater with the default mtu of 1500 bytes because the serialization delay for a 1500-byte frame is less than 19 ms at that speed. The fragmenting gives packet data an ATM-like quality in that all frames are segmented into smaller, more predictable chunks.

This fragmentation would just waste processing power and link bandwidth if it did not include a way to ensure that high-priority traffic was serviced. To transport time-sensitive data, a special queue can be configured which will contain only RTP traffic using the ip rtp reserve command. This queue is similar to priority queuing, but acts at the fragment (subpacket) layer and ensures that RTP packet segments gain access to the line in a timely manner. In practice RTP fragments are sandwiched in-between fragments from a larger frame allowing them access to the line on time, without interrupting other traffic. The receiving router reassembles each datagram and forwards them accordingly. LFI effectively emulates a point-to-point ATM link, but forgoes the structure, signaling, and overhead associated with ATM. Figure 4-6 depicts how LFI works in conjunction with weighted fair queuing.

Configuring Multilink PPP and LFI

Multilink PPP with LFI can be configured for one or more links. That is, it is not necessary to have multiple links bundled together in order to use

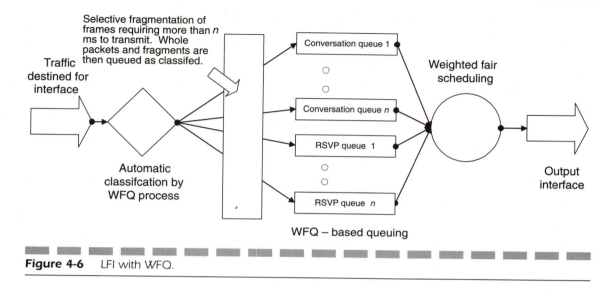

Figure 4-6   LFI with WFQ.

LFI. The basic steps are to enable multilink PPP, enable LFI, and then finetune its performance.

To enable MLPPP on a standard serial interface, first define a virtual template and virtual template interface:

```
!
interface Virtual-template1
 ip address 192.168.1.1 255.255.255.0
 multilink virtual-template 1
```

Then add the `ppp multilink interface` commands for LFI, including reducing the fragment delay and enabling the RTP interleaving using the following commands:

```
ppp multilink
ppp multilink interleave
ppp multilink fragment-delay 20
ip rtp reserve 16384 100 1000
```

where

`ppp multilink interleave` enables the fragment interleaving
`ppp multilink fragment-delay` sets the maximum fragment size in ms
`ip rtp reserve` sets the base UDP port for VoIP traffic
  100 = the range of port numbers
1000 = the maximum bandwidth in kbps allocated for the RTP traffic

EXAMPLE   An MPP with LFI example follows, showing a voice-enabled 3600 router connected to another 3600 router over a fractional T1 link. The configuration excerpt for one 3600 is

```
!
hostname 3600A
!
multilink virtual-template 1
!
interface Virtual-template1
  ip address 192.168.1.1 255.255.255.0
  ppp multilink
  ppp multilink interleave
  ppp multilink fragment-delay 20
  ip rtp reserve 16384 100 384
!
interface serial0/0
  bandwidth 512
  encapsulation ppp
  no ip address
  ppp multilink
  multilink-group 1
!
```

Traffic Shaping

With IOS v11.2, Cisco introduced generic traffic shaping to help control the rate of traffic flow through the router. Generic traffic uses a basic token-bucket mechanism to limit the output rate of traffic. Generic traffic shaping operates at the interface descriptor block (IDB) level within the software, making it applicable to both physical and logical interfaces. This means that it can be used on subinterfaces, as well as physical interfaces. It can be applied to all traffic through the interface or to a select set of traffic identified by an access list.

The token-bucket algorithm is defined by an average bit rate, a traffic burst size, and a time interval. The three are bound by the equation

$$\text{Average bit rate} = \text{burst size} / \text{time interval}$$

This means that for any time interval, the output traffic should not exceed the average bit rate.

By default, the burst size is set to the bit rate divided by 8. Solving the above equation for the time interval, we can see that this makes the default time interval $\frac{1}{8}$ of a second or 125 ms. Given that the average bit rate is measured over a time period and is not an instantaneous value, the actual transmission rate of the traffic can vary significantly as long as the actual amount of data transferred over the time interval is not greater than the burst size. The following example illustrates this.

EXAMPLE

Generic traffic shaping is configured to limit outbound traffic on a frame relay subinterface to 64 kbps. The port rate for the interface is 256 kbps. Since outbound traffic must be transmitted at the port rate, traffic shaping slows the output of packets every time interval. In this example the burst size is set to 64 kbps/8 s, or 8000 bits. Accordingly, the time interval is ⅛ s or 125 ms. This means that every 125 ms, the interface transmits 8000 bits of data over the PVC. However, since the interface is transmitting at the 256-kbps port rate, it takes only 31.25 ms to transmit the allotted 8000 bits. This means that every 125 ms, the router transmits 8000 bits of data for 31.25 ms and then waits 93.75 ms before transmitting more data over the PVC. The graph in Figure 4-7 represents this.

While policing traffic over 125-ms intervals is effective for most purposes, you may want more control over the rate of traffic flow. An increase in control can be accomplished by specifying smaller burst sizes, because these will mandate a higher sampling frequency or shorter time intervals.

It is important to note that the router completes transmission of frames regardless of whether the remaining bits in the frame have exceeded the burst size. In other words, if the burst size is 8000 bits, and the router has already transmitted 7500 bits during the current time interval and the next frame is a 1500 bytes long, the router will transmit the 1500-byte frame before waiting for the next time interval.

Figure 4-7
Generic traffic shaping.

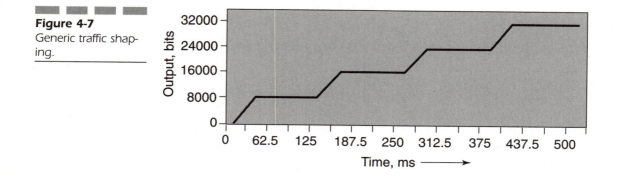

Generic traffic shaping can be configured on a per-interface basis using the traffic-shape interface command described below:

```
traffic-shape rate bit-rate [burst-size [excess-burst-size]]
```

where

bit-rate = the desired output rate. It is specified in bits per second, so 64 kbps must be entered as 64000.

burst-size = the number of bits allowed to be transmitted during a time interval. Specifying the burst-size parameter is optional. If it is not specified, the router derives its value by dividing the bit rate by 8.

excess-burst-size = the maximum number of bits that can exceed the burst size in the first interval in a congestion event.

When applying generic traffic shaping to a frame-relay interface or subinterface, the bit rate should be set to the PVC's CIR, the burst size should be set to committed burst size B_c, and the excess burst size should be set to the excess burst size, or B_e, for the PVC.

EXAMPLE

The following is an example of generic traffic shaping for frame-relay PVC. To apply generic traffic shaping to a 32-kbps PVC on a 56-kbps circuit with a B_c of 16 kb, and a B_e of 4000 kb, the configuration would be as follows:

```
interface serial0/0
 description Frame Relay circuit XXX
 encapsulation frame-relay
 frame-relay lmi-type ansi
 no ip address
 bandwidth 56
!
interface serial0/0.1
 description Subinterface to site Y (DLCI-365)
 ip address 192.168.1.1 255.255.255.0
 bandwidth 32
 traffic-rate 32000 16000 4000
 frame-relay interface-dlci 365
!
```

The traffic-rate command mirrors the frame-relay class of service parameters agreed to by the network provider. In practice, the router would transmit an average of 16,000 bits over half-second intervals and, when extra traffic was present, transmit up to 20,000 bits ($B_c + B_e$) every half-second. When applied to frame-relay interfaces, generic traffic shaping will respond to BECNs by reducing the output rate to the committed information rate. This is discussed in more detail in the chapter on frame relay QoS.

In designing voice networks, the goal is to avoid both congestion and dropped frames. Therefore, it is a good practice to set the excess burst size to 0. This limits traffic rates to the committed rate and avoids packet loss within the frame-relay network.

Generic traffic shaping can also limit the rate at which traffic is transmitted to a specific destination through an interface using access lists to classify the traffic. In voice networks, generic traffic shaping can be effective at limiting the rate of nonvoice traffic. The interface command `traffic-shape group` in conjunction with an access list is used to accomplish this. The interface command syntax is

```
traffic-shape group access-list bit-rate [burst-size [excess-burst-
size]]
```

where `bit-rate`, `burst-size`, and `excess-burst-size` maintain the same definitions as with the traffic-rate command.

EXAMPLE

The following is an example of a traffic group. In order to ensure that there are 24 kbps of bandwidth available for two VoIP sessions, an administrator may wish to limit other traffic to 32 kbps on a 56-kbps dedicated circuit. The configuration would be as follows:

```
!
interface serial 0/1
 description 56 kbps link to site B circuit ID:
 encapsulation ppp
 ip address 172.16.0.1 255.255.255.0
 bandwidth 56
 traffic-shape group 140 32000 4000 0
!
!
access-list 140 deny udp any any range 16384 16624
access-list 140 permit ip any any
!
```

The traffic-shape group command uses the filter created by access list 140 to determine which packets are shaped by the token-bucket shaper. Access list 140 simply tells the shaper to exclude all RTP voice packets from the filter, but to include all other outbound IP traffic in the filter. In practice, this example may not be optimum because it limits data traffic to 32 kbps, even when voice traffic is not present.

Generic traffic shaping is an effective tool for smoothing out traffic bursts and subsequently minimizing congestion and packet loss in the network. In voice networks, it is often combined with another QoS technique because although it provides a means for controlling congestion, it does not address latency issues.

Resource Reservation Protocol

Resource Reservation Protocol (RSVP) is an IETF standard for the dynamic setup of quality of service reservations from source to destination through an IP network. It differs from the most other QoS mechanisms in that it is requested by the end systems and that QoS is dynamically allocated by RSVP-capable devices in the network. RSVP support involves the signaling and queuing functions to honor the QoS requests. RSVP is requested on a per-flow basis, which means it is application specific and is unidirectional in nature.

Cisco routers support host-based RSVP requests and can also act as proxy and reserve bandwidth on behalf of non-RSVP-capable applications. Router-based RSVP support includes two decision components. The first is admission control, which determines whether the router is capable of supporting the requested QoS. The second is policy control, which verifies whether the requesting user is allowed to make a reservation.

Signaling

RSVP senders initiate the process by sending an RSVP path message to the receiver(s). The path messages are processed by each intermediary router and forwarded to the next hop toward the receiver. In processing the message, the RSVP-enabled router stores the IP address of the previous hop's router as a path state in memory. This enables the path state to contain the return path for traffic associated with the sender, which is important because RSVP reservation requests are made by the receivers and must follow the same path the data will use. The path messages include a sender tspec defining the characteristics of the traffic to be sent and an adspec which is optional, allowing the intermediary router to "advertise" its resource availability.

Upon reception of an RSVP path message, receiving hosts issue a RSVP resv message to reserve the appropriate QoS within the forwarding path. The resv message includes a filterspec and a flowspec. The filterspec provides the information the router needs to distinguish traffic for the reservation from all other traffic. It contains source and destination IP addresses, protocol type (TCP/UDP), and transport-layer source and destination port numbers. The flowspec specifies the type of traffic reservation requested including the bit rate and QoS type of service.

QoS Types and Queuing

The two types of QoS in RSVP are *guaranteed service* and *controlled load*. Guaranteed service specifies a bit rate for the flow and defines the maximum tolerable queuing delay and is analogous to ATM's constant bit rate. However, it does not specify or control the variability in packet delivery, just the maximum time between packet delivery. Controlled load service ensures that a very high percentage of the traffic conforming to the negotiated bit rate will be delivered and that the transit delay will be roughly equivalent to the delay experienced on an unloaded network. In other words, controlled load service requests priority for the specified traffic. It attempts to mirror the performance the specified traffic would receive if it were the only traffic on the network.

Cisco married these service types to the two queuing methods best capable of delivering them. Weighted fair queuing is mated to guaranteed service because of its ability to both classify/queue flows and schedule their output in a prioritized, but fair manner. Weighted random early detection is mated to controlled load service because of its ability to provide prioritized and reasonable service expectations through queue management.

Implementation Guidelines

Where to Configure RSVP

RSVP should be enabled on all WAN links involved in transporting voice traffic. While it is possible to enable RSVP on LAN interfaces, it is not recommended since the router has no control over the traffic on the shared medium and the processing required to implement the necessary queuing may degrade throughput on the interface, and thus the performance of the entire router. RSVP does not have to be enabled on the Ethernet interface of a router facing a VoIP source for that router to honor RSVP reservations over its serial interface.

Frame-Relay Considerations

When configuring RSVP on frame-relay interfaces, several considerations must be made.

1. The bandwidth available to RSVP must be configured on both the physical interface (i.e., serial 0) and each subinterface (i.e., serial 0.2) where RSVP will run. The router will permit reservations on a per-subinterface basis providing that the total number of reservations from all of the subinterfaces on a physical interface do not exceed the reservation limit of the entire interface.

2. Multipoint interfaces and subinterfaces do not work well with RSVP because RSVP has no means for distinguishing which dlci the traffic is being reserved for. In other words, RSVP will know only the bandwidth for the entire interface or subinterface and will allow reservations based upon that knowledge. This exposes the risk of RSVP allowing reservations which exceed the capacity of the PVC over which they must be transmitted.

3. RSVP is currently incompatible with frame-relay traffic shaping. If RSVP is enabled for even a single subinterface, frame-relay traffic shaping cannot be used on the entire interface. A workaround for this is to use generic traffic shaping.

Scalability

The scalability of RSVP is suspect, and to date no large-scale implementations exist. Given this, care should be taken to control the size and scope of RSVP's deployment. Given the stringent delay requirements of voice traffic, it is doubtful whether these limits will ever be reached, but care should be taken so that RSVP routers are not subject to an excessive amount of reservations.

Security

To prevent reservations from any unwanted sources, the `ip rsvp neighbor` command should be used to limit the neighbors who are allowed to make reservations. Without this control, any RSVP-capable device may reserve the bandwidth which was planned for voice traffic.

Voice-Specific Reservation Issues

When configuring RSVP for a VoIP dial peer, the dial-peer construct, discussed in a later chapter, makes bandwidth reservations based upon the amount of data which it is providing to the network. This calculation includes the voice traffic plus the IP, UDP, and RTP headers and the frame rate using the following formula:

$$\text{bps} = \text{packet\_size} + \text{IP/UDP/RTP header size} * 50/\text{s}$$

Using the numbers available to dial peer, the equation becomes

$$\text{bps} = (20 \text{ bytes} * 8 \text{ bits/byte}) + (40 \text{ bytes} * 8 \text{ bits/byte}) * 50 \text{ packets/s}$$

which is equal to 24,000 bits/s. Even though G.729 compression brings the payload size down to 8 kbps, the IP overhead is 16 kbps.

However, as discussed earlier, compressed RTP can shrink the 40-byte header to 4–5 bytes. Using CRTP, the equation becomes

$$\text{bps} = (20 \text{ bytes} * 8 \text{ bits/byte}) + (5 \text{ bytes} * 8 \text{ bits/byte}) * 50 \text{ packets/s}$$

which is equal to 10,000 bits/s. Given that all RTP headers cannot be compressed, the value used for planning is usually 11 kbps.

The disparity between the amount of bandwidth the dial peer is reserving and the amount which is actually sent can falsely limit the number of reservations that can be made for VoIP traffic.

Reservation Workaround

A workaround to this problem is to falsely set the interface bandwidth to a number that is greater than the actual bandwidth. An example of this problem and its resolution are presented as follows.

EXAMPLE   A 56-kbps link configured to allow up to 48 kbps for RSVP would allow only two VoIP sessions. In reality, those sessions would only consume 22 kbps of bandwidth and unfairly prevent a third session from being granted a reservation over the link.

Three sessions will consume 33 kbps, so we know that the link is capable of supporting them without consuming the entire link's bandwidth. However, three RSVP requests from dial peers at 24 kbps would require 72 kbps to be allocated to RSVP for the connections to be accepted. By default, RSVP permits only 75 percent of the link's bandwidth to be reserved so the link's bandwidth would have to set 100 kbps to accept all three sessions.

This workaround can have serious effects on other aspects of the network. Specifically, routing protocols such as OSPF and EIGRP use the link's bandwidth to determine optimal routing paths. In simple hub-and-spoke configurations, this may not be an issue, but in more elaborate configurations, improper routing may occur. If this workaround is to be used, the routing topology should be studied to ensure that the modification will not adversely affect operation. Also, if CRTP is disabled for any reason, the link will be oversubscribed.

Non-RSVP Intermediary Routers

RSVP can be implemented within a network where all routers do not support RSVP or all links are not configured for RSVP, but the obvious caveat is that bandwidth allocation and congestion cannot be controlled over those links. Simply put, if the non-RSVP routers and links are fast and lightly loaded, then there's a good chance the reservation will be met. If, however, the non-RSVP links are slow and/or heavily loaded, then there's a good chance that the reservation will not be met.

Configuring RSVP

RSVP is enabled on a per-interface basis and allows for the setting of a maximum reservable bandwidth and a single-reservation maximum bandwidth. The interface command for enabling RSVP is

```
ip rsvp bandwidth [interface-kbps] [single-flow-kbps]
```

where `interface-kbps` represents the maximum bandwidth which can be reserved on the interface and `single-flow-kbps` represents the maximum amount any one reservation will be granted. By default, `interface-kbps` is set to 75 percent of the configured bandwidth for the interface and `single-flow-kbps` is set to `interface-kbps`. If the defaults are used, it is important that the interface bandwidth be accurately configured using the interface command: `bandwidth`. On serial interfaces, the bandwidth defaults to T1 speeds (1536 kbps) so it must be manually configured for subrate interface speeds.

EXAMPLE

An example configuration for a Cisco 3600 connected to a fractional T1 link running at 1024 kbps is presented below.

```
!
interface Serial0/0
 description Fractional T1 to NY
```

```
    ip address 10.3.1.2 255.255.0.0
    ip rsvp bandwidth 768 768
    bandwidth 1024
    ipx network 100
    fair-queue 64 256 1000
    !
```

NOTE: *The router automatically fills in the values for* `interface-kbps` *and* `single-flow-kbps`. *The* `fair-queue` *command is automatically configured by the router to provide up 1000 reservable (RSVP) conversations and limit dynamic conversations (other routed traffic) to 256. These numbers can be modified using the same command, if required.*

To enable RSVP and WRED (discussed later), the interface command `random-detect` must be used. For example,

```
    !
    interface Serial0
     description Fractional T1 to NY
     ip address 10.3.1.2 255.255.0.0
     ip rsvp bandwidth 768 768
     bandwidth 1024
     random-detect
    !
```

EXAMPLE

The following example includes the relevant RSVP configurations for the involved routers. The network comprises a Cisco 3600 voice-enabled router communicating with an AS5300 voice-enabled access server over a T1 link service by the 3600 and a Cisco 4500 at the AS5300 site. The diagram in Figure 4-8 helps clarify the design.

As a review of RSVP operation, Figures 4-9 and 4-10 indicate the setup as messages are communicated. They depict the signaling used when a call is initiated from the 3600.

First, the 3600 sends out the RSVP path message to the AS5300 including the bandwidth requirements in the message. The intermediary 4500 stores the IP address of the 3600's serial port in memory as part of the path state. It then forwards the RSVP path message to the AS5300.

The AS5300 receives the RSVP path, interprets the information, and issues an RSVP reservation request using an RSVP resv message. The intermediary 4500 processes the reservation request, sets up the appropriate filter and bandwidth reservation on serial 0, and forwards the

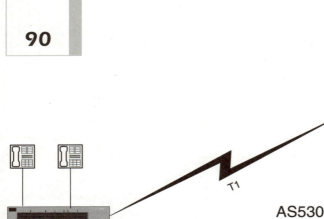

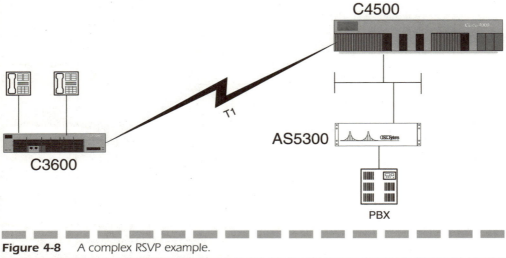

Figure 4-8 A complex RSVP example.

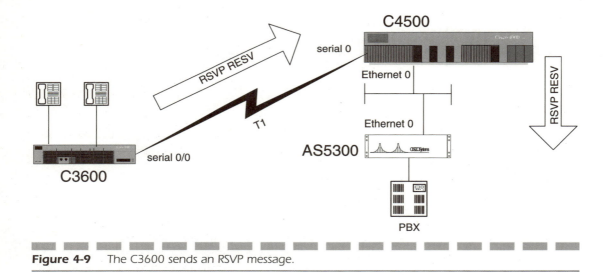

Figure 4-9 The C3600 sends an RSVP message.

RSVP resv message to the 3600. The 3600 processes the reservation request and sets up the appropriate filter and bandwidth reservation on serial 0/0.

Figure 4-9 represents a unidirectional reservation from the C3600 to the AS5300. A second reservation will be made in the opposite direction

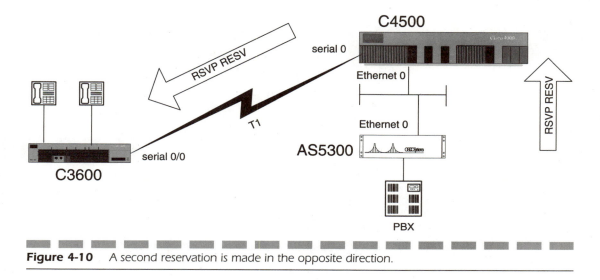

Figure 4-10   A second reservation is made in the opposite direction.

so that bandwidth may be reserved from the AS5300 to C3600. (See Figure 4-10.)

The relevant configurations are provided below:

Router C3600

```
!
interface Serial0/0
 description T1 link to Headquarters
 ip address 172.16.1.2 255.255.255.0
 ip rsvp bandwidth 1152 1152
 bandwidth 1536
 fair-queue 64 256 1000
!
Voice-configuration supporting RSVP
!
```

Router C4500

```
!
interface Ethernet0
 description Ethernet link to AS5300
 ip address 192.168.2.1 255.255.255.0
!
interface Serial0
 description T1 link to Branch Office
 ip address 192.168.1.1 255.255.255.0
 ip rsvp bandwidth 1152 1152
 bandwidth 1536
 fair-queue 64 256 1000
!
```

Access Server AS5300

```
!
interface Ethernet0
 description Ethernet link to C4500
 ip address 192.168.2.2 255.255.255.0
!
Voice-configuration supporting RSVP
!
```

NOTES:

- *The Ethernet ports do not require RSVP configuration.*
- *The serial ports have the bandwidth manually configured to ensure proper reservation limits.*
- *Both serial ports implement RSVP because reservations will be made in both directions.*
- *Details for configuring RSVP-enabled voice traffic will be covered in the chapter on dial peers.*

IP Precedence

Cisco has been leading the charge to enable end-to-end network QoS for IP networks. One of the techniques developed is the utilization of the TOS field within the IP header to provide class of service (CoS). More specifically, the first three bits of the TOS field, called the *IP precedence,* are manipulated. Using these bits, six different classes of service can be defined (actually eight, but two are reserved). Once set, queuing and traffic management functions such as weighted fair queuing, and weighted random early detection interpret and react to these bits in order to provide differentiated service levels. Given that WFQ and WRED are commonly deployed within network backbones, their response to IP precedence-based classifications helps enable network-wide class of service.

The three-bit precedence field provides eight possible settings. The highest two priorities are reserved for use by the internetworking components to ensure priority for routing updates and other important control messages. Most IP end stations ignore the precedence and fill in the fields with zeroes. By default, Cisco routers do not interpret or modify the precedence bits when forwarding IP datagrams. The values for the precedence fields are listed in Table 4-2 in order of increasing priority.

TABLE 4-2

Values for the
Precedence Field

Value	Definition
0	Routine (normal traffic)
1	Priority
2	Immediate
3	Flash
4	Flash override
5	Critical
6	Internet (for network control traffic)
7	Network (for network control traffic)

IP Precedence bits can be set by the source or sending station, or by internetworking equipment transporting the IP packets (routers or advanced switches). Internetworking systems may override the precedence assignment on any or all traffic. This enables network service providers to control the use of IP precedence within their network, and allows enterprise network administrators to gain more control over QoS within their network.

IP Precedence with Voice Traffic

Since a voice-enabled router is the source station for voice over IP traffic, Cisco included a simple mechanism for setting the IP precedence bit for VoIP traffic originating from the router. To accomplish this, Cisco added the command `ip precedence` to the VoIP dial-peer configuration. This allows the precedence bit and, therefore, the network class of service to be set on an individual VoIP session basis. Here is the syntax for the dial-peer command

```
ip precedence n
```

where n is a number from 0 to 5 representing the desired setting. Here is a sample configuration using `ip precedence`.

```
dial-peer voice 99 voip
  destination-pattern 5551234
  ip precedence 5
  session target ipv4:172.16.150.10
 !
```

Policy-Based Routing

Traffic-based control of the IP precedence bits is not quite as easy. It requires the use of either policy-based routing or Cisco's committed access rate features. Policy-based routing provides a means for controlling the flow of traffic through the router based upon predefined policies. Committed access rate is a method of classifying traffic and then limiting its input or output rate through the router interface. CAR is an effective tool for service providers wanting to offer variable access rates to their network and is supported on only the 7200-, 7500-, and RSP7000-based routers. For these reasons we will not discuss CAR in this book.

Policy-based routing has been available since IOS v11.0. Its original intention was to provide a means of selectively overriding the router's normal routing tables and forwarding traffic based upon a router-defined policy. This is helpful in scenarios where an administrative policy or service-level agreement may dictate that a given source's traffic is to transit a specific path, regardless of the lowest cost information provided by the routing protocol. Traffic is classified using extended IP access lists, and therefore policies can be applied based upon source addresses, source/destination address pairs, TCP or UDP port numbers, packet lengths, or a combination of these parameters.

Policy-based routing has now evolved to support classification by and assignment of IP precedence bits. This allows routers to assign the class of service for traffic based upon extended access list criteria.

Configuring Policy-Based Routing

Configuring policy routing involves three steps.

1. Define the traffic to be serviced by the policy.
2. Define the policy to apply to the selected traffic.
3. Determine which router interface(s) to apply the policy to.

Step 1 is done by creating standard or extended IP access lists. Multiple access lists can be applied to a single policy, but one should be sufficient. Alternatively, traffic can be classified by packet length. Once the method of classification is determined, a route map must be created. Route maps are commonly used to perform complex route filtering for routing protocols, but they also provide the mechanism for performing policy-based routing. Route maps require a tag and a sequence number. The tag simply identifies the route map and the sequence number allows for multiple policies to be part of the same route map by specifying the sequence in which they should be inspected. Within the route-map paragraph the `match` command is used to match traffic by either IP address or by length. The syntax for route-map creation is

```
route-map tag [permit / deny] [sequence-number]
match ip address {access-list-number [... access-list-number]}
match length min max
```

where

$$tag = \text{tag or name of the } route\ map$$
$$sequence\text{-}number = \text{desired sequence number. It must fall between 1 and 255.}$$
$$access\text{-}list\text{-}number = \text{access list or lists used to classify the traffic}$$
$$min \text{ and } max = \text{minimum and maximum byte lengths of the packets to match the filter}$$

NOTE: *It is useful to remember that*

■ *Multiple route map paragraphs with the same tag may be used. Care must be taken to assign the sequence number properly so that they execute in the proper order.*

■ *Multiple access lists can be matched within one match statement.*

■ *The route map can match by IP address, length or both.*

Step 2 completes the route map by using the set command to apply the desired policy. The set command can set the next-hop address for forwarding traffic, the desired output interface, and/or the IP precedence value. The correct syntax for this route map command is

```
route-map tag permit 10
...
  set ip next-hop a.a.a.a
  set ip precedence n
  set interface type num
```

where   *a.a.a.a* is the IP address of the desired adjacent router, and *n* is the desired precedence level. Acceptable numbers are 0–5.

Step 3 applies the policy to the proper input interface. This is done with the IP policy route-map command.

The proper syntax is

```
interface x n
  ip policy route-map tag
```

where `tag` is the tag used in the route-map statement created in steps 1 and 2. For improved performance and reduced CPU strain policy routing can be fast switched using the interface command:

```
ip route-cache policy
```

An example of policy-based routing follows. (See Figure 4-11.)

EXAMPLE   The Ethernet segment serviced by Ethernet 0/0 contains multiple IP workstations. The administrator wants the large FTP transfers between workstation 10.1.1.3 and workstation 10.2.1.3 to transit an Internet Virtual Private Network (VPN) accessed via Ethernet 0/1. The administrator would also like other intersite traffic to transit a 56-kbps link

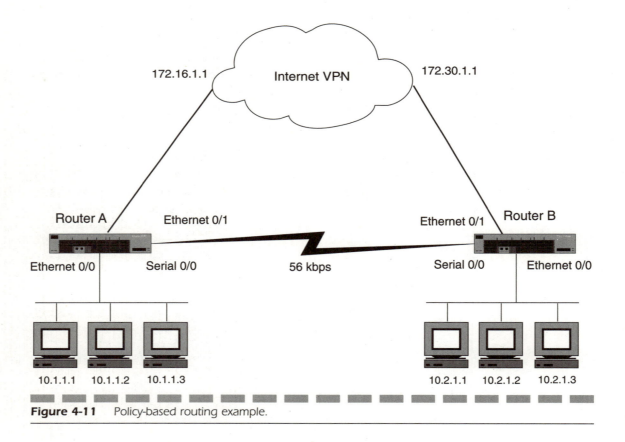

Figure 4-11   Policy-based routing example.

between the sites and for the VoIP traffic to receive a precedence of 5 for preferential treatment by weighted fair queuing.

First, the potential FTP sessions between hosts 10.1.1.3 and 10.2.1.3 need to be identified using an extended IP access list.

Router A

```
access-list 150 permit tcp host 10.1.1.3 host 10.2.1.3 eq ftp
access-list 150 permit tcp host 10.1.1.3 host 10.2.1.3 eq ftp-data
```

Router B

```
access-list 150 permit tcp host 10.2.1.3 host 10.1.1.3 eq ftp
access-list 150 permit tcp host 10.2.1.3 host 10.1.1.3 eq ftp-data
```

Second, the VoIP traffic needs to be identified using a separate extended IP access list.

Router A

```
access-list 151 permit udp any any range 16380 16480
access-list 151 permit tcp any any eq 1720
```

Router B

```
access-list 151 permit udp any any range 16380 16480
access-list 151 permit tcp any any eq 1720
```

Third, the route map needs to match the criteria.

Router A

```
! Match the FTP access-list
!
route-map vpn1 permit 10
 match ip address 150
!
! Match the V/IP access-list
!
route-map vpn1 permit 20
 match ip address 151
!
```

Router B

```
! Match the FTP access-list
!
route-map vpn1 permit 10
 match ip address 150
!
! Match the V/IP access-list
!
route-map vpn1 permit 20
 match ip address 151
!
```

Fourth, the actions must be set for each match.

```
!
route-map vpn1 permit 10
 match ip address 150
 set ip next-hop 172.16.1.1
!
route-map vpn1 permit 20
 match ip address 151
 set ip precedence 5
!
```

Router B

```
!
route-map vpn1 permit 10
 match ip address 150
 set ip next-hop 172.30.1.1
!
route-map vpn1 permit 20
 match ip address 151
 set ip precedence 5
!
```

Lastly, the policy needs to be applied to the input interface on both routers.

Router A

```
interface Ethernet 0/0
 ip address 10.1.1.254 255.255.255.0
 ip policy route-map vpn1
 ip route-cache policy
```

Router B

```
interface Ethernet 0/0
 ip address 10.2.1.254 255.255.255.0
 ip policy route-map vpn1
 ip route-cache policy
```

TIP: *If you are connecting to an unknown network or one which is out of your direct control, it is a good idea to reset the precedence bit for all nonvoice traffic. In the above example this can be accomplished by using a third route-map paragraph. For example, if Router A connected to an insecure LAN, the following statements could be added to Router A's configuration to ensure that only voice over IP traffic received a precedence of 5.*

```
access-list 152 deny udp any any range 16380 16480
access-list 152 deny tcp any any eq 1720
access-list 152 permit ip any any
!
route-map vpn1 permit 30
 match ip address 152
 set ip precedence 0
!
```

Access-list 152 excludes the voice over IP traffic with the first two lines and includes all other traffic with the third line. The route map then assigns a precedence of zero to the included traffic (all non-VoIP). Security in the example could be enhanced by using specific host IP addresses in the access lists instead of the "any" wildcard.

Why Did I Set the Precedence Bit?

The setting of IP precedence bits is important because it enables the easiest method of implementing QoS: the automatic method. Both weighted fair queuing and weighted random early detection automatically respond to precedence bits and allocate greater priority to packets with higher precedence. This means that you do not have to go through special machinations, such as policy routing or custom queuing, in each router the voice traffic will pass through. This is good because it simplifies network design and support efforts and pushes QoS classification to the network edge where it belongs.

WFQ Interaction

As mentioned above, WFQ automatically provides priority to IP datagrams with a higher precedence. Flows with higher precedence values are given $p + 1$ times higher bit rates than traffic with a precedence of 0 where p is the precedence value for the datagram. In other words, a datagram with an IP precedence of 5 will be given 6 times the bandwidth of normal packets.

Cisco's 75xx backbone routers offer additional enhancements including precedence-based WFQ and additional parameters for finetuning WFQ. A brief description of these features is provided below.

If desired, WFQ can be configured to provide precedence-based queuing. This causes WFQ to use a single queue for each precedence level instead of allocating a queue for every active flow. The benefit to this is that it provides a greater distinction between the precedence queues since there are only 8 as opposed to the default of 256 per interface. The drawback is that all traffic is now in a FIFO queue within each precedence level. In other words, weighted fair queuing is only occurring for the 8 precedence queues. The packets within each of these 8 queues are serviced in order of delivery. Hierarchical WFQ solves this, but is not yet available in the IOS. This makes TOS-based queuing advantageous in very low bandwidth environments or environments requiring a high level of differentiation among the classes of service.

In addition to offering multiple queuing strategies, WFQ also allows an administrator to adjust the number and depth of queues available. This is an area where experimentation may lead to improved results, but, more often than not, has a negative impact. With TOS-based queuing, the weights assigned to the each precedence level may also be adjusted. This allows for greater control over the differentiation between each class of service, but again, the defaults work well in most environments. Here is the syntax for the WFQ modifications.

To enable TOS-based WFQ use the interface command:

```
fair-queue tos-based
```

To adjust the total queue space available for all queues use the interface command:

```
fair-queue aggregate-limit n
```

To adjust the total queue space available for any single queue use the interface command:

```
fair-queue aggregate-limit n
```

Weighted Random Early Detection

Random early detection (RED) is a congestion avoidance technique developed in the 1980s to overcome the congestion collapse issues associated with TCP/IP traffic. RED guards against extreme congestion conditions by proactively managing queue depths within the router. This results in better link utilization, improved throughput, and more graceful traffic reduction under congestion conditions.

Operation of TCP

To understand RED, a brief review of TCP's congestion control is required. TCP is dynamic in that it reacts to changing network latency and throughput conditions. TCP measures the time intervals between transmitting a segment of data and the associated acknowledgment from the receiving station. This provides an estimate of network latency and host response times which TCP uses to vary the size of the send window. The size of TCP's send window controls the rate at which TCP transmits because it dictates how many unacknowledged datagrams may be sent at any one time. Under normal conditions the window size is not varied, rather minor variations in round-trip time cause TCP to adjust its thresholds for minimum and maximum round-trip times.

When Does TCP React?

1. If the maximum round-trip time threshold is exceeded before receiving an acknowledgment, TCP will assume that the packet has been delayed or lost and will retransmit the lost information, set the congestion window to 1 segment, and then implement slow start.

2. If the receiving station indicates to TCP that it is missing one datagram of a segment, TCP will retransmit and back off by halving the congestion window and performing congestion avoidance.

Slow Start

Slow start seeks to optimize TCP throughput by increasing the size of TCPs congestion window upon receipt of successful ACKs from the receiver. At session startup and after a timeout, the congestion window is set to 1. Slow start increases the transmission rate almost exponentially until either the advertised window (the one negotiated by the receiver at session startup) is reached or more congestion is experienced. The exponential ramp up makes the term slow start a bit of a misnomer.

Congestion Avoidance

Congestion avoidance occurs in response to lost network datagrams and is more cautious than slow start in that it increases TCP's transmission rate linearly. After a lost datagram is identified, TCP cuts the congestion window in half. This will usually decrease the transmission rate by half. Congestion avoidance then increments the congestion window with a conservative linear scale until it equals the advertised window size or further congestion is experienced.

In summary, dropping packets associated with TCP flows is a way of informing TCP that it needs to slow down. TCP reacts by slowing its transmission rate through shrinking its transmit window size, usually by one half, and retransmitting the lost data. One of two methods is then employed to increase the transmission back to its optimal rate. On its own, this scenario is both benign and common.

Congestion Collapse

Congestion collapse occurs when traffic overwhelms a link bringing about the following chain of events.

- Router buffers begin to fill up.
- Packets are delayed, increasing latency and sometimes causing retransmissions.
- Retransmissions add to the traffic level.
- Router buffers overflow and arriving traffic is dropped.
- Dropped traffic causes more retransmissions.
- Source stations initiate slow start or congestion avoidance.
- Source stations ramp up transmission rates once again leading to overflowing buffers.
- Larger numbers of packets are dropped and the scenario starts again.

The chain of events above indicates a cyclic event where traffic continually rises, then drops off severely, then rises again. This is demonstrated in Figure 4-12 representing the traffic pattern over a link when congestion collapse is being experienced.

The steep drop off after buffer overflow is due to packets being simultaneously dropped from many different TCP sessions. As a result slow start is initiated and the sessions ramp up again. The massive drop off in traffic is called *tail drop* because all of the packets that could not fit into the overflowing queue are dropped.

Synchronization

Congestion collapse is exacerbated by a tendency for all flows over the link to synchronize and experience congestion at the same time. This

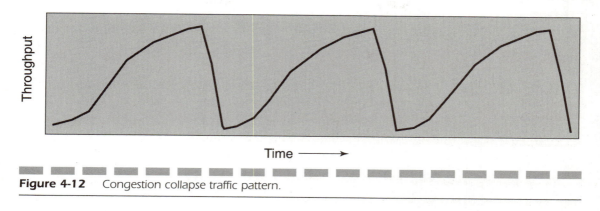

Figure 4-12   Congestion collapse traffic pattern.

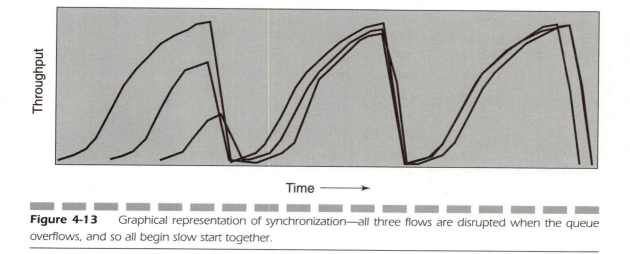

Figure 4-13   *Graphical representation of synchronization—all three flows are disrupted when the queue overflows, and so all begin slow start together.*

produces the uneven traffic pattern shown in Figure 4-13; this traffic pattern does not make efficient use of the available bandwidth. This problem is caused by the fact that massive congestion causes large buffer overruns resulting in the loss of packets from many different flows simultaneously. The flows that experienced packet loss then all begin slow start and quickly overwhelm the link again. This time, packets from newer streams may be lost, and they too will become part of the same pattern. This coming together of flows is called *synchronization*.

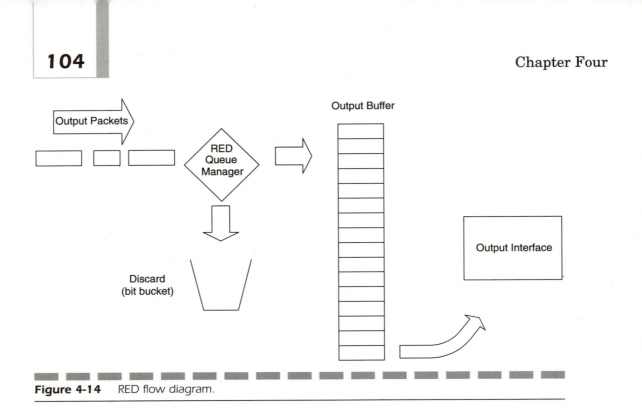

Figure 4-14   RED flow diagram.

RED

Random early detection addresses these problems by monitoring output queue depths and dropping packets from random sessions in order to limit the depth of the queue. This has two important effects. The first is that congestion collapse is avoided because the queues aren't allowed to overflow. The second is that the flow synchronization is avoided because packets from multiple flows aren't dropped at once. The random nature of the drops also ensures that the same streams aren't continually penalized. Figure 4-14 is a graphical depiction of packet flow with RED enabled.

RED Algorithm

The RED queue manager function in the diagram above uses the following algorithm for directing packets.

Packet arrives at interface queue
If current average queue size is less than the minimum threshold
    Then queue the packet
Else if the current average queue size is between the minimum and maximum
thresholds

Then calculate the probability for dropping the packet
If yes
Then Drop the packet
Else if no
Then queue the packet
Else if the current average queue size is above the maximum threshold
Then drop the packet

The computation of average queue size and probability directly affect the behavior of RED. Average queue size is computed using an exponential weighting factor. A larger weighting factor causes RED to react more slowly to queue-size changes, while a smaller weighting factor causes RED to react more quickly to queue-size changes.

The probability associated with dropping a packet is controlled by the current queue size and a mark-probability denominator. Larger values of the mark-probability denominator allow more packets to be queued before discards occur. Lower values of the mark-probability denominator make RED more aggressive at packet discard.

Why Use RED ?

RED is specifically designed to work with TCP flows, so how can it be effective in UDP-based VoIP networks? For the answers we look to WRED. Cisco's implementation of RED includes a feature called weighted RED. Weighted RED provides differentiated packet-drop thresholds for the different IP precedence-based classes of service and RSVP. This means that voice traffic tagged with a precedence of 5 or controlled by RSVP will enjoy much higher discard thresholds than normal traffic. WRED parameters can be further tuned to provide even higher levels of differentiation among the different classes of service. Also, WRED does not place a significant strain on router resources (memory or CPU) and is supported by all IOS-based router platforms; therefore it is easy to deploy throughout most networks.

WRED Details

WRED queues traffic according to precedence values. Once queued, the RED algorithm is run against each queue. Different thresholds are set for each queue so that preferential service can be provided by discarding lower-priority traffic first. More aggressive discard thresholds are applied to the lower-precedence queues. WRED operation is depicted in Figure 4-15.

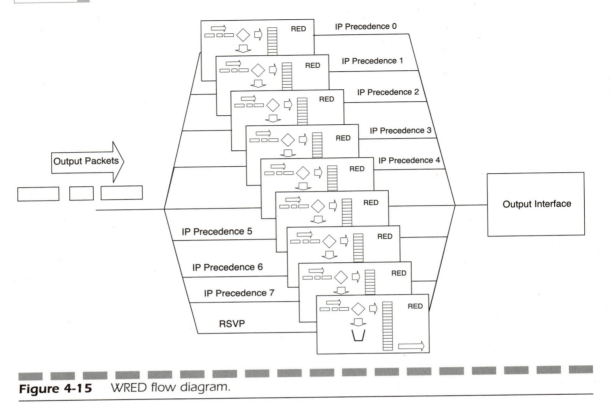

Figure 4-15 WRED flow diagram.

By default, the maximum queue-depth threshold is determined by a function of the interface speed and the output buffers available for the interface. The default values for the minimum queue-size threshold are based upon a fraction of the maximum threshold. The default values used for each class of service are presented in Table 4-3.

Configuring WRED

WRED is enabled using the interface command:

```
random-detect
```

The default value for the exponential weighting factor which affects the responsiveness of WRED is 9. The configurable range is 1 to 16, with 16 making RED the least responsive to queue-depth changes and provid-

TABLE 4-3

Default Values for Queue-Size Threshold

Class of Service	Default Minimum Threshold (Fraction of Max)
IP precedence 0	9/18
IP precedence 1	10/18
IP precedence 2	11/18
IP precedence 3	12/18
IP precedence 4	13/18
IP precedence 5	14/18
IP precedence 6	15/18
IP precedence 7	16/18
RSVP	17/18

ing smoothest response. The command to modify the exponential weighting factor is

```
random-detect exponential-weighting-constant n.
```

where n is the desired value for the constant. Valid numbers are 1–16.

The default value for the mark-probability denominator is 10. To modify the minimum and maximum thresholds and mark-probability denominator for different classes of service, the following interface command is used:

```
random-detect precedence p min-threshold max-threshold mark-prob-
denominator
```

where

p = IP precedence tag. Valid values are 0–7 and rsvp.

min-threshold = lowest queue size at which RED will begin random discards. Valid values are 1–4096.

max-threshold = largest queue size before RED begins dropping all packets. Valid values are from min-threshold–4096

mark-prob-denominator = mark-probability denominator which influences the number of packets that can be queued before discards occur. Valid values range from 1 to 65535.

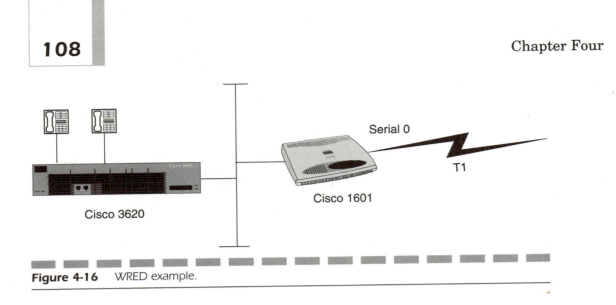

Figure 4-16   WRED example.

EXAMPLE   When configuring WRED on an intermediary router in a VoIP network, we want to prioritize voice packets and aggressively and discard lower-precedence traffic (Figure 4-16).

To enable WRED on the 1601 router, the configuration would be:

```
interface serial0
 ip address 10.1.1.1 255.255.0.0
 random-detect
 !
```

The 3620 sets the IP precedence bit to 5 for all VoIP packets so, by default, WRED will prioritize these packets. In order to tweak its priority slightly, the minimum threshold can be increased using the random-detect precedence commands. Similarly, low-priority traffic can be more aggressively discarded by lowering the mark-probability denominator for the routine precedence level.

Since the IOS calculates the value for maximum threshold automatically, it is a good idea to use the value it computed. To do this, enable WRED using just the commands shown above. Then use the command show queueing red to reveal the values computed by the IOS. Sample output follows:

```
R5#sh queueing red int s 0
Current RED queue configuration:
 Interface: Serial0 Exp-weight-constant: 9
  Class  Min-th  Max-th   Mark-prob
   0      20      40       1/10
   1      22      40       1/10
   2      24      40       1/10
```

```
3      26     40     1/10
4      28     40     1/10
5      31     40     1/10
6      33     40     1/10
7      35     40     1/10
rsvp   37     40     1/10
```

Using the precomputed value for `max-threshold`, the interface parameters can be adjusted more intelligently to support the goals of increased priority for voice traffic and more aggressive discarding of lower-priority traffic. The interface commands for this are presented below with the changes in bold.

```
random-detect precedence 0 20 40 6
random-detect precedence 1 22 40 10
random-detect precedence 2 24 40 10
random-detect precedence 3 26 40 10
random-detect precedence 4 28 40 10
random-detect precedence 5 37 40 12
random-detect precedence 6 33 40 10
random-detect precedence 7 35 40 10
random-detect precedence rsvp 37 40 10
```

SUMMARY

This chapter discussed a number of techniques of which IP traffic can take advantage to receive preferential service, reduced jitter, reduced packet loss, and lower end-to-end delay. These benefits all enable the more efficient transport of voice traffic across existing IP networks. In future chapters we will discuss how to select the appropriate features and combine them with voice-specific features to provide a solid network for the transport of voice over IP traffic.

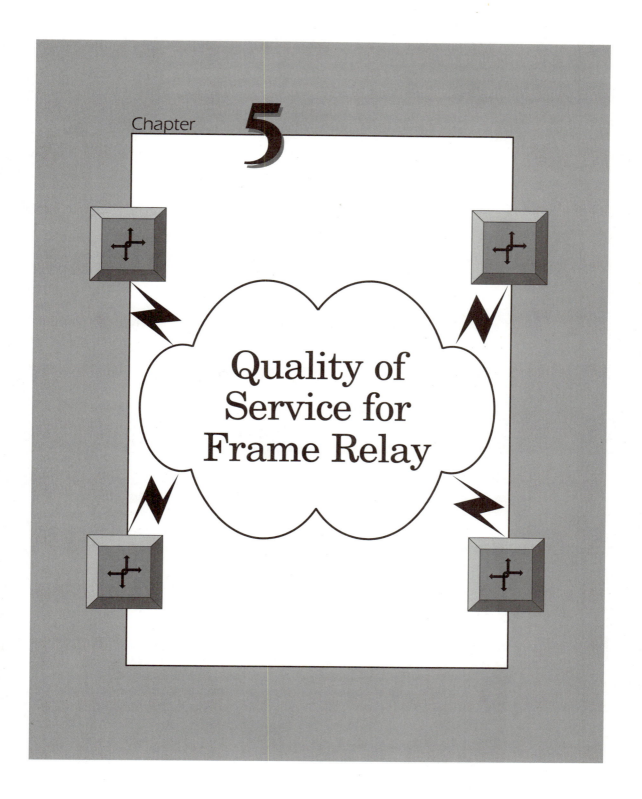

Chapter **5**

Quality of
Service for
Frame Relay

Introduction

This chapter will cover the following:

- Frame-relay QoS: class of service and congestion management
- Router-based frame-relay quality of service configuration
- Challenges for frame-relay networks and QoS
- Future alternatives

Quality of service for frame relay is another challenge in the networking field. Different WAN switch vendors and different carriers provide different levels of support for frame-relay QoS, depending upon their switch architecture and network design. Router-based frame-relay QoS mechanisms are important because they enable the router to intelligently interface with the frame-relay network and provide a more solid platform for enabling the transport of voice traffic over the network. This chapter provides a brief review of frame-relay-specific QoS mechanisms, router-based traffic management techniques, and a guideline for implementing the various schemes.

Frame-Relay Quality of Service

Frame-relay-based QoS can be divided into two categories: class of service and congestion management. *Class of service* (CoS) is the ability of the network to provide differentiable levels of network performance, while *congestion management* proactively and reactively controls network traffic flow by monitoring and reacting to congestion situations in switches and links.

Class of Service

The frame-relay standards define several classes of service parameters to provide a common base upon which frame-relay networks can be designed and implemented. Frame-relay classes of service parameters deal primarily with bandwidth availability and do not directly address latency or variability. The frame-relay standards also define a rudimentary traffic management scheme to help control and shape the flow of traffic through frame-relay networks. These class of service and congestion management techniques are defined below.

Standards-based class of service is defined on an individual PVC basis. This means that each PVC on a physical port may have a different class of service assignment. The standards-based CoS parameters deal with bandwidth and bandwidth availability. Measurement and policing of latency or delay variability are not part of the frame-relay standards. Some carriers, however, do offer latency guarantees for their domestic and international networks. The three frame-relay class of service parameters are: CIR, B_e, and B_c.

Committed burst size, or B_c, defines the amount of data that the network will accept during a given period of time. B_c is measured in bits and is used along with a time interval to determine the value for CIR. Both the time interval and CIR are described below. The use of the word "burst" in the title can be misleading. It is important to remember that traffic is transmitted at the actual physical line access rate or port rate. Each packet represents a burst of information onto that line. This should not be confused with the concept of bursting above a PVC's committed rate.

B_e defines the amount of data, beyond B_c, which the network will attempt to transfer during a given period of time. Like B_c, B_e is measured in bits, but unlike B_c, B_e traffic is not guaranteed to be transferred. When traffic exceeds the agreed-on value for B_c, it is then measured against B_e. Excess traffic will be transferred on a best-effort basis.

Committed rate measurement interval, or T_c, specifies the period at which traffic is measured. T_c is defined in fractions of seconds. Typical rates for T_c are from 0.5 to 2 s. Higher values for T_c allow for greater variability in latency and traffic rate, while lower values of T_c provide more consistent traffic delivery rates.

Committed information rate, or CIR, specifies the minimum transmission rate between PVC endpoints supported by the network. CIR is measured in kilobits per second (kbps) and is the ratio of B_c to T_c. It serves as a lower bound for communication supported by the network under normal conditions.

Excess information rate, or EIR, specifies the amount of traffic above CIR that the network agrees to transport for a period of time. The length of that period varies from implementation to implementation. Nominally it is one interval of T_c. EIR is derived from the slope of B_e over T_c and, accordingly, is measured in kbps. The addition of CIR and EIR represents the maximum transient capacity for a PVC. Traffic exceeding CIR + EIR may be transported, but there are no guarantees.

To better understand these parameters, let's look at the following equations:

$$\text{CIR} = B_c/T_c$$

Solving for T_c yields

$$T_c = B_c/\text{CIR}$$

Solving for B_c yields

$$B_c = T_c * \text{CIR}$$

B_e is calculated using

$$\left(\frac{[B_c + B_e]}{B_c}\right) \times \text{CIR} \leq \text{link access rate}$$

$$\text{EIR} = B_e/T_c$$

The relationship among CIR, B_c, B_e, and T_c is important. The following facts and observations are drawn from these relationships:

1. Decreasing T_c (to provide more granular measurements) requires that B_c be reduced, which in turn limits the buffering capability of the network.
2. Similarly, increasing B_c to allow more burstiness requires that T_c be increased, resulting in less granular measurements and, therefore, more variability in frame delivery.
3. $B_c + B_e$ represents the maximum amount of information the network agrees to accept during any period of T_c.
4. The sum of $B_c + B_e$ must be less than or equal to the port access rate.

Congestion Management

Standards-based congestion management in frame-relay networks is handled in two ways: the setting of explicit congestion notification bits within frames and the marking of discard eligible bits within frames. The congestion notification bits signal to the frame-relay terminal equipment (the routers) that there is congestion somewhere along the path of the PVC, while the setting of discard eligible bits identifies traffic which a switch will drop first during periods of congestion. Figure 5-1 identifies

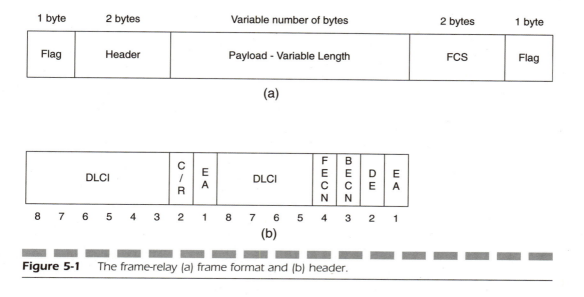

Figure 5-1   *The frame-relay (a) frame format and (b) header.*

both the frame-relay frame format and the position of these bits within the header.

The forward explicit congestion notification (FECN) bit can be set by a frame-relay switch when the switch or the network is experiencing congestion over the links which support the virtual circuit. FECNs notify the receiving endpoint about congestion within the network. Ideally, the receiving station would recognize the FECN and slow down the transmitter by shrinking the window size, delaying the sending of ACKs, or other higher layer function. Unfortunately, the mapping of the layer 2 FECN to an upper-layer equivalent is only done for DECNET and CLNS traffic, so, in practice FECNs serve little purpose outside of statistical.

Switches can also set the backward explicit congestion notification bit on frames returning to a transmitting station to indicate congestion in the network. Of the two, BECNs are more useful since they notify the transmitting station responsible for the congestion. As with FECNs, the setting of BECNs does not map well to upper-layer protocols, so the congestion information does not make it back to the source station. However, since the transmitting router can interpret the BECNs, it is well positioned to respond to the congestion situation. In the absence of a standards-defined response to BECN reception, router and frame-relay access device (FRAD) vendors have implemented their own responses. By default, Cisco routers ignore the bit. However, once frame-relay traffic shaping is enabled, the router will automatically slow down transmission to the PVC's CIR.

Unlike FECN and BECN bits which are usually only set by switches, the discard eligible bit may be set by either the switches or terminal equipment (routers). When excessive switch or link congestion occurs, switches must drop frames to operate effectively. The discard eligible bit identifies frames which, under periods of switch or link congestion, would be dropped by the switch before nonmarked frames. This allows noncritical frames to be identified and discarded before critical traffic. In this case, the terminal equipment (router) must identify the traffic appropriately and set the DE bit before transmitting it through the frame-relay network. The discard eligible bit is often set by a switch when frames are in excess of the committed class of service for a PVC. In this scenario, the switch passes those frames which are within contract unchanged, but sets the DE bit on all frames which are above the contracted rates, thereby reducing their probability of successfully transiting the frame-relay network.

While the frame-relay standards offer recommendations for the handling of FECN/BECN bits on both network and user sides, few implementations are in line with these recommendations. This provides a disparity in the carriers' offerings and requires the consumer to review each offering in detail to fully understand the services being offered. FRAD and router vendors have devised several ways of responding to congestion management signals and their implementations vary from vendor to vendor as well. Similarly, vendors have not all followed the standards' recommendations for the setting of the discard eligible bit by switches or access devices. A description of how Cisco routers handle these parameters follows.

Router-Based Frame-Relay QoS Configuration

The frame-relay QoS functions are described above for a better understanding of how Cisco routers interact with these layer 2 functions. The router's interaction with these functions enables it to more effectively transport high-priority/low-latency traffic, such as voice, over frame-relay networks.

By default, Cisco routers do not interact with frame relay's QoS functions, nor do they perform any traffic prioritization of their own. A frame-relay-connected Cisco router need only know the DLCI of each PVC and what protocols to transmit and receive over the interface. The router does not take into account a PVC's CIR or B_e, nor does it pay attention to the FECN and BECN bits in incoming frames, except for DECNET Phase IV and CLNS traffic where Cisco routers set a congestion-experienced bit in the transport-layer header. Ignoring FECN and BECN bits minimizes processing overhead and allows the routers to operate more efficiently. Unfortunately, it is unacceptable when transporting delay-sensitive voice traffic.

To help address the issue of frame-relay QoS, Cisco has incorporated several features into the IOS. These include discard eligible lists, DLCI prioritization, priority queuing, custom queuing, generic traffic shaping, and frame-relay traffic shaping.

Discard Eligible Tagging

Discard eligible lists classify traffic using standard or extended access lists and then selectively set the DE bit in the frame-relay headers before transmitting the data over the frame-relay network. As described earlier, traffic with the DE bit set will be dropped first by a switch experiencing congestion. This enables an administrator to create a scenario where low-priority traffic will be dropped first by the network, thereby improving the odds that the higher-priority traffic will transit successfully.

Configuring Discard Eligible Tagging

Traffic can be classified by using generic protocol identifiers, access lists, or by input interface. The `de-list` command used to classify traffic follows.

```
frame-relay de-list list-number {protocol protocol | interface type
number } characteristic
```

where the `list number` is a number from 1 to 10 uniquely identifying the list.

If `interface type` is selected, the `de-list` only operates on packets input through the specified interface.

If `protocol` is selected, the list can be more discriminating. The options for the protocol field include all of the layer 3 protocols supported by the router. For an IP network, the choice would be IP.

The `characteristic` field allows for refinement beyond layer 3 protocol. Options include: specifying a minimum or maximum frame size using the lt (less than) or gt (greater than) operators followed by the size; specific TCP or UDP ports using the TCP or UDP operators followed by the port; or more granular definition with an access list using the list operator.

To apply the `de-list` to an output interface, the following interface command is used:

```
frame-relay de-group group_number dlci
```

where `group number` refers to the de-list defined using the `frame-relay de-list` command and `dlci` refers to the output dlci associated with the desired PVC.

EXAMPLE   The following example of discard eligible tagging implements a basic de-list which marks all nonvoice traffic as discard eligible (see Figure 5-2). The relevant discard eligible commands are in bold.

```
!
hostname Router A
!
frame-relay de-list 1 protocol ip list 100
!
...
!
```

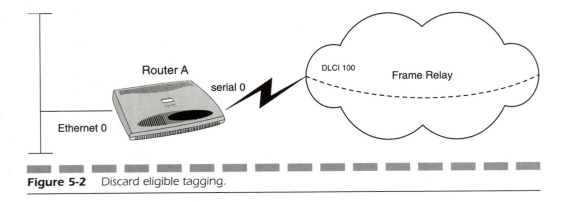

Figure 5-2   Discard eligible tagging.

```
interface Serial0
 bandwidth 512
 no ip address
 no ip directed-broadcast
 encapsulation frame-relay
 frame-relay lmi-type ansi
!
interface Serial0.1 point-to-point
 bandwidth 192
 ip address 192.168.1.1 255.255.255.0
 no ip directed-broadcast
 frame-relay de-group 1 100
 frame-relay interface-dlci 100
!
...
!
access-list 100 deny tcp any any eq 1720
access-list 100 deny udp any any range 16384 16484
access-list 100 permit ip any any
!
```

Generic Traffic Shaping

Generic traffic shaping is a mechanism for controlling the rate at which a router interface transmits outbound traffic. Generic traffic shaping was added to the IOS in version 11.2 to enable a network administrator to specify the maximum traffic rate for outbound transmission through an interface. When applied to frame-relay (sub-) interfaces, generic traffic shaping can be made adaptive in that it will respond to the reception of frames with the BECN bit set by lowering the transmission rate toward the rate specified as the minimum rate. This enables the router to adapt to congestion conditions and throttle traffic flow back to the interface's CIR, which the network should honor. An additional frame-relay feature of generic traffic shaping is the ability to "reflect" FECNs as BECNs. That is, with *fecn-adaptive* enabled, the router will set the BECN bit in frames returning to the source of the traffic which arrived with the FECN bit set. This enables the routers to respond more quickly to congestion conditions in that they do not have to wait for the frame-relay switches to set the BECN bit before throttling traffic. The ultimate goal of generic traffic shaping is rate-control output traffic in an effort to avoid congestion and to intelligently react when congestion arises.

Generic traffic employs a token-bucket approach for rate control. The algorithm allows for the specification of a traffic rate, burst size, and excess burst size. When used with frame relay, these parameters map directly to CIR, B_c, and B_e, respectively.

Configuring Generic Traffic Shaping

Generic traffic shaping is configured on an individual (sub-) interface basis. Access lists can be used if rate control is only desired for a subset of the interface's traffic. The interface command used to enable generic traffic shaping is

```
traffic-shape rate bit-rate [burst-size [excess-burst-size]]
```

where `bit-rate` specifies the desired output bit rate. It should be sent to the CIR of the DLCI which it is being applied to.

`burst-size` is optional, but should be used with frame-relay interfaces. It should be set to the B_c value used by the frame-relay network provider.

`excess-burst-size` is also optional and should be set the B_e value used by the frame-relay network provider.

EXAMPLE   An example configuration implementing generic traffic shaping is shown in Figure 5-3. A voice-enabled router connects to a frame-relay network using a single port. That port uses two PVCs. One of those PVCs will carry voice traffic, while the other PVC will carry only data traffic. To avoid congestion and congestion-related packet loss, generic traffic shaping is configured for the voice-bearing PVC. The bit rate is set to the CIR, burst size set to the B_c, and excess burst size set to the B_e for the PVC. The initial configuration is as follows:

```
!
hostname routerA
!
interface Serial0/0
 bandwidth 512
 no ip address
 ip directed-broadcast
 encapsulation frame-relay
 frame-relay lmi-type ansi
!
interface Serial0/0.1 point-to-point
 description Voice-bearing PVC
 bandwidth 128
 ip address 192.168.1.1 255.255.255.0
 no ip directed-broadcast
 traffic-shape rate 128000 64000 32000
 frame-relay interface-dlci 100
!
interface Serial0/0.2 point-to-point
 description data-only PVC
 bandwidth 128
 ip address 192.168.2.1 255.255.255.0
```

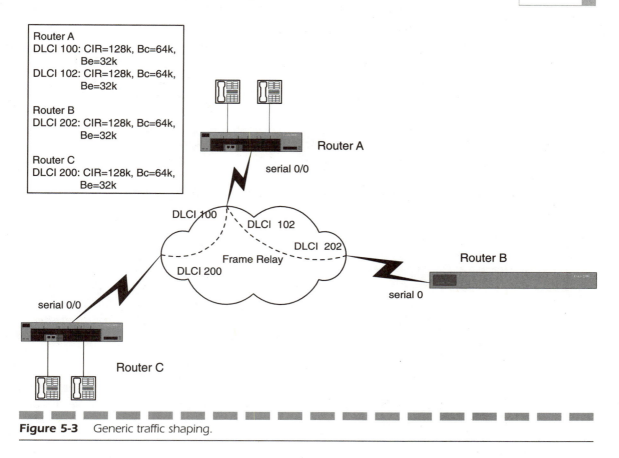

Figure 5-3 Generic traffic shaping.

```
no ip directed-broadcast
frame-relay interface-dlci 102
!
```

The values for B_c and B_e are obtained from the provider. In this example, it is assumed that the provider configured a T_c of 0.5 s. Using the formula

$$\text{CIR} = B_c/T_c$$

or

$$B_c = \text{CIR} * T_c$$

B_c then becomes 64000.

Since the data-only PVC will be transmitting bursty traffic, it needs to be controlled so that it will not unfairly grab bandwidth from the voice bearing PVC. However, the goal is to still allow the interface to take advantage of the frame relay's ability to deliver bursts of traffic. To accomplish this, generic traffic shaping will be configured with a peak rate equal to that of the link bandwidth minus the voice bearing PVC's bandwidth.

$$512 \text{ kbps} - 128 \text{ kbps} = 384 \text{ kbps}$$

To prevent significant data loss as well, each PVC should be configured to react to frame-relay congestion notifications. The interface command to allows generic traffic shaping to react to BECNs is

```
traffic-shape adaptive [bit-rate]
```

where `bit-rate` represents the minimum value traffic should be shaped to on reception of BECNs. In most situations, this value should be set to the CIR associated with the PVC. By using the PVC's CIR, the router can scale back transmission to a rate that is supported by the frame-relay network.

In the example, applying this command to the data-only PVC will force the router to back off its transmission rate on the subinterface to the PVC's CIR when BECNs are received. The modified configuration then becomes the following:

```
!
hostname routerA
!
interface Serial0/0
 bandwidth 512
 no ip address
 ip directed-broadcast
 encapsulation frame-relay
 frame-relay lmi-type ansi
!
interface Serial0/0.1 point-to-point
 description Voice-bearing PVC
 bandwidth 128
 ip address 192.168.1.1 255.255.255.0
 no ip directed-broadcast
 traffic-shape rate 128000 64000 32000
 frame-relay interface-dlci 100
!
interface Serial0/0.2 point-to-point
 description data-only PVC
 bandwidth 128
```

```
    ip address 192.168.2.1 255.255.255.0
    no ip directed-broadcast
    traffic-shape rate 384000 192000 192000
    traffic-shape adaptive 128000
    frame-relay interface-dlci 102
   !
```

As a result of this configuration, the router can use most of the link's bandwidth for the data-only PVC, but is forced to back-off its transmission rate to the CIR when congestion occurs.

The last refinement is to enable more responsive congestion identification, by configuring the data-only PVC's remote peer to reflect FECNs back to the source as BECNs. The BECNs are sent using Q.922 test response messages. This is helpful in that the downstream router can notify the upstream router of congestion in an almost out-of-band manner. The intermediary frame-relay switches can only set the BECN bit in frames returning to the offending source router. If there are no immediate return frames, as there often are with windowing protocols such as TCP, then the source router will continue to overwhelm the network and, perhaps, cause additional congestion. The following interface command should be configured on both sides of the PVC in order to enable the reflection of FECNs as BECNs.

```
    traffic-shape fecn-adapt
```

To complete this example, a subset of the configuration for data-only router B and complementary voice-enabled router C is included in addition to the updated router A configuration.

Router A

```
   !
   hostname routerA
   !
   interface Serial0/0
    bandwidth 512
    no ip address
    ip directed-broadcast
    encapsulation frame-relay
    frame-relay lmi-type ansi
   !
   interface Serial0/0.1 point-to-point
    description Voice-bearing PVC
    bandwidth 128
    ip address 192.168.1.1 255.255.255.0
    no ip directed-broadcast
    traffic-shape rate 128000 64000 32000
    frame-relay interface-dlci 100
```

```
!
interface Serial0/0.2 point-to-point
 description data-only PVC
 bandwidth 128
 ip address 192.168.2.1 255.255.255.0
 no ip directed-broadcast
 traffic-shape rate 384000 192000 192000
 traffic-shape adaptive 128000
 traffic-shape fecn-adapt
 frame-relay interface-dlci 102
!
```

Router B

```
!
hostname routerB
!
interface Serial0
 bandwidth 512
 no ip address
 ip directed-broadcast
 encapsulation frame-relay
 frame-relay lmi-type ansi
!
interface Serial0.1 point-to-point
 description data-only PVC
 bandwidth 128
 ip address 192.168.2.2 255.255.255.0
 no ip directed-broadcast
 traffic-shape rate 384000 192000 19200
 traffic-shape adaptive 128000
 traffic-shape fecn-adapt
 frame-relay interface-dlci 202
!
```

Router C

```
!
hostname routerC
!
interface Serial0/0
 bandwidth 256
 no ip address
 ip directed-broadcast
 encapsulation frame-relay
 frame-relay lmi-type ansi
!
interface Serial0/0.1 point-to-point
 description Voice-bearing PVC
 bandwidth 128
 ip address 192.168.1.2 255.255.255.0
 no ip directed-broadcast
 traffic-shape rate 128000 64000 32000
 frame-relay interface-dlci 200
!
```

Monitoring Generic Traffic Shaping

To verify that the traffic shaping is operational, the command show traffic-shape can be used. Here is sample output from Router A:

```
RouterA#sh traffic-shape
        Access Target Byte  Sustain   Excess    Interval Increment Adapt
I/F     List   Rate   Limit bits/int  bits/int  (ms)     (bytes)   Active
Se0.1          128000 12000 64000     32000     500      8000      -
Se0.2          384000 48000 192000    192000    500      24000     BECN
```

Note that the time interval (500 ms) is automatically derived by the router based upon the target rate and the burst size. Additionally, the activity of generic traffic shaping can be monitored using the show traffic-shape statistics command. Sample output follows:

```
RouterA#sh traffic-shape statistics
        Access Queue   Packets   Bytes     Packets  Bytes    Shaping
I/F     List   Depth                       Delayed  Delayed  Active
Se0.1          25      4460      500413    100      28455    yes
Se0.2          0       1384      194366    0        0        no
```

At this point, traffic shaping is active on subinterface 0.1 with 25 currently queued and inactive on subinterface 0.2. The other values are cumulative so a total of 4460 packets containing 500,413 bytes have passed through subinterface 0.1 since traffic shaping was configured and of those, 100 packets containing 28,455 bytes have been delayed due to excess rate conditions.

Frame-Relay Traffic Shaping

Frame-relay traffic shaping is a feature which was added to the IOS in version 11.2. It is significant because it enables the router to intelligently allocate bandwidth on a per-PVC basis and control the rate of traffic flow into the network. Frame-relay traffic shaping introduced three new QoS functions which had previously been absent from Cisco's frame-relay implementation. They are per-PVC rate limiting, per-PVC dynamic throttling, and per-PVC custom or priority queuing.

Rate Limiting

Rate limiting is similar to generic traffic shaping in that it adapts output traffic rates. Frame-relay traffic shaping, however, uses a leaky-bucket algorithm which provides a more controlled, smoother traffic pattern.

Using rate limits, an administrator can specify the rate at which the router will transmit traffic over each individual PVC. Currently, average and peak rates can be specified. The average rate should be set to the PVC's CIR, while the peak rate is usually set to one of the following three values: the interface's port speed, the PVC's maximum throughput (CIR + EIR), or the remote end's access rate.

Setting the peak rate to the interface's port speed is the most aggressive scheme. It works well with bursty data traffic because it provides access to the most bandwidth possible. The average rate and frame-relay traffic shaping's ability to respond to the reception of BECNs limits the risks of data loss since the interface will buffer data and reduce their output rate during congestion conditions.

Setting the peak rate to the PVC's maximum rate (CIR + EIR) allows the interface to transmit up to the maximum rate supported by the network for the PVC and is a more conservative approach. It provides a more consistent, predictable traffic flow since the output rates are tightly controlled. The CIR + EIR upper bound ensures that the router interface will not overwhelm the network, while the average rate of CIR ensures that the router transmits at a rate which the network can support under normal conditions.

The third approach of setting the peak rate to the remote end's access rate ensures that traffic from the local router will not overwhelm the remote end's local loop and is the most conservative approach. This is important because in most hub-and-spoke configurations, the hub site transmits at a much higher access rate than the spokes. In the United States, it's common to provide T1 access at the hub site and 56-kbps access at the smaller spoke sites. Without traffic shaping, the router transmits bursts of data at the T1 line rate. These data then transit the carrier's network links at that rate until they reach the termination switch connected to the spoke site. At this point, the switch is receiving data at near T1 rates, but can only forward them over a single 56-kbps port which forces the switch to buffer the excess traffic. Since the switch's buffers have been allocated based upon the 56-kbps access rate and the PVC's CIR, it is easy for large volumes of T1 rate data to overflow the output buffers at the switch. This is depicted in Figures 5-4 and 5-5.

If router A transmits 128 kilobytes (1024 kilobits) of data at T1 rate, it would require approximately ⅔ of a second to transmit the entire burst. That same burst would require approximately 18.3 s to transmit at 56 kbps. Assuming that the frame-relay backbone transmits the data at or close to T1 rate, switch B then must buffer almost the entire burst for up

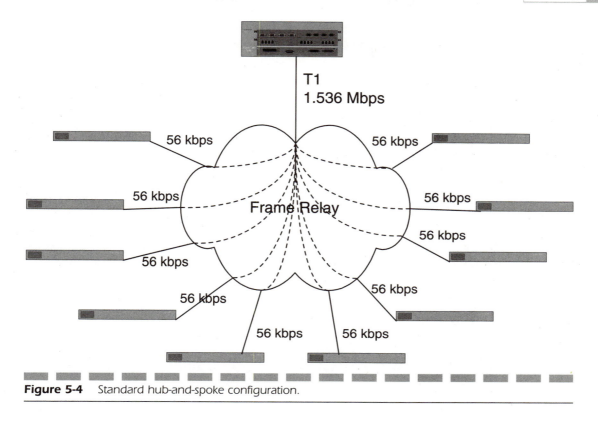

Figure 5-4   Standard hub-and-spoke configuration.

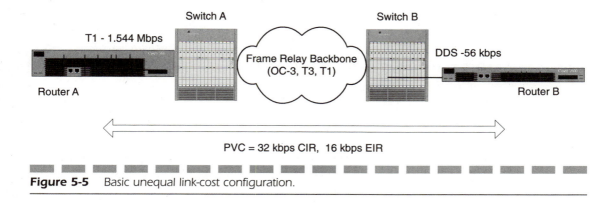

Figure 5-5   Basic unequal link-cost configuration.

to 18 s while it transmits the burst over the 56-kbps local loop. Depending on the network configuration, switch architecture, and switch configuration, this may be possible, but it is easy to see how situations like this can cause problems.

To prevent this condition, frame-relay traffic shaping can control the hub site's output along the PVC destined for the spoke site(s) and limit it to a 56-kbps maximum. A sample router configuration for this scenario will be presented later in the chapter.

Congestion Management

Dynamic throttling can occur either reactively or proactively. The default is reactive once frame-relay traffic shaping has been enabled. In reactive mode, the router responds to the BECNs it receives by stepping down the transmission rate over the appropriate PVC. To enable proactive mode, the router must be connected to a Cisco-Stratacom WAN switch running ForeSight traffic management. In IOS release 11.3 and higher, the command `frame-relay adaptive-shaping foresight` enables the router to listen to ForeSight messages from a directly connected Cisco WAN switch. These ForeSight messages contain congestion information about each DLCI on the port that is derived from StrataCom's closed loop congestion management. If congestion exists along the path of a particular PVC, the ForeSight message will indicate congestion for the associated DLCI and the router will activate its traffic-shaping function and decrease the output rate.

ForeSight-based traffic shaping is considered proactive because the router is made aware of network congestion before transmitting data along a PVC. With this knowledge, the router will transmit data at a lower rate and not exacerbate the congestion condition. In contrast, BECN-based traffic shaping requires that the router downstream from the offending source transmit data back toward that source router. Only when the return traffic is present does an intermediary switch have an opportunity to set a BECN bit. After this point the router receives the BECN and begins to reduce its transmission rate.

Shaping

Configuration of frame-relay traffic shaping requires a new construct called a frame-relay map class. The map class is simply a paragraph within the router configuration that specifies frame-relay class of service parameters and special queuing techniques. Since a frame-relay map class is a global construct, it may be applied to multiple interfaces or subinterfaces.

Frame-relay traffic shaping must be enabled on the physical interface before it can be applied to individual subinterfaces. This is done with the following interface command:

```
frame-relay traffic-shaping
```

Once enabled on the physical interface, traffic shaping and per-VC queuing is automatically enabled for all PVCs on the interface. All of the subinterfaces for an interface inherit the shaping and queuing parameters of the main interface. If all or most of the PVCs on the interface are configured the same, it makes sense to configure a default mapping for the main interface. Individual subinterfaces can override this default by defining their own mappings.

Queuing and shaping parameters are defined with the map class mentioned above. Each map class requires a name to uniquely identify it, and one or more queuing or shaping commands. To define a map class, use the following global command:

```
map-class frame-relay map-class-name
```

where *map-class-name* is a unique character string.

Underneath the map class, the specific features are configured. The definable shaping parameters are output rates and congestive notification methods. The following map-class commands are used:

```
frame-relay traffic-rate average [peak]
```

and

```
frame-relay adaptive-shaping {becn | foresight}
```

where *average* represents the desired average output rate in bits per second and the peak value represents maximum desirable output rate. In general practice, these are set to the PVC's CIR and CIR + EIR, respectively. The adaptive-shaping options relate to the reactive and proactive congestion-management options discussed above. BECN configures the router to respond to BECNs sent from the network and reduce its traffic rate accordingly. The foresight option can be enabled if the router is connected to a Cisco-Stratacom-based WAN switch which is configured to communicate foresight messages with the router.

To apply a map class to a frame-relay interface or (sub)interface, the following interface command is used:

```
frame-relay class map-class-name
```

where map-class-name corresponds to the appropriate map-class.

EXAMPLE   In a simple frame-relay traffic shaping example, the map class which would be built for the previous hub-and-spoke scenario would be

```
map-class frame-relay frts_ex1
frame-relay traffic-rate 32000 48000
frame-relay adaptive-shaping becn
```

This defines the CIR and peak rate for the PVCs. To apply it, the following configuration text would required:

```
hostname hubrouter
!
interface serial 1/0
 bandwidth 1536
 no ip address
 ip directed-broadcast
 encapsulation frame-relay
 frame-relay traffic-shaping
 frame-relay class frts_ex1
 frame-relay lmi-type ansi
!
interface Serial1/0.1 point-to-point
 description PVC to spoke 1
 bandwidth 32
 ip address 192.168.1.1 255.255.255.0
 no ip directed-broadcast
 frame-relay interface-dlci 100
!
interface Serial0/0.2 point-to-point
 description PVC to spoke 2
 bandwidth 32
 ip address 192.168.2.1 255.255.255.0
 no ip directed-broadcast
 frame-relay interface-dlci 102
!
...
interface Serial1/0.10 point-to-point
 description PVC to spoke 10
 bandwidth 32
 ip address 192.168.2.1 255.255.255.0
 no ip directed-broadcast
 frame-relay interface-dlci 110
!
...
!
map-class frame-relay frts_ex1
 frame-relay traffic-rate 32000 48000
 frame-relay adaptive-shaping becn
!
```

In this example, the map class specified on the main interface is automatically applied to all subinterfaces. A possible improvement on this would be to increase the peak rate to 56 kbps. This will still prevent the hub router from overwhelming the spokes and also allow it to access the full-link bandwidth. The configuration would be same except for the frame-relay traffic rate statement in the map class which would become

```
frame-relay traffic-rate 32000 56000
```

NOTE: *It is important to configure at least a base traffic rate for the interface, because the default traffic rates may not be applicable to your configuration. Once frame-relay traffic shaping is enabled, the router applies the following default parameters to all PVCs:*

$$CIR = 56000, B_c = 56000, B_e = 0$$

EXAMPLE

In the following complex frame-relay traffic shaping example, multiple map classes are used to support PVCs of differing rates. The diagram below represents the logical layout of the network. (See Figure 5-6.)

The hub router at the top connects to all sites using a single T1 interface. The hub router also connects to an AS5300 which interfaces with a PBX. All sites have a single PVC which connects them to the hub. The four 3600 series routers at the bottom all support voice and connect to the network with 256-kbps port speeds and 160-kbps CIRs. The five routers on the left carry only low-speed data traffic, and have a 56-kbps port speed with 32-kbps CIR on their PVCs back to the hub. The five routers on the right carry higher volumes of data and use a 256-kbps port speed with 128-kbps CIRs. The challenge is to ensure consistent WAN performance for the four voice-enabled routers while providing the most bandwidth flexibility with the data remote sites.

Frame-relay traffic shaping provides the per-VC queuing at the hub site to isolate voice traffic from other traffic. Three map classes will be created on the hub router to address each type of site's needs. For the low-bandwidth data sites, the map class will limit the peak output to 48 kbps (CIR + EIR) and set the average to their CIR of 32 kbps. For the higher-speed data sites, the map class will limit the output to 256 kbps (port rate) and set the average to their CIR of 128 kbps. For the voice routers, the map class will limit output to 192 kbps (CIR + EIR) and set the average to their CIR of 160 kbps.

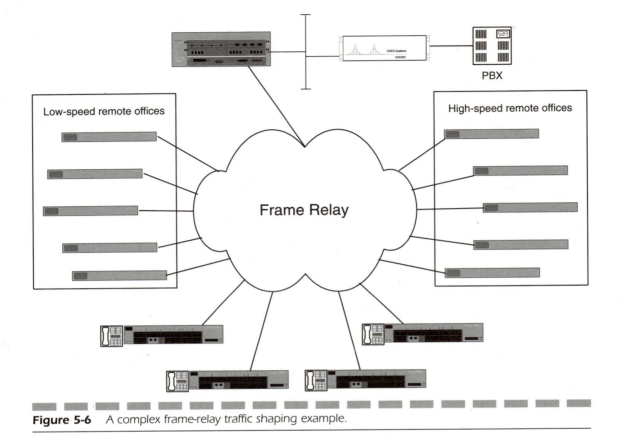

Figure 5-6 A complex frame-relay traffic shaping example.

The sum total of the average rates is 1440 kbps, or just below the T1's 1536-kbps capacity. The sum total of the peak rates is 2288 kbps, which oversubscribes the T1 port by a factor of about 1.5. This is usually reasonable presuming that the data applications are bursty and that all sites will not require maximum transfer rates at all times. Adaptive shaping with BECN response also helps reduce congestion conditions.

In addition to shaping the output from the hub to the remote sites, each remote site must also shape its traffic sent from the remote to the hub. This helps avoid congestion issues along the return path and better enables the voice traffic to grab its fair share of the input link bandwidth.

The configuration excerpt for the hub router follows. Only one subinterface for each type of remote site is included to save space.

```
!
hostname hubrouter
!
...
!
interface Serial2/0
 bandwidth 1536
 no ip address
 ip directed-broadcast
 encapsulation frame-relay
 frame-relay traffic-shaping
 frame-relay lmi-type ansi
!
interface Serial2/0.1 point-to-point
 description low speed data site 1
 bandwidth 32
 ip address 192.168.1.1 255.255.255.0
 no ip directed-broadcast
 frame-relay class lowspeeddata
 frame-relay interface-dlci 100
!
...
!
interface Serial2/0.6 point-to-point
 description voice router site 1
 bandwidth 160
 ip address 192.168.101.1 255.255.255.0
 no ip directed-broadcast
 frame-relay class voice
 frame-relay interface-dlci 201
!
...
!
interface Serial2/0.10 point-to-point
 bandwidth 128
 ip address 192.168.201.1 255.255.255.0
 no ip directed-broadcast
 frame-relay class highspeeddata
 frame-relay interface-dlci 301
!
...
!
map-class frame-relay lowspeeddata
 frame-relay traffic-rate 32000 48000
 frame-relay adaptive-shaping becn
!
map-class frame-relay voice
 frame-relay traffic-rate 160000 192000
 frame-relay adaptive-shaping becn
!
map-class frame-relay highspeeddata
 frame-relay traffic-rate 128000 256000
 frame-relay adaptive-shaping becn
!
```

The configurations of each remote site are provided below. Again, only one site of each type is included to save space.

Low-Speed Data Site

```
!
hostname lowspeeddata1
!
...
!
interface Serial0
 bandwidth 56
 no ip address
 ip directed-broadcast
 encapsulation frame-relay
 frame-relay traffic-shaping
 frame-relay lmi-type ansi
!
interface Serial0.1 point-to-point
 description connection to hub
 bandwidth 32
 ip address 192.168.1.2 255.255.255.0
 no ip directed-broadcast
 frame-relay class lowspeeddata
 frame-relay interface-dlci 500
!
...
!
map-class frame-relay lowspeeddata
 frame-relay traffic-rate 32000 48000
 frame-relay adaptive-shaping becn
!
```

High-Speed Data Site

```
!
hostname highspeeddata1
!
...
!
interface Serial0
 bandwidth 256
 no ip address
 ip directed-broadcast
 encapsulation frame-relay
 frame-relay traffic-shaping
 frame-relay lmi-type ansi
!
...
!
interface Serial0.1 point-to-point
 description connection hub
 bandwidth 128
 ip address 192.168.201.2 255.255.255.0
 no ip directed-broadcast
 frame-relay class highspeeddata
 frame-relay interface-dlci 500
!
...
!
```

```
map-class frame-relay highspeeddata
 frame-relay traffic-rate 128000 256000
 frame-relay adaptive-shaping becn
```

Voice-Enabled Site

```
!
hostname voicerouter1
!
...
!
interface Serial0/0
 bandwidth 256
 no ip address
 ip directed-broadcast
 encapsulation frame-relay
 frame-relay traffic-shaping
 frame-relay lmi-type ansi
!
interface Serial0/0.1 point-to-point
 description connection to hub
 bandwidth 160
 ip address 192.168.101.2 255.255.255.0
 no ip directed-broadcast
 frame-relay class voice
 frame-relay interface-dlci 500
!
...
!
map-class frame-relay voice
 frame-relay traffic-rate 160000 192000
 frame-relay adaptive-shaping becn
```

Queuing

The queuing options definable under the map class will be discussed in a forthcoming section of this chapter.

Cisco-Stratacom Integration

If the router is connected to a Cisco-Stratacom-based frame-relay network, then the QoS parameters can be automatically sensed using Cisco's Enhanced-Local Management Interface or E-LMI. E-LMI communicates the values of CIR, B_c, and B_e for all PVCs on the port. The router can then automatically apply them to the traffic-shaping mechanism. This simplifies the router configuration significantly and has the added benefit of not requiring router configuration changes when frame-relay parameters are modified.

The configuration of a router connected to a Cisco-Stratacom switch follows:

```
!
interface serial0/0
 no ip address
 encapsulation frame-relay
 frame-relay traffic-shaping
 frame-relay qos-autosense
!
interface serial0/0.1 point-to-point
 ip address 192.168.10.1 255.255.255.0
 frame-relay interface-dlci 101
!
```

Generic Traffic Shaping versus Frame-Relay Traffic Shaping

At first glance, the two techniques seem very similar. They both limit output rates, they both react to frame-relay congestion notifications, and they both support per-VC operations. The difference lies in the underlying algorithm which performs the traffic shaping. Generic traffic shaping uses a token-bucket algorithm and frame-relay traffic shaping uses a leaky-bucket approach.

Token-Bucket Algorithm

The token-bucket approach creates an abstract bucket. The size of the bucket is equivalent to the maximum burst size. The algorithm adds tokens to the bucket at the specified data rate. When the bucket is full, additional tokens are discarded. In order to transmit a packet, there must be an available token in the bucket, so each packet that is transmitted uses a token from the bucket. If the tokens are exhausted, incoming packets must wait for a token to be allocated before they can be transmitted.

Figure 5-7 depicts the operation of the token bucket in generic traffic shaping.

Leaky-Bucket Algorithm

The leaky-bucket approach also creates an abstract bucket. It's size is limited to prevent excessive latency. The algorithm creates a "hole" in the bottom of the bucket which is large enough to let packets "leak" out at the specified rate. All incoming packets must pass through the bucket before transmission. If the bucket is empty, the packets head directly to the bottom and are transmitted at the specified rate controlled by the size of the hole in the abstract bucket. If traffic arrives at a rate which is

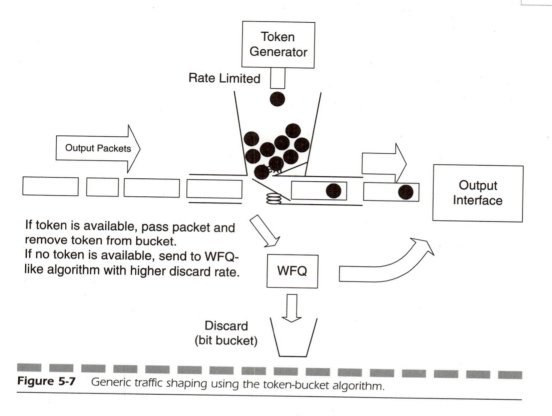

Figure 5-7 *Generic traffic shaping using the token-bucket algorithm.*

faster than the leak rate, then it is buffered in the bucket until it may be transmitted. The adaptive nature of frame-relay traffic shaping allows the leak rate to be modified dynamically. This allows the router to transmit at burst rates, but back-off to the PVC's CIR, when congestion occurs. Figure 5-8 shows the operation of the leaky-bucket algorithm in frame-relay traffic shaping:

Conclusions

In comparing the two algorithms, the following conclusions can be drawn:

1. Generic traffic shaping does not require all traffic to be buffered.
2. Generic traffic shaping enables bursty traffic by allowing the token bucket to fill when no traffic is present.
3. Generic traffic shaping is less processor-intensive than the leaky-bucket approach.

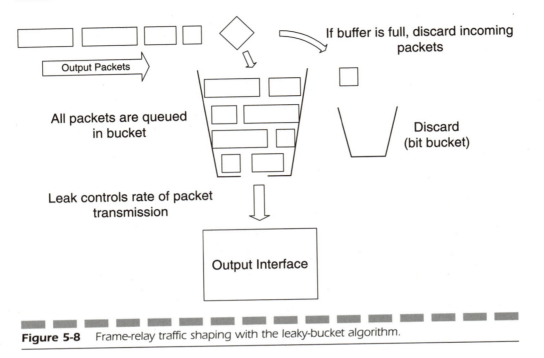

Figure 5-8 Frame-relay traffic shaping with the leaky-bucket algorithm.

4. Frame-relay traffic shaping buffers all traffic before transmission.

5. Frame-relay traffic shaping does not allow bursts beyond the defined traffic rates.

6. Frame-relay traffic shaping consumes more resources, but smooths traffic output.

Priority and Custom Queuing

Priority and custom queuing are some of the oldest router-based QoS mechanisms, with priority queuing predating custom queuing by several releases. However, it was not until IOS release 11.2 that these features were applicable to frame-relay PVCs.

Priority queuing classifies traffic and then assigns it to one of four priority queues. Traffic flows are identified by input interface or through access lists. Each of the higher-priority queues must be completely emptied before traffic in a lower priority queue will be processed. This technique ensures that higher-priority traffic is always processed, but does so with the liability that lower-priority traffic may never get serviced. Priority queuing is applied to outbound traffic only and its use disables weighted fair queuing.

Custom queuing is an enhanced priority queuing strategy where limits can be placed on the amount of traffic serviced at each priority level. This overcomes the low-priority queue starvation problem because the higher-priority queues must cede to the lower-priority queues after transmitting the maximum amount permitted. Additionally, custom queuing provides up to 16 queues (priority levels) as opposed to priority queuing's four. Frame-relay traffic shaping allows these techniques to be applied on a per-PVC basis.

Configuring Priority and Custom Queuing

Configuring priority and custom queuing on frame-relay interfaces is similar to the configuration on regular interfaces. The classification and queue mapping are performed the same way. Only the mapping of the queues to the interface is different. Frame-relay traffic shaping uses the following map class commands to accomplish this:

```
frame-relay custom-queue-list list-number
```

and

```
frame-relay priority-group list-number
```

where `list-number` refers to the priority of custom queue list developed.

For details on creating queue lists refer to the chapter on quality of service for IP.

Challenges for Frame Relay

Frame-relay networks introduce many design and implementation challenges for transporting VoIP traffic. These challenges and their resolutions are listed below.

1. Prioritizing voice traffic

2. Preventing nonvoice traffic from delaying voice traffic

3. Minimizing delay and delay variance without effecting other network-layer protocols

4. Enabling QoS functions without degrading performance on the frame-relay connected routers

5. Enabling QoS functions without affecting the traffic over other PVCs

6. Identifying all routers in all paths between source and destination

7. Ensuring that voice traffic does not exceed the network's capacity to deliver frames to the remote end

8. Ensuring that nonvoice traffic is discarded before voice traffic in the event of network congestion

9. Frame-relay traffic shaping and RSVP are not compatible and cannot be run simultaneously

10. Maintaining frame relay's cost-effectiveness and high voice quality

11. Minimizing and/or preventing interference from other network-layer protocols

12. Managing the provider's QoS delivery

Tackling these challenges, in order:

1. *Challenge number 1* is not a new one, but its implementation on frame-relay interfaces is slightly different. In order to enable priority queuing on a per-PVC basis, frame-relay subinterfaces must be used. This is not a major problem, but may require router configuration and network addressing modifications in certain scenarios. Also, in order to enable priority queuing, frame-relay traffic shaping must also be enabled, which, in turn, requires that RSVP be disabled on the interface. Other methods of prioritization including the use of IP precedence bits are discussed in the chapter on quality of service for IP.

2. *Challenge number 2* is a difficult one to tackle when low-speed links are in use. The serialization delay associated with low-speed links results in long transmission times for large frames. For example, it takes over 200 ms to transmit a 1500-byte frame over a 56-kbps circuit. Voice traffic will exceed its delay budget if it has to wait for such a large frame to be transmitted. Several protocols and applications call for the use of such large frames, and sharing low-speed links with them is an extreme challenge. One method of overcoming this is to lower the mtu for the serial interface. This limits the size of the frames which can be

transmitted over the link, resulting in a lower transmission time for the smaller frames. A priority-queuing mechanism then enables voice traffic to be interleaved within the other traffic. As we will soon see, this technique is not a panacea for frame-relay related issues.

3. *Challenge number 3* is the result of our quick fix from challenge 2. Shrinking the mtu on an interface can have an adverse effect on other protocols. When the mtu for an interface is less than the datagrams which must be transmitted over the interface, the datagrams must be fragmented into smaller datagrams which can later be reassembled. While IP has a facility for this, IPX does not. Therefore, reducing the mtu size on an interface can, in effect, prevent large IPX frames from being transmitted through the interface. Additionally, fragmenting traffic does increase overhead on both the router and the receiving host and will limit the actual amount of data transmitted over the link (due to the additional headers required for the fragmented datagrams). This will cause a slight reduction in performance.

4. *Challenge number 4* is a result of the additional processing required to implement router-based QoS mechanisms. While a few of these techniques are supported by the fast-switching software, most are not. Performing the necessary queuing, traffic shaping, and header compression will increase the processor utilization which can adversely affect all communications through the router. This may cause problems on some of the older access routers such as the 2500 and 4000, as well as RP-based 7000 routers. The newer, more powerful routers such as the 2600, 3600, 4500, 4700, 7200, and 7500 series can generally handle these functions without significantly impacting performance. Regardless of the router platform, its relative performance should be measured and monitored before applying these processor intensive tasks.

5. *Challenge number 5* is also a side effect of the quick fix applied in challenge 2. Changing the mtu must be done on the main interface with all of the subinterfaces inheriting the mtu change. It is not possible to change the mtu on a single subinterface. Often, routers positioned at the central site will support multiple remote sites and often multiple protocols to each site. Since adjusting the mtu can have an adverse effect on other protocols, you must be careful when modifying it on an interface with multiple PVCs, because while mtu change may work for intended PVC, it may also disrupt traffic on other PVCs.

6. *Challenge number 6* is usually not a major issue, but can become an issue in rerouting conditions. It's usually easy to identify the path between source and destination and apply the necessary QoS techniques along that path under normal conditions. However, the path which may be used during a link or router failure condition is often ignored. Care should be taken to ensure either that the backup data paths are configured properly to support voice traffic or that phone systems and/or voice routers are configured to use an alternate path, like the PSTN, under failure conditions.

7. *Challenge number 7* is a simple sanity check. In the data world, we got spoiled with frame relay's ability to handle bursty data traffic. When voice traffic is being considered, care must be taken to ensure that the peak amount of voice traffic does not exceed the network's ability to deliver it to the remote destination. Proper calculations should be made for voice traffic, including framing and protocol overhead.

8. *Challenge number 8* helps ensure the end-to-end delivery of voice traffic. As discussed earlier, frame-relay switches will drop frames under congestion conditions. The switch's selection process can be influenced through the setting of the discard eligible (DE) bit. In order to protect voice traffic from discard, you may wish to mark some or all other traffic as discard eligible using the `de-lists` command.

9. *Challenge number 9* is a caveat which limits the administrator's options when selecting QoS mechanisms for frame-relay-based VoIP networks. If RSVP is strongly desired, then the administrator must forgo the use of priority queuing, custom queuing, and ForeSight-based adaptive shaping. Generic traffic shaping can be used to provide rate control, but priority and custom queuing will not be possible with RSVP enabled. Ostensibly, RSVP should provide the necessary bandwidth and delay variance required, but RSVP queues at the datagram level, so it is unable to overcome problems caused by large frames and high serialization delays.

10. *Challenge number 10* refers to the provisioning requirements for transporting voice over frame-relay networks. Cisco's documentation suggests the separate PVCs be configured: one for voice traffic and one for data traffic. Alternatively, Cisco recommends provisioning the CIR at, or close to, the link's access rate. While both of these suggestions go a long way toward providing improved QoS, they also incur more expense. Frame-relay pricing is usually broken into two components, a local loop charge and a per-PVC charge. Given this, it's easy to see how adding a PVC would increase cost. The second suggestion causes the frame-relay circuit to behave more like a private line. This is good for voice, since performance is more predictable and there is less probability of the router's output overwhelming the network. However, it diminishes some of the advantages network designers have come to expect from frame relay. More specifically, if the CIR is close to the link-access rate, then there is little room to burst above CIR. Frame relay's burstiness allows network managers to provision circuits to handle the normal traffic flow, knowing that traffic bursts will be handled by the network. Removing bursting means that circuits must be provisioned to better support peak periods, and that means higher CIRs and, in turn, higher costs.

11. *Challenge number 11* has been touched on before, only we focused more on voice traffic's effect on other protocols. We must also be careful of what effects these protocols may have on voice traffic. The periodic RIP and SAP updates required by IPX are an example of the interference which can be caused. Another example is the IP-routing protocol Integrated IS-IS, which sends periodic hello packets that are the length of the interface's mtu. These and other protocol behaviors must be considered when designing a voice-enabled frame-relay network.

12. *Challenge number 12* has been around for a long time. The ability to measure the performance or service levels delivered by your provider is important when considering whether a network will meet voice's low-latency requirements. Management packages have been developed to measure performance using a number of techniques. Some applications poll SNMP MIBs in the routers and do a fair job of reporting throughput. Others use specialized hardware to accurately measure both throughput and latency. Yet others use specialized processes on RMON/RMON2 devices to monitor the response time to particular traffic patterns and attempt to characterize the latency of the network as well as the devices supporting the applications running over the network. Cisco has recently introduced the *response time reporter* function, which is used to measure the response time for traffic sent from the router to an IP host and back to the router. This is an automated equivalent to pinging hosts from the router console and recording the round trip times. Whatever method of measurement is chosen, one must be implemented to not only verify the network's ability to support voice traffic, but to ensure that these service levels are being met during normal operating conditions.

Future Alternatives

Cisco will soon support Frame Relay Forum's FRF.12 specification for frame-relay fragmentation. This technique provides a standardized method for fragmenting large frames into a sequence of shorter frames before transporting them through the frame-relay network. Frame fragmenting is important to voice implementations because it helps control delay and delay variance across the network by allowing the interleaving of voice frames within streams of larger data frames.

FRF.12 defines the process of fragmentation and reassembly by both DTE devices (routers) and DCE devices (frame-relay switches). The DTE operation is analogous to what is attempted when lowering the mtu on frame-relay interfaces. However, FRF.12 performs fragmentation and reassembly at the data-link layer. This enables it to transport all network-layer protocols regardless of whether or not they support fragmentation. It is also more efficient than IP fragmentation because only a single 2-byte fragmentation header is added to each fragment instead of the 20-byte IP header which IP requires.

The Forum leaves several implementation details open including the method used by the DTE for interleaving real-time data, and fragment-size specifications. Interleaving of data will probably occur in a manner similar to the one implemented in Multilink PPP link fragment interleaving where a special queue for real-time data is reserved. The FRF.12 Implementation agreement does no specify or recommend fragment sizes. It only points out the UNI link speed as well as the speeds of the NNI links that should be considered when determining fragment sizes. In all likelihood Cisco will recommend sizes similar to those used on their MC3810.

SUMMARY

The protocols, algorithms, and features discussed in this chapter all help to make frame relay a more capable platform for carrying voice over IP traffic. The building blocks of these techniques are classification methods, queuing methods, and traffic-shaping methods. All of these techniques must integrate with the frame-relay network's built-in QoS and congestion-management mechanisms, as well as those of IP to form a more seamless voice-capable network. In the upcoming chapters, these techniques will be combined with the IP QoS techniques and enhanced voice-processing features to build solid, high-quality voice-enabled data networks.

Chapter

6

Understanding
Voice Ports and
Dial Peers

Introduction

This chapter covers two essential components for the configuration of VoIP networks, the voice port and the dial peer. These constructs isolate physical-layer functions from logical functions and call routing to maintain flexibility in configuring voice networks. Voice ports deal primarily with physical-layer functions while dial peers deal primarily with logical functions like QoS, call routing, and even voice encoding. Dial peers logically link the physical voice ports and together they provide an end-to-end voice network.

Voice Ports

Voice ports are the physical interfaces on the voice-enabled router which connect to telephony devices. The router's voice ports handle all of the physical-layer functions between the router and phone device. This includes such functions as providing power to an analog phone, detecting off-hook conditions, generating the ring signal, receiving and transmitting analog or digital voice calls, and receiving or transmitting dialed digits for call routing.

Physical Interfaces and Signaling

Analog and digital voice ports differ greatly in both transmission characteristics and signaling. To more clearly address the needs of both analog and digital ports, they are presented separately.

Analog Voice Ports

There are three types of signaling used with analog systems today: FXS, FXO, and E&M. On a Cisco router, you must be careful to match the right voice-interface card (VIC) with the requirements of your application. A brief review of the signaling types follows.

FXS

FXS stands for Foreign eXchange Station. Standard residential phone lines are configured as FXS, and thus it is the interface with which we are most familiar. FXS ports are useful when the router will be connecting to a standard analog phone, a fax machine, a trunk port on a key system, or, possibly an external port on a PBX. FXS interfaces supply ring, line voltage, and dialtone. The physical interface is the common RJ-11 receptacle.

FXO

FXO stands for Foreign eXchange Office and can be considered the opposite of the FXS port. FXO ports can connect to the PSTN or an analog station line of a PBX. FXO interfaces function somewhat like a standard phone, in that they expect dialtone and use dialed digits to initiate phone calls. The physical interface is the common RJ-11 receptacle.

E&M

E&M is often called "ear and mouth" and is the type of signaling used for network to network, like linking PBX systems over trunk lines or switch-to-switch connections. There are five types of E&M signaling, and they are generally represented with roman numerals. (i.e., E&M type I, E&M type II, or E&M type V). To complicate matters further, there are 2- and 4-wire implementations. E&M signaling is sometimes referred to as receive and transmit because the E lead is used for inbound signaling and the M lead is used for outbound signaling relative to the PBX. The physical interface for E&M ports is an RJ-48 receptacle. Cisco currently supports E&M types I, II, III, and V in both 2- and 4-wire implementations.

When ordering and configuring voice-enabled routers it is important to select the proper interface types. Table 6-1 lists some common telephony devices and identifies the type of voice port required to communicate with them.

Cisco currently offers VoIP-capable analog interfaces on its 2600 and 3600 series routers. Each signaling type requires a different voice-interface card. As discussed earlier, there are two voice-network modules (VNMs) available for the 2600/3600 routers. The NM-1V with 1 slot for a VIC and the NM-2V which supports two VICs. This method decouples the VoIP-specific functions (performed by the network module) from the physical-layer functions (performed by the VICs). All current VICs contain two ports, and both ports must perform the same signaling type. That is, if the 2-port FXS VIC (part number: VIC-2FXS) is in use, both ports on that VIC will only perform FXS interface functions. The available VICs are presented in Table 6-2.

TABLE 6-1

Analog Interface Types for Common Applications

Phone Device/Port Type	FXS	FXO	E&M
Standard phone	X		
Fax machine	X		
PBX—analog external line	X		
Key system—external line	X		
PSTN—analog line		X	
PBX—analog station line		X	
PBX—trunk or tie line			X

TABLE 6-2

Voice-interface Cards (VICs)

VIC	Description
VIC-2FXS	2-port FXS interface card
VIC-2FXO	2-port FXO interface card for use in the U.S., Canada, and Mexico
VIC-2FXO-EU	2-port FXO interface card for use in Europe
VIC-2FXO-M3	2-port FXO interface card for use in Australia
VIC-2E/M	2-port E&M interface card—supports 2- and 4-wire types I, II, III, and V

Configuring Analog Voice Ports

Voice-port configuration paragraphs show up in the router configuration automatically. They are referenced by their slot number in the router, the VIC slot number on the voice-network module, and then the port number on the VIC. This is analogous to the way that IOS handles standard interfaces such as Ethernet or Token Ring. For example, Figure 6-1 represents a 3640 router with an NM-2V in slot 0 and 2 FXS VICs installed in the NM-2V. The 3640 also contains an NM-2E2W in slot 1. Figure 6-2 is an excerpt from the router configuration file showing the voice ports.

FXS and FXO Interfaces

As mentioned earlier, FXS interfaces must provide line voltage, ring generation, off-hook detection, call-progress indicators (ring-back, busy sig-

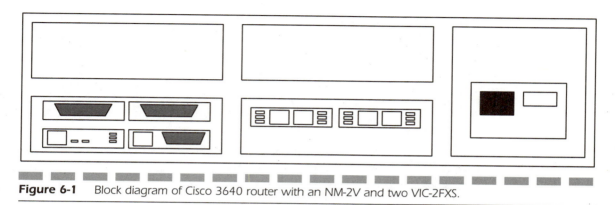

Figure 6-1 Block diagram of Cisco 3640 router with an NM-2V and two VIC-2FXS.

Figure 6-2
Voice port configuration excerpt.

```
!
voice-port 0/0/0
!
voice-port 0/0/1
!
voice-port 0/1/0
!
voice-port 0/1/1
!
...
!
interface Ethernet1/0
 no ip address
 shutdown
!
interface Ethernet1/1
 no ip address
 shutdown
!
interface Serial1/0
 no ip address
 shutdown
!
interface Serial1/1
 no ip address
 shutdown
!
```

nal, etc.), and recognize dialed digits for call routing. Similarly, FXO interfaces interface with the PSTN, or possibly station lines on a PBX and therefore require dialtone for dialing, ring indication, line power, and call-progress indicators. These functions are provided by default on FXS and FXO interfaces, but may require some customization to work in specific environments. The following voice-port parameters and configuration commands are common to both FXS and FXO interfaces.

Off-hook signaling on FXO and FXS interfaces can be performed using either loop start or ground start. For most applications, the default of loop start is appropriate. The voice-port command for setting the off-hook signaling type is the following:

```
signal {loop-start | ground-start}
```

Call-progress tones are transmitted by the local interface to indicate ringing and other call-status events. Since these tones vary from country to country, voice ports are customizable on a per-region basis. The default setting is us for United States. To change a voice port to use tones from a different locale use the following command:

```
cptone locale
```

where locale is selected from Table 6-3.

TABLE 6-3

Call-Progress Tone Locale Keywords

Keyword	Locale	Keyword	Locale	Keyword	Locale
ar	Argentina	is	Iceland	pl	Poland
au	Australia	in	India	pt	Portugal
at	Austria	id	Indonesia	ru	Russian Federation
be	Belgium	ie	Ireland	sg	Singapore
br	Brazil	il	Israel	sk	Slovakia
ca	Canada	it	Italy	si	Slovenia
cn	China	jp	Japan	za	South Africa
co	Columbia	kr	Korea Republic	es	Sweden
cz	Czech Republic	lu	Luxembourg	ch	Switzerland
dk	Denmark	my	Malaysia	tw	Taiwan
fi	Finland	mx	Mexico	th	Thailand
fr	France	nl	Netherlands	tr	Turkey
de	Germany	nz	New Zealand	gb	Great Britain
gr	Greece	no	Norway	us	United States
hk	Hong Kong	pe	Peru	ve	Venezuela
hu	Hungary	ph	Philippines		

Private-Line Automatic Ring Down

Automatic ring down circuits have statically configured endpoints and do not require user dialing to connect calls. When the phone on one end of the circuit is taken off-hook, the call is automatically connected and the phone on the remote end begins to ring. Examples of private-line automatic ring down (PLAR) applications are connections between brokers and trading floors for time-sensitive transactions where dialing time is considered costly or even the famous "bat phone" which automatically linked Batman to Commissioner Gordon's office. Voice ports configured for PLAR map to a single destination which is specified by a dial string. The command to configure a voice port for PLAR operation follows:

```
connection plar string
```

where `string` is the phone number or dial string of the destination

FXS Specific Command

FXS interfaces are responsible for generating ring signals when incoming calls are present. Since some electronic ringers may not respond to certain frequencies, Cisco includes a command to adjust the frequency of the ring tone it generates on a per-voice-port basis. The default value of 25 Hz works for most devices, but it can be modified with the command:

```
ring frequency {25 | 50}
```

where 25 and 50 Hz are the only two frequencies supported.

FXO Specific Commands

FXO interfaces are responsible for receiving calls from and dialing to the PSTN or another switched network. This means that the router must answer calls and also effectively communicate dial strings with the external voice network. Cisco allows for administrators to adjust the number of rings required before the router answers an incoming call. Cisco also supports touch-tone and pulse for outbound dialing. By default, the router answers after one ring and dials using tone dialing also known as Dual-tone Multiple Frequency (DTMF). The following voice port commands can be used to change this behavior.

```
ring number number
```

and

```
dial-type dtmf | pulse
```

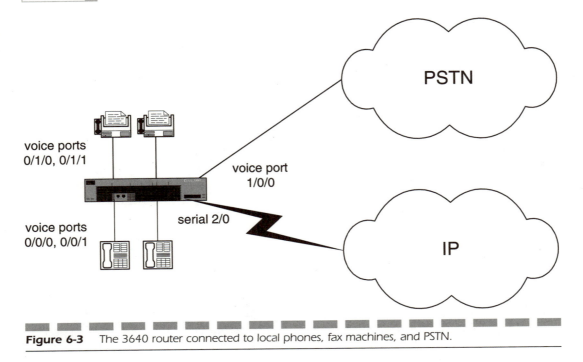

Figure 6-3   The 3640 router connected to local phones, fax machines, and PSTN.

where `number` is the number of rings required before the router will answer and `dtmf` stands for *dual tone multiple frequency* dialing which is more commonly known as touch-tone.

EXAMPLE   In an FXO Voice Port Configuration, Figure 6-3 shows a 3640 voice-enabled router connected to the PSTN via an FXO port and four local phones using FXS ports. The PSTN requires pulse dialing with ground start and the two fax machines require 50-Hz ring tones. Figure 6-4 shows an excerpt of the router configuration containing the voice-port details.

E&M Interfaces

Some of the parameters for FXO/FXS interfaces also apply to E&M interfaces. However, additional parameters are required to support the different E&M's types, wiring configurations, and off-hook detection schemes.

Figure 6-4

FXO voice port con-
figuration example—
router configuration.

```
!
hostname vp_ex_1
!
...
!
voice-port 0/0/0
!
voice-port 0/0/1
!
voice-port 0/1/0
 ring frequency 50
!
voice-port 0/1/1
 ring frequency 50
!
voice-port 1/0/0
 dial-type pulse
 signal ground-start
!
voice-port 1/0/1
!
interface Ethernet2/0
 no ip address
 shutdown
!
interface Ethernet2/1
 no ip address
 shutdown
!
interface Serial2/0
 ip address 192.168.1.1 255.255.255.0
!
interface Serial2/1
 no ip address
 shutdown
!
```

The wide range of configuration possibilities and larger variance in vendor implementations make it unlikely that the default values will work
for all parameters. This section presents the basic configuration parameters for E&M interfaces.

Off-hook signaling for analog E&M interfaces is explained in detail in
Chapter 3. The three different methods, wink start, immediate start, and
delay start, are all configurable and should be matched with the device
to which the router is connecting. The voice port command which accom-
plishes this is the following:

```
signal { wink-start | immediate | delay-dial }
```

where the default is wink-start.

The dial method can be set to touch-tone (DTMF) or pulse and should match the expectations of the system to which the router is connecting. The appropriate voice-port command is

```
dial-type { dtmf | pulse }
```

where `dtmf` stands for Dual Tone Multiple Frequency dialing, which is more commonly known as touch tone. DTMF is the default.

The details of call progress tones are standardized within geographic regions. Cisco routers support several regional call progress tones. Unlike FXS/FXO interfaces, regional support is limited to a few regions. These are configured with the following voice-port command:

```
cptone region
```

where `region` can be: `australia`, `brazil`, `china`, `finland`, `france`, `germany`, `japan`, `northamerica`, or `unitedkingdom`.

E&M interfaces can work in 2-wire or 4-wire configurations. The number refers to the number of wires used for voice transmission, not the total number of wires used on the interfaces. The following voice-port command is used to establish the number of wires to be used for the interface.

```
operation { 2-wire | 4-wire}
```

where 2-wire is the default.

The different physical wiring and signaling methods used for E&M are grouped into 5 types, E&M I through V. These types are discussed in detail in Chapter 3. The router should be configured to comply with the type of E&M signaling used by the external system it is connecting to. Cisco currently supports all types except for type IV. The voice-port command used to set the E&M type is

```
type { 1 | 2 | 3 | 5 }
```

where type I is the default and the rest are dynamically configurable with the command above.

The terminating impedance of the voice port must be set properly to prevent undue echo. The PBX or other system which is connecting to the router should specify the impedance required. Mismatched impedance settings will cause voice signals to be reflected at the interface and cause a significant amount of echo. PBX systems and central office switches in the United States usually run at 600 real ohms (600 r). The two ports on a VIC must be set to the same impedance and the ports must be reset by shutting it down and reenabling it before a new impedance setting will take effect. The voice-port command for setting the impedance follows:

```
impedance {600c | 600r | 900c | complex1 | complex2 }
```

where

600c **represents 600 ohms complex**

600r **represents 600 ohms real**

900c **represents 900 ohms complex**

complex1 **and** complex2 **are as written**

The default value is 600r.

Private-line-automatic-ring-down (PLAR) circuits can also be set up over E&M interfaces. Voice ports configured for PLAR automatically connect to a fixed destination as soon as the off-hook condition is detected. PLAR is configured using the following command:

```
connection plar string
```

where string is the phone number or dial string of the destination.

EXAMPLE   In this example of an E&M Voice Port Configuration, Figure 6-5 depicts a PBX connected to a 3640 which uses a company's IP infrastructure to transport voice traffic to the central site. The PBX requires 4-wire E&M type V with wink start and specifies an impedance of 900c. Figure 6-6 is a configuration excerpt from the 3640 router connected to the PBX.

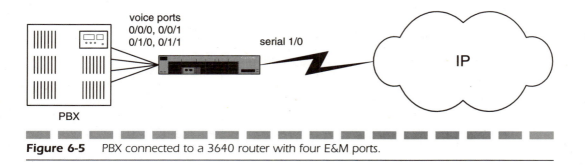

Figure 6-5   PBX connected to a 3640 router with four E&M ports.

■■ ■■ ■■ ■■
Figure 6-6
E&M voice port configuration example router configuration excerpt.

```
!
hostname vp_ex_2
!
...
!
voice-port 0/0/0
 operation 4-wire
 type 5
 impedance 900c
!
voice-port 0/0/1
 operation 4-wire
 type 5
 impedance 900c
!
voice-port 0/1/0
 operation 4-wire
 type 5
 impedance 900c
!
voice-port 0/1/1
 operation 4-wire
 type 5
 impedance 900c
!
!
interface Ethernet1/0
 ip address 172.16.1.0 255.255.255.0
!
interface Ethernet1/1
 no ip address
 shutdown
!
interface Serial1/0
 ip address 192.168.1.1 255.255.255.0
!
interface Serial1/1
 no ip address
 shutdown
!
```

Additional Voice-Port Parameters

In addition to the basic parameters presented above, additional voice-port parameters allow for the tweaking of voice-port sensitivity, timing values, and for the enabling of echo cancellation. The adjustment of these parameters helps fine tune the voice-port interface to better interact with the connected telephony device. The following parameters are configurable on all analog interfaces.

Gain and Loss Parameters

To control the input sensitivity of the voice port, the input gain parameter can be adjusted. It amplifies or reduces the voice signal based upon the factor specified. Input gain can increase the signal by as much as 14 decibels and decrease it by as much as 6 decibels. Adjusting the input gain may be required to maintain consistent volume levels throughout the voice network. The voice-port command for adjusting the input gain is

```
input gain n
```

where n is an integer between -6 and 14 representing the desired decrease or increase in decibels. The default is 0.

The voice-enabled routers also allow for control over the output levels of voice traffic through a voice port. Reducing the voice signal at the output port allows for an otherwise standard signal to be reduced in order to adapt to a specific system receiving the signal from that port. The command which controls the level at which signals are reduced at the output voice port is

```
output attenuation n
```

where n is an integer from 0 to 14 and the default value is 0. Note that the output level cannot be increased.

Echo Cancellation

Echo caused by impedance mismatches impacts the perceived quality of voice traffic and can render the connection unusable. Echo is essentially the electrical voice signal reflected back from an end system. To counteract echo, an echo canceler can be placed inline between the codec transmitting to the voice port and the end system. Echo cancelers operate by storing samples of voice signals in one direction and waiting for the reflection of the stored signal to be received on the return path. At this point the canceler combines the echoed signal with the inverse of the memorized signal and effectively eliminates the echo. The length of time which an echo canceler remembers traffic patterns is sometimes called its *coverage*. To enable echo cancellation and adjust its coverage, the following voice-port commands are used:

```
echo-cancel enable
```

and

```
echo-cancel coverage time
```

where time is in milliseconds and configurable to 16, 24, or 32 ms. The default value is 16 ms.

Timing Parameters

To enable voice ports to interoperate with a wide array of systems, various timing parameters are configurable on a per-voice-port basis. These parameters control timing for the transmission and duration of both dialed digits and signaling transitions.

Dialing Specific Timers

The amount of time a voice port waits for digits to be dialed after the connected device goes off-hook can be adjusted. To change this timeout from the default value of 10 seconds, the following voice-port command is used:

```
timeouts initial n
```

where n is the desired timeout in seconds. Acceptable values are from 0 to 120 seconds.

The amount of time the voice port will wait for the next digit to be dialed is configurable as well. If the timeout is exceeded, a tone is sent to the user and the call is terminated. The default of 10 seconds can be changed using the following voice-port command:

```
timeouts interdigit n
```

where n is the desired timeout in seconds. Acceptable values are from 0 to 120 seconds.

When configured for DTMF dialing, the duration of individual digit tones and the time in between subsequent digits can be configured. The voice-port commands used for this are

```
timing digit m
timing inter-digit n
```

where m and n are in milliseconds between 50 and 100 ms and the default for each is 100 ms.

When configured for pulse dialing, the duration of the individual pulses is configurable and so is the time that the voice port waits in between digits. Note that with pulse dialing, digits are comprised of multiple pulses. The default-time pulse duration is 20 ms and the default time in between digits is 500 ms. The appropriate voice-port commands to modify these attributes are

```
timing pulse-digit m
timing pulse-inter-digit n
```

where m and n are in milliseconds; m is configurable between 10 and 20 ms and n is configurable between 100 and 1000 ms. FXS interfaces do not support these commands since they do not perform outbound dialing.

E&M-Specific Signaling Commands

E&M interfaces support additional timing commands which relate to E&M specific signaling procedures. These commands are extremely valuable for fine-tuning E&M connections to PBX systems.

The duration between the voice port receiving an inactive seizure signal and then clearing the call can be adjusted from the default time value of 400 ms using the following command:

```
timing clear-wait n
```

where n is in milliseconds and may be any value between 200 and 2000 ms.

Delay Dial Commands

To adjust the delay signal duration the following voice-port command is used:

```
timing delay-duration n
```

where acceptable values for n are from 100 to 5000 milliseconds and the default is 2000 ms.

To adjust the minimum delay before line seizure for outbound calls on delay-dial voice ports, the following voice-port command is used:

```
timing delay-start n
```

where acceptable values for n are from 20 to 2000 milliseconds and the default is 300 ms.

Wink Start Commands

To adjust the duration of the "wink" from its default setting of 200 ms, the following voice-port command is used:

```
timing wink-duration n
```

where acceptable values for n are from 100 to 400 milliseconds.

To adjust the amount of time which the voice port waits for a wink from a connected system, the following voice-port command is used:

```
timing wink-wait n
```

where acceptable values for n are from 100 to 5000 milliseconds and the default is 200 ms.

Digital Interfaces

Digital voice telephony was introduced to overcome some of the limitations of analog circuits including line noise and long-distance transmission. Since voice is inherently an analog signal, it must be adapted for transmission over a digital network. Pulse code modulation was developed to perform this task.

Signaling in digital networks is performed somewhat differently than in analog networks. There are two methods of signaling for T1 circuits, and they depend upon which type of circuit is provisioned.

Channelized T1 circuits use *channel-associated signaling*, which is sometimes called *robbed-bit signaling*. CAS steals a bit from every 6th frame and uses it to convey messages between the end systems. For telephony, CAS is capable of sending the following signals: ringing, hang-up, wink, pulse digit dialing, DNIS, ANI, as well as E&M and FXS ground start.

PRI circuits perform all signaling out of band on the D channel. The Q.931 protocol is used to communicate call setup, call supervision, call teardown, and supplementary services. Unlike CAS, ISDN signaling does not steal any bits from the voice channels. Instead, it allocates an entire channel for signaling. This reduces the number of channels available for voice calls from 24 to 23.

Cisco Digital Interface Support

The AS5300 supports both T1/E1 PRI and T1 CAS for connecting to PBXs or the PSTN. The type chosen depends entirely on the interfaces available from both your service provider and the PBX. The AS5300 is software configurable to support either configuration.

The digital interfaces on the AS5300 do not generate voice-port constructs within the configuration; rather the standard controller-interface construct is used. This is consistent with the ISDN and channelized T1 configuration methods used throughout Cisco's product lines.

Configuring PRI Interfaces

To configure the controller for primary rate ISDN operation, several tasks must be performed. First the standard physical-layer parameters such as framing, encoding, and timing must be configured. Then the interface must be configured to forward ISDN calls marked as voice bearer to the voice-processing software and hardware.

Controller Commands

To establish the ISDN switch type with which the port will be communicating, the following command is entered on the controller interfaces:

```
isdn switch-type switch-type
```

where *switch-type* is one of primary-5ess, primary-4ess, primary-dms100, primary-ni, primary-net5, primary-ntt, or primary-ts014. The most common are 5ess and dms100.

The framing and line encoding should be configured with the following controller commands:

```
framing esf
encoding b8zs
```

The timing or clock source for the interface is set using the following controller command:

```
clock source [line | internal]
```

The last controller configuration step is to assign all of the 24 channels to a PRI group using the following command:

```
pri-group timeslots 1-24
```

This command generates a new interface construct within the router. The new interface will show up as a serial interface referencing channel

23, the D channel. The syntax uses a colon to designate the channel after the interface number. Since the D channel handles all signaling for ISDN circuits, it is the appropriate place for signaling related commands. For incoming voice calls to be routed to the AS5300's voice-processing subsystem, the following interface commands are used:

```
interface serial0:23
 isdn incoming-voice voice
```

The above commands are condensed into the configuration excerpt shown in Figure 6-7.

Configuring T1 CAS

To configure the AS5300 to support channelized T1 interfaces with CAS, you must first determine the type of signaling it will support. The available options are represented below:

E&M Feature Group B. E&M fgb implements wink start. In order to let the originating system know that the terminating system is ready to receive dialing digits, the terminating system responds to the originating system's off-hook signal with a quick on-hook, off-hook, on-hook sequence. The quick transition is called a wink.

E&M Feature Group D. E&M fgd performs the wink start as in E&M feature group B, but also adds a second wink after receiving the dialing digits. This is called wink start with acknowledgment.

E&M Immediate Start. With E&M immediate start, the originating system simply goes off hook and sends dialing digits. The terminating system goes off hook after receiving the digits.

Figure 6-7

ISDN port configuration.

```
!
controller T1 0
 isdn switch-type primary-5ess
 framing esf
 clock source line primary
 linecode b8zs
 pri-group timeslots 1-24
 !
 !
interface Serial0:23
 isdn incoming-voice voice
 !
```

FXS Ground Start. FXS ground start provides immediate off-hook line seizure from the network by dropping the A bit in the ESF frame to 0 and simulates ringing by toggling the B bit.

The router's signaling type must be matched up with the PBX system's signaling type for proper operation.

The next step is to configure the physical-layer parameters on the router's controller interface. This is done the same way as it is on other channelized interfaces within IOS-based routers. The common steps as outlined below are performed.

1. The framing and line encoding should be configured with the following controller commands:

```
framing esf
encoding b8zs
```

2. The timing or clock source for the interface is set using the following controller command:

```
clock source [line | internal]
```

3. The last controller configuration step is to assign all of the 24 channels to a channel-associated signaling group using the following command:

```
cas-group n timeslots range type signal [[tone] [service]]
```

where

n is a channel group number and should be unique within the router; valid channel group numbers are from 0 to 23.

range specifies the timeslots to be used for the channel group; usually 1–24, but may be configured to support fewer channels

signal specifies the type of signaling being used between the telephony system and the router; valid signal keywords are e&m-fgb, e&m-fgd, e&m-immediate, fxs-loop-start, and fxs-ground-start

tone is either dtmf or mf

service is either dnis or ani-dnis

An example of a CAS digital interface configuration is provided in Figure 6-8. This is all that is required to enable the physical-layer functions of a digital-voice interface. The details of ring parameters, off-hook signaling, and dialed digits are handled by either the signaling type

Figure 6-8
Sample CAS inter-
face.

```
controller t1 0
 framing esf
 linecode b8zs
 clock source line
 cas-group 0 timeslots 1-24 type e&m-fgb dtmf dnis
```

(E&M or FXS) or the interface type (CAS/PRI). The details of these signaling methods are discussed in Chapter 3.

Dial Peers

Dial peers are an important construct within Cisco's voice-networking
software. Dial peers specify a call endpoint or destination. This endpoint
can be a physical port or remote destination. Each dial peer represents a
discrete call leg. Multiple dial peers are required to receive and forward
a call through a voice-enabled router.

EXAMPLE
To help understand dial peers, a basic example will be utilized. It is a
simple voice over IP network composed of two Cisco 3620 routers connected over a T1 WAN link. The phone devices are standard analog
phones. The example will be built upon throughout the remainder of the
chapter, and is depicted in Figure 6-9.

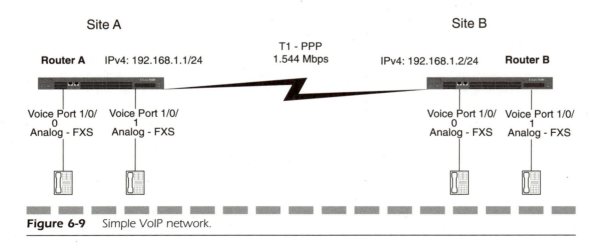

Figure 6-9   Simple VoIP network.

Call Legs

Voice calls can be broken down into discrete segments referred to as *call legs*. The connection from the voice device to the voice port on the router is a single call leg and the VoIP call from the router to another VoIP router is a call leg. When put together, they form a connection between the source caller and the destination VoIP router. In order the complete the call, two more call legs would be required. First, the destination router must understand the incoming call leg and terminate the VoIP session; second, the destination router must have a connection to the receiving phone device. This is summarized in Table 6-4 and Figure 6-10.

The first two call legs are defined by the originating router, router A. From router A's perspective, it receives an inbound call on a voice port and then packetizes and routes that call to a foreign voice over IP destination. Similarly, the second two call legs are defined by the terminating router, router B. From router B's perspective, it receives voice-over-IP call, depacketizes it, and then routes it to a directly connected voice port.

Dial Peers

In order to model these call legs in the router configuration, Cisco created a configuration object called dial peers. An individual dial peer is associated with a single call leg. Given the call legs described above, we can see that there are two types of call legs: one associated with the router to telephony device and another associated with the router-generated voice call over the network. In associating these call legs with dial peers, Cisco refers to the first type as a POTS (Plain Old Telephone Service) dial peer and the second as a VoIP (voice over IP) dial peer. With this knowledge, we can identify the type of dial-peer associated with each leg in our table. This is demonstrated in Table 6-5.

TABLE 6-4

Call Legs for Simple VoIP Call

Call Leg	Description
Call leg 1	Phone to VoIP router A
Call leg 2	VoIP call from router A to router B
Call leg 3	VoIP session termination by router B
Call leg 4	Router B to destination phone

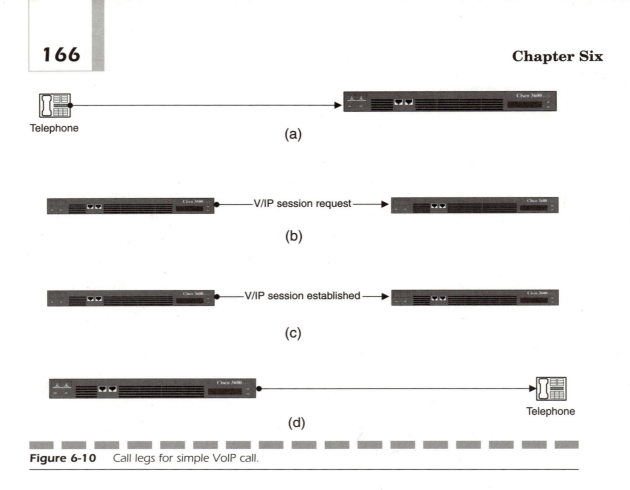

Figure 6-10   *Call legs for simple VoIP call.*

Now that the type of each call leg is identified, we need to start associating the dial peers with physical ports and voice-over-IP peers. Dial peers handle this, as well as the addressing of voice ports and the routing of voice calls. They are roughly analogous to the assignment of IP addresses and static IP routes within the router. The obvious difference is that addressing in the voice world is done with phone numbers or dial strings, while addressing in the IP world is done with IP addresses.

TABLE 6-5

Call Legs with Dial Peer Types

Call Leg	Description	Type
Call leg 1	Phone to VoIP router A	POTS
Call leg 2	VoIP call from router A to router B	VoIP
Call leg 3	VoIP session termination by router B	VoIP
Call leg 4	Router B to destination phone	POTS

POTS Dial Peers

Physical-voice ports can only be associated with POTS dial peers. To accomplish this, a POTS dial peer must be created using the global command:

```
dial-peer voice n pots
```

where n is a dial-peer tag and can be any number from 1 to 2147483647.

Dial-peer tags must be unique within the same router. However, they are only locally significant, so the same dial-peer tags can be used in other routers within the network. In an effort to provide some consistency, we will use the call-leg number in our example as the dial-peer tag. To assign the physical-voice ports to a POTS dial peer, the following configurations would be used in routers A and B:

Router A:

```
dial-peer voice 1 pots
 port 1/0/0
```

Router B:

```
dial-peer voice 4 pots
 port 1/0/1
```

This indicates to the router's voice software that dial peer 1 in router A is linked to physical-voice port 1/0/0 and that dial peer 4 in router B is linked to physical-voice port 1/0/1. The next step is to provide the router with addressing information so that the voice software can route calls to the appropriate ports.

When we want to assign an address to an interface in the IP world, we simply enter interface configuration mode and assign it using the `ip address a.a.a.a mask m.m.m.m` command. In the voice arena, we assign a dial string (phone number) to individual dial peers. Underneath the POTS dial-peer statement, the statement `destination-pattern` is used to associate a phone number with a given POTS voice port. To continue our example, we will add extension numbers to the phones in our simple VoIP network. For simplicity we will assign the extensions 11 and 12 to the voice ports in router A and 21 and 22 to the voice ports in router B. Also, to continue our example, we will update our table and network diagram with Table 6-6 and Figure 6-11.

TABLE 6-6

Dial Peers with
Destination
Patterns and Ports

Call Leg	Description	Type	Destination Pattern	Voice Port
Call leg 1	Phone to VoIP router A	POTS	11	1/0/0
Call leg 2	VoIP call from router A to router B	VoIP		
Call leg 3	VoIP session termination by router B	VoIP		
Call leg 4	Router B to destination phone	POTS	22	1/0/1

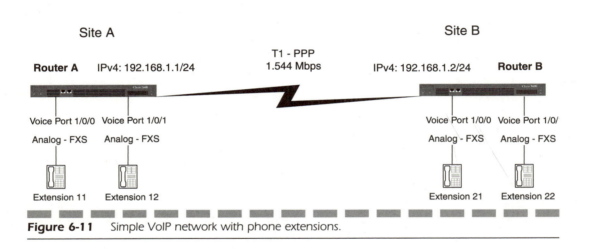

Figure 6-11   Simple VoIP network with phone extensions.

Applying the destination-pattern command in our example yields the
following configuration for routers A and B.

Router A:

```
dial-peer voice 1 pots
  port 1/0/0
  destination-pattern 11
```

Router B:

```
dial-peer voice 4 pots
  port 1/0/1
  destination-pattern 22
```

The destination-pattern command will be described in more detail later in this chapter, but for now let's move on to configuring the dial peers for call legs 2 and 3.

VoIP Dial Peers

In order to route IP packets, the router must have a routing table. The basic elements of a routing table entry are the destination network and the next-hop-IP-address. In other words, a routing table entry includes the ultimate destination for the packet and where the router needs to send the packet it to get it to that destination. Cisco's voice-over-IP software works similarly in that it creates call-routing tables based upon destination phone numbers and the IP address of the voice-over-IP router servicing the destination phone number.

To manually create IP routing tables in a Cisco router, static routes are entered into the configuration with the `ip route` command. To manually create a voice routing entry, a VoIP dial peer must be created. The VoIP dial peer simply associates a destination phone number or pattern with a voice-over-IP target. The `destination-pattern` command is used to identify the remote phone number and the `session target` command is used to identify the IP address of the remote voice-over-IP router. Again, these commands will be discussed in more detail later, but first let's see how they apply to our example. Here are the VoIP dial-peer statements associated with call legs 2 and 3 in our example.

Router A:

```
dial-peer voice 2 voip
  destination-pattern 22
  session target ipv4:192.168.1.2
```

Router B:

```
dial-peer voice 3 voip
  destination-pattern 11
  session target ipv4:192.168.1.1
```

This means that when router A receives the digits 22 from a voice port, it will match those digits to dial peer 2 which instructs the router to forward the call to voice-over-IP peer 192.168.1.2. Implicit in the VoIP dial peer is the router's need to packetize the data. Similarly, router B matches the digits 11 and then invokes dial peer 3 to forward the call to router A.

The prefix ipv4: is added to the IP address of the remote router to indicate that the destination is a version 4 IP address and not a hostname to be resolved through DNS.

Finishing the Dial-Peer Statements

In order to enable the second phone at each site, additional dial-peer statements must be configured. To enable the voice port and assign it a phone number, we create another POTS dial-peer statement.

In order to make the second phone at each site reachable from the remote site, we will enable one of the wildcard features associated with the destination pattern command. For our immediate purposes, we will use the . wildcard which represents a single digit wildcard. The use of a period in a destination pattern allows for any single digit to be used in its place. For our example, the phone extensions for router A begin with a 1 and the phone extensions for router B begin with a 2. To identify all two-digit calls beginning with a 1, we can use the notation: 1. Similarly, the notation: 2. will identify all two-digit calls beginning with a 2.

This allows us to make the following changes to our example:

Router A:

```
dial-peer voice 5 pots
   destination-pattern 12
   port 1/0/1
!
dial-peer voice 2 voip
   destination-pattern 2.
   session target ipv4:192.168.1.2
```

Router B:

```
dial-peer voice 6 pots
   destination-pattern 21
   port 1/0/0
!
dial-peer voice 3 voip
   destination-pattern 1.
   session target ipv4:192.168.1.1
```

The session target field is added to the dial-peer table and included in Table 6-7.

To help organize this information better, Cisco suggests creating a dial-peer configuration table containing the pertinent information. The recommended columns are dial-peer tag, extension, destination-pattern, type, voice port, session target, CODEC, and QoS. Reorganizing the table from our example into Cisco's recommended format yields Table 6-8.

TABLE 6-7

Dial-Peer Table
with Session
Targets

Call Leg	Description	Type	Destination Pattern	Voice Port	Session Target
Call leg 1	Phone to VoIP router A	POTS	11	1/0/0	
	Phone to VoIP router A	POTS	12	1/0/1	
Call leg 2	VoIP call from router A to router B	VoIP	2.		192.168.1.2
Call leg 3	VoIP session termination by router B	VoIP	1.		192.168.1.1
Call leg 4	Router B to destination phone	POTS	22	1/0/1	
	Router B to destination phone	POTS	21	1/0/0	

The fields for extension, CODEC, and QoS will all be discussed later in the chapter.

Dial Peer Summary

Before moving on to a more detailed discussion of dial peers, a review of the concepts demonstrated by the example is appropriate:

1. Call legs are discrete segments of an end-to-end call.
2. Call legs are identified relative to a single router and include an inbound call leg and an outbound call leg.

TABLE 6-8

Dial-Peer
Configuration
Table

Dial-Peer Tag	Ext.	Destination Pattern	Type	Voice Port	Session Target	CODEC	QoS
			Router A				
1		11	POTS	1/0/0			
2		2.	VoIP		192.168.1.2	G.729	Best effort
5		12	POTS	1/0/1			
			Router B				
3		1.	VoIP		192.168.1.1	G.729	Best effort
4		22	POTS	1/0/1			
6		21	POTS	1/0/0			

3. Call legs are mapped to the dial-peer router configuration object.

4. POTS dial peers are used to assign addresses to voice ports.

5. VoIP dial peers are used to map phone numbers to voice-over-IP sessions.

6. Dial-peer configuration tables should be generated to document the dial plan and assist in the configuration of voice-enabled routers.

7. Dialed digits are collected by the router and used to route calls by mapping them to the proper dial peer.

8. Wildcards can be used to simplify dialing plans.

Dial-Peer Details

The preceding example presented a simple overview of dial peers and demonstrated how they are used to achieve voice connectivity over the network. This section will discuss additional configuration options for dial peers and show how they can be used in real world scenarios.

As mentioned earlier, dial peers are used to identify individual call legs and to customize each call leg. In addition to simply identifying phone numbers and destinations, dial peers can also specify the type of voice encoding used, IP quality of service mechanisms, and voice-activity detection.

Important Commands

Destination Pattern

The destination pattern dial-peer command assigns phone numbers (patterns) to dial peers. The router's voice software then routes voice calls based upon these patterns. This is loosely analogous to the assigning of IP addresses to a network interface in the router. Wildcards and other operators help to simplify the creation of dial plans. The full syntax for the command follows:

```
destination-pattern [+]string[t]
```

where

A leading + indicates that the string is an E.164 standard number; its use is optional.

string is the dial string or phone number comprised of digits (0–9), the letters A through D, or the * or #; acceptable operators are (1) a comma calls for a 1-s pause in dialing, (2) a period indicates a single digit wildcard (a period within a string matches any valid character for that location).

A trailing *t* indicates that variable-length dial strings are in use and that the router should wait for the interdigit timeout to expire before acting on the string.

To specify a specific phone number for a voice port, the following configuration would be used.

```
destination-pattern 2905000
```

Alternately, the following command could be used:

```
destination-pattern +2905000
```

In a scenario where the voice port was handing off to a PBX system which supported all of the phone extensions from 2905000 through 2905999, the following command would be appropriate:

```
destination-pattern 2905...
```

Session Target

As mentioned previously, the session target command identifies the remote end of the VoIP call. The destination can be specified using an IP address, a DNS name, or a loopback. The use of DNS can help simplify identification of remote peers in some scenarios. The use of loopbacks helps test connectivity and voice quality through different parts of the network. The full syntax for the session target dial-peer command follows:

```
session target target
```

where *target* could be either a remote VoIP peer or a loopback. The keywords and their descriptions are explained below.

Destination Based

ipv4:*address* where *address* is the actual IP address of the remote VoIP peer.

dns:*hostname* where *hostname* is the DNS name for the destination router. For example, the following configuration would be used for the router to route the voice call to the IP address identified by rts36v1.company.com:

```
ip name-server 192.168.1.250
!
...
!
dial-peer voice 669 voip
  session target dns:rts36v1.company.com
!
```

Also, the following operators can be used along with the DNS key-word:

:s specifies that the source pattern be used as part of the DNS name.

:d specifies that the destination pattern be used as part of the DNS name.

This allows an administrator to assign the device's phone number as its DNS name, which can simplify the identification of devices. In a network with multiple remote offices, it may be convenient to enter the remote sites' phone numbers as hostnames in DNS and group their destination patterns such that they could be identifiable with a common pattern prefix that is unique from other elements. The following DNS d example demonstrates the flexibility this introduces.

EXAMPLE

In the network diagram shown in Figure 6-12, the remote sites each have a phone number that begins with 21229051. Therefore, the following configuration would allow the AS5300 at the central site to reach each remote site without requiring a separate dial-peer paragraph.

```
ip name-server 192.168.1.250
ip domain-name company.com
!
...
!
dial-peer voice 99 voip
  destination-pattern 121229051..
  session target dns:$d$.company.com
!
```

The notation u specifies that the unmatched portion of the destination pattern be used as the hostname portion of the DNS name. This is

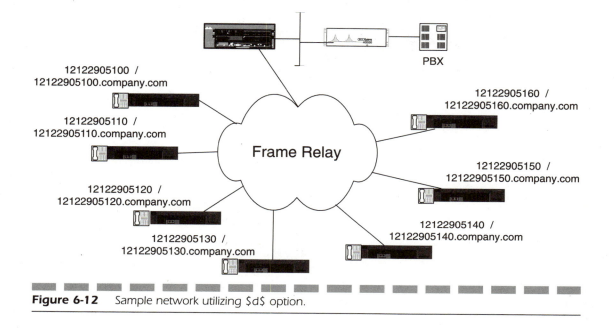

Figure 6-12 *Sample network utilizing d option.*

advantageous for addressing multiple endpoints with a single dial peer and for shortening the DNS names used. The following DNS u example demonstrates this.

EXAMPLE

In the previous example, the only part of the phone number which changed from site to site was the last two digits. This means that each site can be uniquely identified by those digits. Figure 6-13 illustrates this.

In this scenario, only the last two digits are used as the DNS hostname. It provides more of an extension-based DNS naming technique. The configuration excerpt which would support this is as follows:

```
ip name-server 192.168.1.250
ip domain-name company.com
!
...
!
dial-peer voice 99 voip
 destination-pattern 121229051..
 session target dns:$u$.company.com
!
```

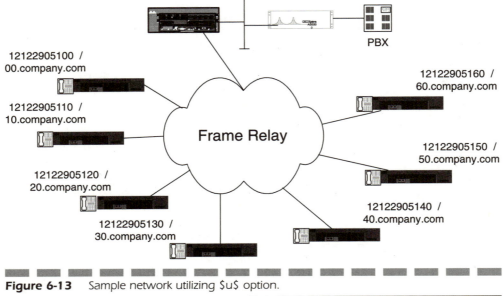

12122905100 /
00.company.com

12122905110 /
10.company.com

12122905120 /
20.company.com

12122905130 /
30.company.com

12122905160 /
60.company.com

12122905150 /
50.company.com

12122905140 /
40.company.com

PBX

Frame Relay

Figure 6-13   Sample network utilizing u option.

Loopback Based

`loopback:rtp` indicates that the VoIP session be looped back to the source at the RTP layer. This attribute is applicable to VoIP peers where the remote peer's traffic is looped back when it reaches the RTP layer. This verifies that the router has received the voice traffic and is capable of processing it as high as the RTP layer. This test verifies that proper network and IP connectivity are established. The path setup by this loopback is depicted in Figure 6-14.

`loopback:compressed` instructs the router to send the voice data through the compression software before looping it back to the source. This attribute is applicable to POTS peers and verifies that the compression/decompression software is working. It also provides a sampling of the representative quality of the voice signal after the compression/decompression cycle. The loopback path for this command is depicted in the left portion of Figure 6-15.

`loopback:uncompressed` instructs the router to loop the traffic back to the source before it reaches the compression software. This attribute is applicable to POTS peers and simply verifies physical connectivity through the voice port. The loopback path for this command is depicted in the right portion of Figure 6-15.

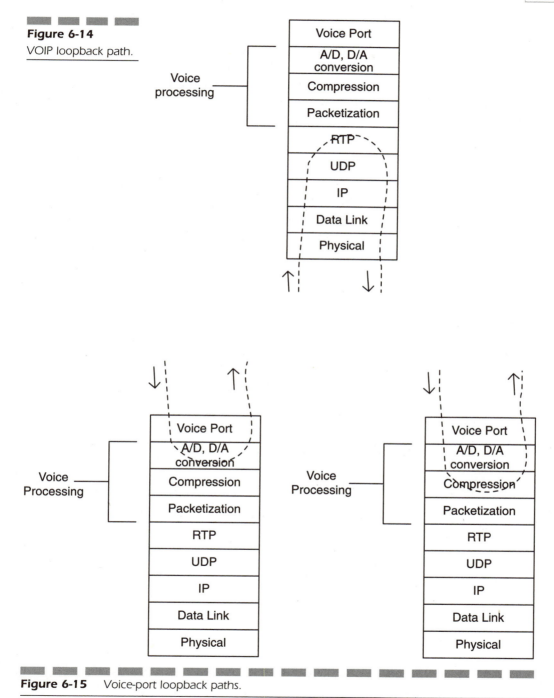

Figure 6-14
VOIP loopback path.

Figure 6-15   Voice-port loopback paths.

Prefix

To add a prefix for outgoing calls through a POTS dial peer, the prefix command is used. This is helpful when the voice-enabled router is connected to a PBX system which requires a 9 for accessing an outside line, or another number for accessing a specific trunk line. It can also be used to prepend an access code for dialed calls such as a 10-10-xxx code. The syntax for the dial-peer command is as follows:

```
prefix string
```

where *string* can be any number of digits or a comma. The comma provides a momentary pause in dialing.

The simple example of prepending 9 for outgoing calls through a PBX follows:

```
!
dial-peer voice 2 pots
 prefix 9,
 dest-pat 1212317....
 port 0:D
!
```

QoS Commands

The dial-peer construct allows for the specification of quality of service techniques including IP precedence and RSVP. This allows QoS mechanisms to be set more granularly.

IP PRECEDENCE   In Chapter 4, it was discussed how the setting of IP precedence bits in the IP header interworks with various IP QoS mechanisms such as weighted fair queuing, weighted random early detection, access lists, and others. One way of setting these bits for outgoing voice-over-IP calls is to set it within the dial-peer paragraph. The syntax for this dial-peer command follows:

```
ip precedence n
```

where n is a digit from 0 through 5. The significance of each IP-precedence value is presented in Table 6-9, but, in general, voice traffic should be given a precedence of 5.

A sample configuration for setting the IP precedence bit follows:

TABLE 6-9

IP Precedence Values

Value	Definition
0	Routine (normal traffic)
1	Priority
2	Immediate
3	Flash
4	Flash override
5	Critical
6	Internet (for network control traffic)
7	Network (for network control traffic)

```
!
dial-peer voice 101 voip
 destination-pattern 140852645..
 session target ipv4:192.168.1.1
 ip precedence 5
!
```

RSVP The use of RSVP for voice traffic can be enabled on a per-call basis by configuring it under the dial peer construct. The dial/peer, when activated, initiates an RSVP request to support the call. Since the request is made at the dial-peer level, it does not account for the bandwidth savings introduced by compressing RTP headers or other external techniques. This results in RSVP requests for 24 kbps when using G.729 compression instead of the actual 11 kbps which is realized when using CRTP.

As discussed in Chapter 4, an RSVP client can request two different types of QoS: controlled load or guaranteed delay. Cisco recommends the controlled-load model for voice traffic. The dial-peer command for enabling RSVP for a given dial peer is the following:

```
req-qos { best-effort | controlled-load | guaranteed delay }
```

where

> The best-effort option is the default and does not make a bandwidth reservation.

> The controlled-load option provides preferential service to the associated RSVP flow such that the performance for the flow mimics that of an unloaded network

> The guaranteed delay option attempts to guarantee queuing delay throughout the network

An example configuration using RSVP at the dial-peer level follows:

```
!
dial-peer voice 25 voip
 destination-pattern 29052..
 req-qos controlled-load
 session target ipv4:10.1.1.254
 !
```

Voice Encoding/Compression

To select the type of voice encoding and compression to be used for voice calls to a given destination, the `codec` command is used. It is configurable on a dial-peer basis so that different compression techniques may be used for different destinations. For instance, in a LAN environment where bandwidth is plentiful, G.711 PCM encoding may be used to achieve slightly higher voice quality. However, for remote calls, G.729 may be selected to conserve bandwidth over WAN links. The dial-peer command to select the voice encoding algorithm is

```
codec { g711ulaw | g711alaw | g729r8 }
```

where

> g711ulaw specifies 64-kbps PCM using the mu-law compander
>
> g711alaw specifies 64-kbps PCM using the a-law compander
>
> g729r8 specifies 8-kbps CS-ACELP compression and is the default

Voice-Activity Detection

As discussed in Chapter 3, voice-activity detection can be used to reduce the amount of bandwidth consumed by the session. Voice-activity detection identifies silent periods when the participant is listening and not speaking, and stops the transmission of voice packets during the silent period. The effectiveness of VAD is limited by its ability to identify the start and stop of conversations. As a result, VAD can sometimes clip voice signals and add a choppy nature to conversations. The dial-peer command used to enable VAD is simply

```
vad
```

One side effect of enabling VAD is that the remote user hears pure silence when silence is detected. This can be disconcerting since users are accustomed to hearing background noise. To combat this, generic noise can be transmitted over the local line to simulate background noise. The dial-peer command to generate the simulated background noise is

```
comfort-noise
```

SUMMARY

This chapter introduced the concepts of voice ports and dial peers. Voice ports handle the physical-layer communications with telephony devices while dial peers handle the logical connections between voice ports and VoIP destinations. It is important to understand the distinction between the two constructs and how the two work together to form an end-to-end voice network.

Chapter

7

Developing
a Dial Plan

Introduction

This chapter will cover the following:

- Issues associated with addressing
- Dial-plan organization
- Dial-plan building blocks creating the basic plan
- Integrating with the external world
- Addressing tools

The first step in planning the voice-specific functions on the routers is to develop a voice-network dialing plan. This plan will map out to the phone numbers associated with each voice port and router, as well as the connectivity and call routing between voice-enabled routers.

It is important that the dial plan be compatible with the other dial plans with which the router-based voice network will integrate. Most commonly, the other plans to consider are the existing private dial plan within the organization and that of the public switched telephone network (PSTN).

Issues Associated with Addressing

Developing dial plans is roughly analogous to developing an IP addressing scheme for IP-based data networks. Many of the same concepts and challenges apply. Some of the more prevalent issues are discussed below.

Dial-Plan Organization

Logical organization of phone numbers aids in management and administration. Phone set extensions can be grouped by floor, department, job function, or other criteria. Having well-defined phone extensions and prefixes eases management and troubleshooting because traffic is easily identified by its address. This provides a sense of consistency which humans both adapt to and come to rely on.

Consider an environment where phone extensions are allocated using the following formula:

The extension consists of four digits. The first digit identifies the location, the second digit identifies the department, and the remaining two digits identify the user. Specific user codes are reserved for functions that are present in each location. For instance, the trailing digits of 00 may identify reception or administrative function, 01 may identify the department head, while a user code of 11 or higher identifies employees of the department. Using this scheme, personnel can be easily identified by their phone extensions. More importantly, specific positions within the organization can be reached by simply applying the formula. To reach the receptionist for a given department within a location, a user dials the location code, followed by the department code, and then the numbers 00.

In the IP world, we often create IP addressing schemes that allocate addresses by location and department or floor. Further, we often reserve specific host addresses for routers and other network components. This helps manage and administer the network. For instance, knowing that the default router for a subnet is always the highest possible host address makes it easy to configure devices for the subnet and for network managers to Telnet to the router for troubleshooting. Applying similar concepts to voice network addressing affords the same benefits.

Scaling Issues

As phone networks grow, the size of their routing tables can grow as well. A phone network with randomly allocated phone numbers will have to maintain larger routing tables because routing information cannot be summarized. In a worst-case scenario, PBX systems would need to know the phone number of every phone in the network. Consider the scenario represented in Figure 7-1. The PBX at site A needs to know the number of each individual phone in the network. In this model, a new entry in each PBX system's routing table is created for every phone that gets added to the network, regardless of which site it is added to. This can become tedious and error prone very quickly. Even if each site had just 20 phones, the routing tables would require 60 entries in addition to the 20 locally attached numbers. This situation is roughly analogous to haphazard IP address assignment in data networks. In small to midsized networks, each router can support a full routing table including all IP network addresses in the network. As the network grows, this becomes more and more tedious and stresses the routing protocol and router resources (memory and CPU), as well as increasing management challenges.

Figures 7-1 and 7-2 depict a poorly planned voice network and a poorly planned IP network which use noncontiguous, nonsummarizable addresses at each site.

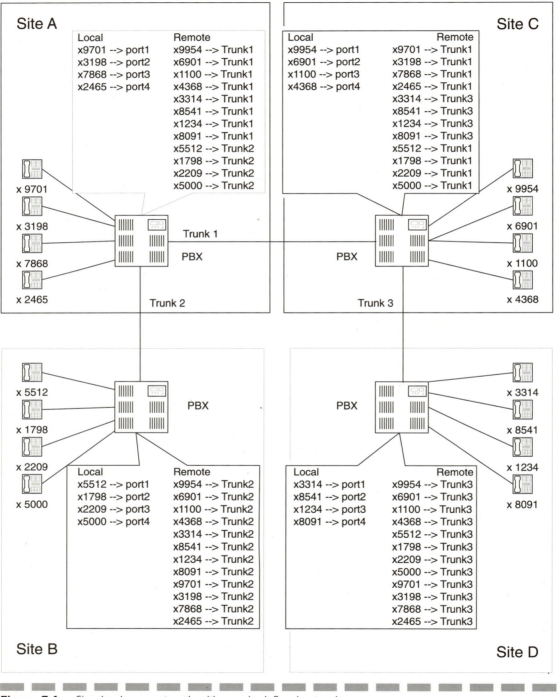

Figure 7-1 Simple phone network with poorly defined extensions.

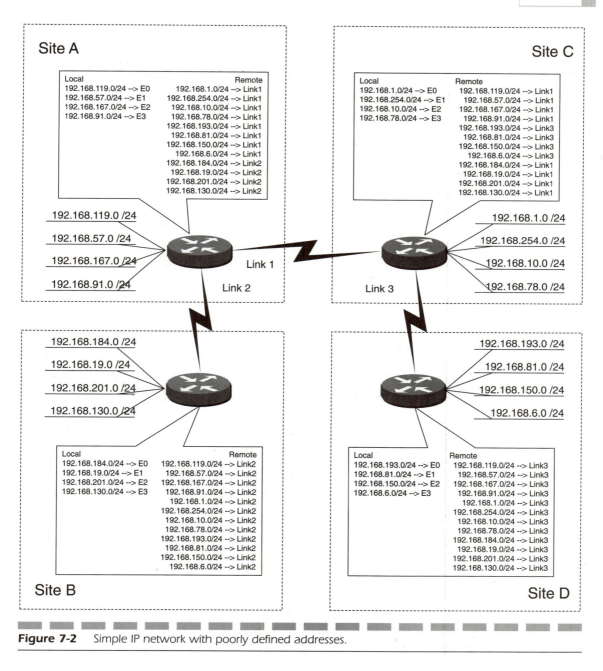

Figure 7-2 Simple IP network with poorly defined addresses.

In both scenarios, the resolution is to summarize routing information at specific boundaries. An example of this would be to use the site code model discussed in the previous section. Using site codes, site A's extensions could begin with a 1, site B's with a 2, site C's with a 3, and site D's with a 4. This would reduce the routing tables in each PBX to just three external entries. Each site also gains flexibility in that as long as the new phone numbers begin with the proper site code, phone numbers can be assigned to phones at a given site without modifying the routing tables at the other sites. This concept of summarizing routes and providing flexibility within a zone is directly analogous to the IP community's classless interdomain routing and its implementations in OSPF and BGP4. These techniques enable phone and data networks to scale while still maintaining flexibility at the local level.

Figures 7-3 and 7-4 demonstrate how an organized addressing scheme can reduce the complexity of the network. In both scenarios, the network is more logically addressed, reducing routing table sizes while easing administration and management.

NOTE: *In Figure 7-3 external routes are summarized and require a single entry in the routing table. In Figure 7-4 the four class C addresses contained at each site are summarized with a single route entry, using a 22-bit netmask.*

Interior/Exterior Routing

In the telephony world, corporations can secure a block of phone addresses from the local telephone company. The local exchange carrier then configures its switches to forward all traffic destined for phone numbers within that block to the corporation's phone systems. The local exchange carrier does not verify the availability of the destination addresses; it merely passes the calls along for the corporation's phone systems to process and route as required. The corporation's phone systems may use whatever means they like to route the calls internally. This operation is somewhat analogous to the interior and exterior routing in the IP world. In most situations, a corporation's ISP provides the corporation with a block of IP address space. The ISP then handles the routing of IP traffic to and from the addresses allocated to the corporation. The ISP's routers merely look at the network portion of the IP address in the data packets and forward relevant packets to the corpora-

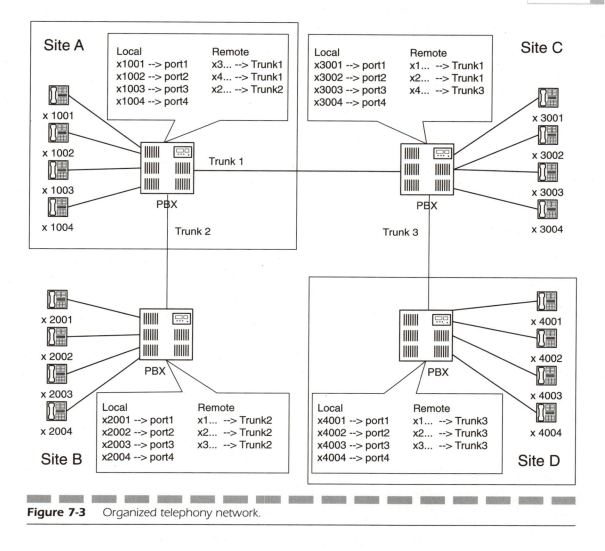

Figure 7-3   Organized telephony network.

tion's Internet-access router. The ISP knows nothing about the status of the particular host, nor does it care. Delivering traffic to the specific host is the job of the routers within the corporation's internal network.

In both the telephony and data scenarios described above, the network provider handles the routing of public traffic to and from the corporation. More importantly, the corporation's network can receive traffic destined for only the public address space that the provider has allocated. Also prevalent in both scenarios is the fact that external

Site A

Site C

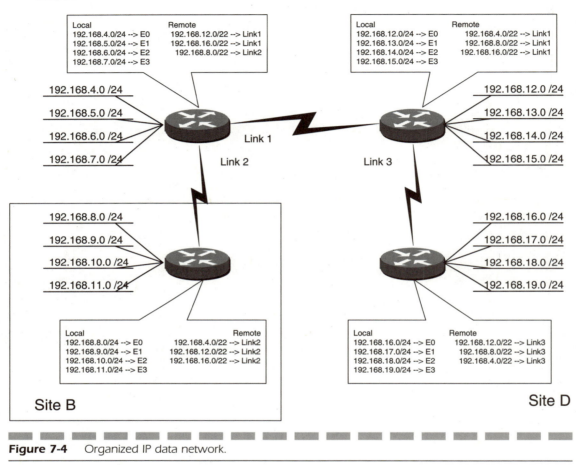

Local	Remote
192.168.4.0/24 --> E0	192.168.12.0/22 --> Link1
192.168.5.0/24 --> E1	192.168.16.0/22 --> Link1
192.168.6.0/24 --> E2	192.168.8.0/22 --> Link2
192.168.7.0/24 --> E3	

Local	Remote
192.168.12.0/24 --> E0	192.168.4.0/22 --> Link1
192.168.13.0/24 --> E1	192.168.8.0/22 --> Link1
192.168.14.0/24 --> E2	192.168.16.0/22 --> Link1
192.168.15.0/24 --> E3	

192.168.4.0 /24

192.168.5.0 /24

192.168.6.0 /24

192.168.7.0 /24

Link 1

Link 2

Link 3

192.168.12.0 /24

192.168.13.0 /24

192.168.14.0 /24

192.168.15.0 /24

192.168.8.0 /24

192.168.9.0 /24

192.168.10.0 /24

192.168.11.0 /24

192.168.16.0 /24

192.168.17.0 /24

192.168.18.0 /24

192.168.19.0 /24

Local	Remote
192.168.8.0/24 --> E0	192.168.4.0/22 --> Link2
192.168.9.0/24 --> E1	192.168.12.0/22 --> Link2
192.168.10.0/24 --> E2	192.168.16.0/22 --> Link2
192.168.11.0/24 --> E3	

Local	Remote
192.168.16.0/24 --> E0	192.168.12.0/22 --> Link3
192.168.17.0/24 --> E1	192.168.8.0/22 --> Link3
192.168.18.0/24 --> E2	192.168.4.0/22 --> Link3
192.168.19.0/24 --> E3	

Site B

Site D

Figure 7-4   Organized IP data network.

routing is performed on an aggregated-route basis and the corporation's network is ultimately responsible for delivery of the call to the end station.

The telephony and data worlds also offer the ability to more intelligently interact with the routing of traffic outside of the private network. The PSTN allows customers the means to obtain SS7 interconnects, while ISPs offer savvy customers to communicate with the ISP using the BGP4 routing protocol. These protocols and connections provide more dynamic connectivity with the public network and afford the customer greater control over routing traffic to and from their network.

Table 7-1 lists some of the issues in network addressing and shows how the telephony community and IP community have addressed them.

TABLE 7-1

Similarities between Telephony and IP Addressing

Issue	Telephony	Data/IP
Random addressing	Standardized phone number scheme using 10 digits (E.164)	Standardized addressing scheme using a 32-bit code (IP address)
User identity	Phone numbers: calling line ID (CLID), dialed number identification service (DNIS)	IP address (source/destination)
User to address resolution	Phone book, online directories	Domain name system (DNS)
Logical organization and grouping	Hierarchical addressing format; area code, CO code, number	Class A, B, C networks; IP subnetting and CIDR blocks
Route table size and complexity	Summarization at specific bit boundaries within the phone number; well-defined network hierarchy	Summarization at specific bit boundaries
Internal summarization and routing	Routing by summarized extensions	OSPF areas, summary routes
External summarization and routing	SS7 point codes and hierarchical network configuration	BGP4 with flexible policies
Single external contact address	Hunt groups, DNIS-based routing	Round-robin DNS, hardware and software load balancing
Intelligent session routing	DNIS/CLID-based routing	Policy-based routing
Security	Filtering by source number, destination number, long distance access, etc.	Filtering by MAC address, IP address, TCP/UDP port, etc.
Dynamic rerouting and policy control	SS7	BGP4
Address translation	A PBX allows many phone sets to use a small number of external trunk lines.	NAT software enables many hosts to use a small amount of publicly routable address space

Dial Plan Building Blocks

Chapter 6 discussed the concepts of voice ports and dial peers. These are the fundamental building blocks required for developing a dial plan. Voice ports identify physical voice interfaces, and dial peers are used to link physical-voice ports and voice over IP destinations. Each of these constructs is now described relative to their role in building voice over IP dial plans.

Voice Ports

Voice ports perform the physical-layer functions for connected telephony devices. They serve as placeholders within the configuration for external connections. Dial peers reference voice ports as POTS (plain old telephone service) ports.

Dial Peers

There are two types of dial peers: POTS and VoIP. POTS dial peers reference physical ports while VoIP dial peers reference voice over IP destinations.

POTS Dial Peers

POTS dial peers are identified by using the POTS keyword after the dial-peer command. The two main components of POTS dial peer are a physical voice port and a phone number. The port command is used to reference the voice port, and the destination-pattern command is used to associate a phone number with that port. Remember that the dial-peer tag is a user-defined number and does not correlate with the voice port in any way.

The following POTS detail peer example demonstrates the interaction between the voice ports and dial peers.

EXAMPLE   A Cisco 3640 router is equipped with a single voice module (NM-2V) and two 2-port FXS voice cards (VIC-2FXS) to provide a total of four voice ports. (See Figure 7-5.) The initial voice-specific configuration is shown in Figure 7-6.

To assign phone numbers to these ports, POTS dial-peer statements

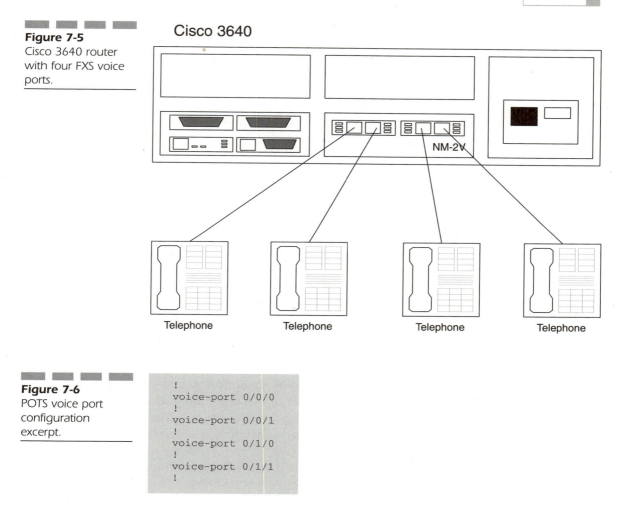

Figure 7-5
Cisco 3640 router
with four FXS voice
ports.

Cisco 3640

NM-2V

Telephone   Telephone   Telephone   Telephone

Figure 7-6
POTS voice port
configuration
excerpt.

```
!
voice-port 0/0/0
!
voice-port 0/0/1
!
voice-port 0/1/0
!
voice-port 0/1/1
!
```

can be used. Figure 7-7 contains the configuration statements that achieve this goal.

The configurations from Figure 7-6 and Figure 7-7 will enable the phones to connected to the router to place calls among themselves. That is, the phone connected to port 1/0/0 can call the phone connected to 1/1/1 by dialing 5555204.

This type of connectivity can be convenient when integrating very small offices where the expense of a small PBX or key system may be hard to justify. However, the router's local call switching functionality is limited and should not be viewed as a PBX or key system replacement.

Figure 7-7
Dial-peer
configuration
excerpt.

```
!
dial-peer voice 1000 pots
  destination-pattern +5555201
  port 0/0/0
!
dial-peer voice 1001 pots
  destination-pattern +5555202
  port 0/0/1
!
dial-peer voice 1010 pots
  destination-pattern +5555203
  port 0/1/0
!
dial-peer voice 1011 pots
  destination-pattern +5555204
  port 0/1/1
```

VoIP Dial Peers

The next step is to enable calls between VoIP devices. VoIP dial peers perform this task by associating a phone number (destination-pattern) with a remote IP address. In addition to this task, VoIP dial peers provide an ability to specify the type of QoS associated with the call. The ability to specify QoS on a per-call basis allows administrators to vary the type of QoS employed based upon destination address and/or traffic path. This provides a method for offering differentiated service levels, as well as a way to avoid the processing overhead of QoS algorithms for traffic that traverses high-speed LAN links. Figure 7-8 demonstrates the use of basic VoIP dial peers.

Figure 7-9 depicts the basic voice-specific configuration for enabling local calling on router C.

Figure 7-10 depicts the VoIP dial-peer statement required to connect calls from router C to routers A and B.

Given that traffic to router B must traverse the T1 link, router D can be configured for RSVP operation and the dial peer associated with calls to router B should be updated to include RSVP support. For consistent performance, the controlled-load model will be requested. As a secondary measure, the IP precedence bits for traffic associated with these calls are set to 5 (critical). This provides preferential treatment from the WRED process invoked by the controlled-load model. The updates for the dial-peer statements are provided in Figure 7-11.

Note that the dial peers for traffic to the AS5300 are not changed since they communicate over high-speed LAN connections that generally do not employ QoS mechanisms.

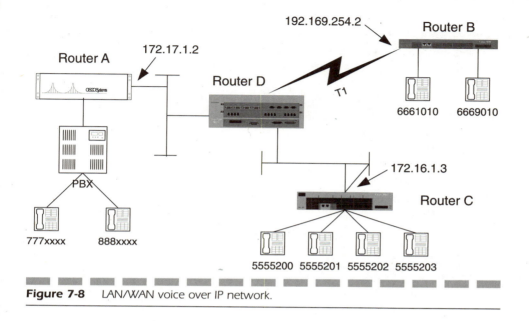

Figure 7-8 LAN/WAN voice over IP network.

Figure 7-9
POTS dial-peer voice
configuration
excerpt.

```
!
voice-port 2/0/0
 output attenuation 3
!
voice-port 2/0/1
 output attenuation 3
!
voice-port 2/1/0
 output attenuation 3
!
voice-port 2/1/1
 output attenuation 3
!
...
!
dial-peer voice 200 pots
 destination-pattern +5555200
 port 2/0/0
!
dial-peer voice 201 pots
 destination-pattern +5555201
 port 2/0/1
!
dial-peer voice 210 pots
 destination-pattern +5555202
 port 2/1/0
!
dial-peer voice 211 pots
 destination-pattern +5555203
 port 2/1/1
!
```

Figure 7-10
VoIP dial-peer voice
configuration
excerpt.

```
!
dial-peer voice 500 VoIP
 destination-pattern +666....
 session target ipv4:192.168.254.2
!
dial-peer voice 501 VoIP
 destination-pattern +777....
 session-target ipv4:172.17.1.2
 !
dial-peer voice 502 VoIP
 destination-pattern +888....
 session-target ipv4:172.17.1.2
 !
```

Figure 7-11
VoIP dial-peer config-
uration with QoS
request.

```
 !
dial-peer voice 500 VoIP
 destination-pattern +666....
 req-qos controlled-load
 ip precedence 5
 session target ipv4:192.168.254.2
!
dial-peer voice 501 VoIP
 destination-pattern +777....
 session-target ipv4:172.17.1.2
 !
dial-peer voice 502 VoIP
 destination-pattern +888....
 session-target ipv4:172.17.1.2
 !
```

Creating the Basic Plan

Voice Network Diagram

As with most network planning tasks, the dial plan starts with a network diagram. The challenge is to provide the appropriate amount of
information in the diagram without cluttering the picture. The focus of
this section is to identify the necessary steps for building a voice dial-
plan-specific diagram.

The first step is to draw a simple logical network diagram, highlight-
ing the planned voice ports and the components they are connecting
to. You can use network drawing packages or simply draw it freehand.
Use common symbols for routers, phones, serial links, PBXs, etc. The use

of common symbols will provide consistency throughout your designs and prevent confusion. Extreme detail within the network diagram is not required when mapping out dial plans. LAN connections, LAN hubs, switches, CSU/DSUs, and other components are probably not important for this task, and may add unnecessary clutter. It is important, however, to represent any and all of the following components:

- Relevant phones and/or fax machines
- Relevant PBX or key systems
- Any other voice device which will connect directly to the voice-enabled router
- All voice-enabled routers

Once the basic diagram is drawn, add detail on the types of connections required at each point in the network. Only include detail for the relevant ports. This will help determine the types of voice interfaces required on the router. During this step, you should

- Identify all physical interfaces between the router and the voice device (i.e., channelized T1, analog)
- Identify the role which each voice port must play
- Provide additional detail for relevant ports on the router
  Relevant LAN ports on router
  Relevant WAN ports on router
  All voice ports on the router
- Provide additional detail for relevant WAN links between voice-enabled routers
  WAN type (frame relay, PPP)
  Relevant PVCs including DLCI and CIR for frame relay
  Link access rates (port speed for frame relay)

The final network diagram step is to begin assigning phone numbers or extension numbers to each voice port. These numbers should be in accordance with any existing private dial plan and should also be compatible with external dialing schemes. The phone numbers and extensions should be placed on the diagram as close to the actual phone as possible.

Review your work, verifying all connections and the accuracy of the information. If everything is in order, the next step is to create a peer configuration table.

Create a Configuration Table

The dial-peer configuration table summarizes voice connectivity between the routers. It serves as a quick reference for both phone numbers and dial-peer configurations. The table should be periodically reviewed and updated to ensure that it is well maintained. Table 7-2 is a sample dial-peer configuration table template.

The dial-peer configuration table is a big jump from simply assigning phone numbers to a diagram. It organizes information and provides a template from which router configurations can be built. Additional information such as CODEC and QoS type not only make building the configuration easier, but are a helpful reference when diagnosing connectivity issues. The organization of dialing information in this manner also helps to identify inconsistencies in the design or configuration before placing it into production.

Dial Plan Diagram Examples

The following examples are provided to help understand the process of mapping out a dial plan. The emphasis is on creating the diagrams, so the phone numbers are kept simple.

TABLE 7-2

Dial-Peer Configuration Table Template

Dial-Peer Tag	Ext.	Dest-Pattern	Type	Voice Port	Session Target	CODEC	QoS
			Router 1				
			Router 2				
			Router *n*				

EXAMPLE

The basic VoIP network example demonstrates the steps for adding VoIP to a simple network with a 3620 series router at each site connected over a point-to-point T1 link. In both cases, the routers connect via Ethernet to switched LANs at each facility. It is assumed that all of the equipment, excluding the router-voice interfaces, was in place before voice was added to the environment.

There are two standard analog phones at each site. Each connects directly to the routers and is used for communication between the sites. The administrator wants to be able to call either phone at site A from either phone at site B, and vice versa.

Step 1: Basic Diagram

Figure 7-12 represents the basic diagram including the routers, the WAN link, and the phones.

Note that the details for the LAN environment are omitted because they are not relevant to the voice network.

Step 2: Include relevant details

This step adds detail for the WAN link, the phone connections, and the IP addresses. Figure 7-13 shows the results of step 2.

Step 3: Assign phone numbers

Since the voice network is private and not linked to any other system, simple extensions are given to each voice port. The use of a common leading digit at each site helps reduce routing information for intersite communications. The results of step 3 are displayed in Figure 7-14.

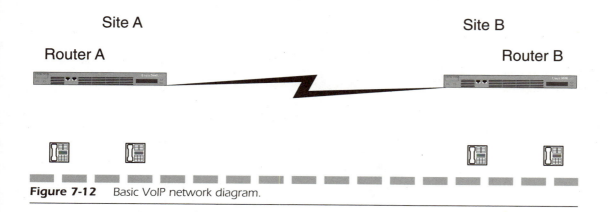

Figure 7-12   Basic VoIP network diagram.

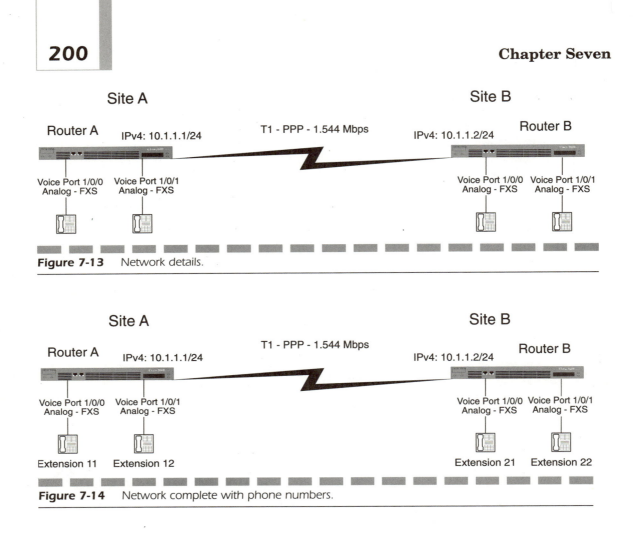

Figure 7-13   Network details.

Figure 7-14   Network complete with phone numbers.

The final step in the dial plan process is to create the dial peer configuration table using the information from Step 3's diagram as shown in Table 7-3. The combination of the final diagram and the dial peer configuration table should provide sufficient information for generating the voice-specific sections of the router configuration file. These diagrams are intended for that purpose only and are not meant to document the complete network.

EXAMPLE   The environment for this frame-relay-based network example is as follows:

Three remote sites are linked to a hub site using a frame-relay network. The hub site uses an AS5300 for voice traffic, while each of the

TABLE 7-3

Dial-Peer
Configuration
Table for Basic VoIP
Network Example

Dial-Peer Tag	Ext.	Destination Pattern	Type	Voice Port	Session Target	CODEC	QoS
			Router A				
100		11	POTS	1/0/0			
101		12	POTS	1/0/1			
200		2.	VoIP		10.1.1.2	G.729	Best Effort
			Router B				
50		21	POTS	1/0/0			
51		22	POTS	1/0/1			
60		1.	VoIP		10.1.1.1	G.729	Best Effort

remote sites use Cisco 2600 series routers. In this scenario, a 7200 series router is functioning as the main router for the hub site and each of the 2600 routers at the remote sites is being upgraded to support voice. The AS5300 is given a dedicated Ethernet port off of the main router at the hub site.

Step 1: Basic Diagram

The first step includes just the basic components: relevant routers, WAN links, LAN devices, and telephony components. All extraneous routers, WAN links, and LAN components are left out. (See Figure 7-15.)

Step 2: Include Relevant Details

The second step adds a significant amount of information as shown in Figure 7-16. First, all IP address related to IP telephony are added. Second, all frame-relay links are identified including the port speeds and the CIR of each PVC. Third, the relevant voice, LAN, and WAN ports are identified. And lastly, the type of voice interface is identified for each voice port.

Step 3: Assign Phone Numbers

Figure 7-17 shows the assignment of phone numbers and Table 7-4 the dial-peer configuration table. As noted previously, phone numbers are assigned in this example without serious consideration of the existing dial plan. This topic will be discussed later in the chapter.

TABLE 7-4

Dial-Peer
Configuration
Table for Frame-
Relay-Based
Network Example

Dial-Peer Tag	Ext.	Destination Pattern	Type	Voice Port	Session Target	CODEC	QoS
			AS5300-A				
4000		4...	POTS	0:D			
3000		30..	VoIP		172.16.30.2	G.729	FRTS w/priority queuing (on 7200)
3100		31..	VoIP		172.16.30.6	G.729	FRTS w/priority queuing (on 7200)
3200		32..	VoIP		172.16.30.10	G.729	FRTS w/priority queuing (on 7200)
			Router A				
1		3001	POTS	1/0/0			
2		3002	POTS	1/0/1			
3		3003	POTS	1/1/0			
4		3004	POTS	1/1/1			
4000		4...	VoIP		172.16.10.10	G.729	FRTS w/priority queuing
			Router B				
1		3101	POTS	1/0/0			
2		3102	POTS	1/0/1			
3		3103	POTS	1/1/0			
4		3104	POTS	1/1/1			
4000		4...	VoIP		172.16.10.10	G.729	FRTS w/priority queuing
			Router C				
1		3201	POTS	1/0/0			
2		3202	POTS	1/0/1			
4000		4...	VoIP		172.16.10.10	G.729	FRTS w/priority queuing

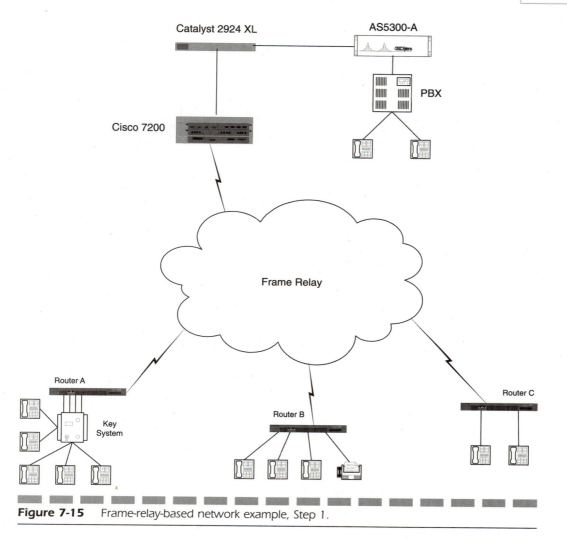

Figure 7-15 Frame-relay-based network example, Step 1.

NOTES:

1. *Dial-peer tags (numbers) are only significant within the router and are reused in each router.*

2. *Dial string wildcards reduce the number of dial peers required.*

3. *Frame-relay traffic shaping with priority queuing is used to provide better service for voice traffic.*

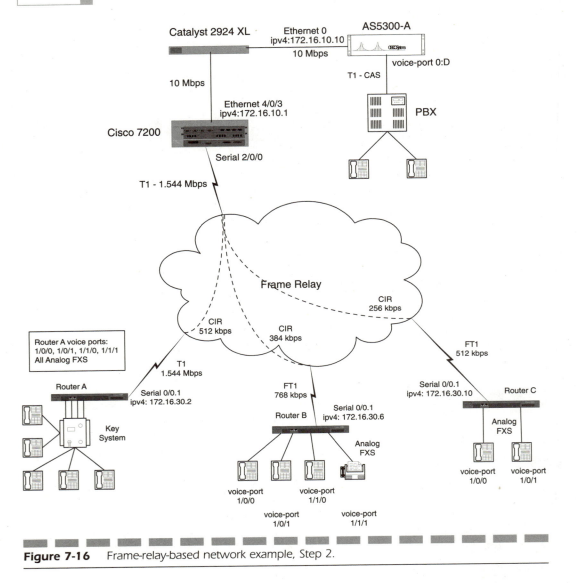

Figure 7-16   Frame-relay-based network example, Step 2.

Integrating with the External World

In order for voice over IP networks to successfully integrate with external corporate and public networks, they must conform to the established standards. Most of these standards are well known, for example, country

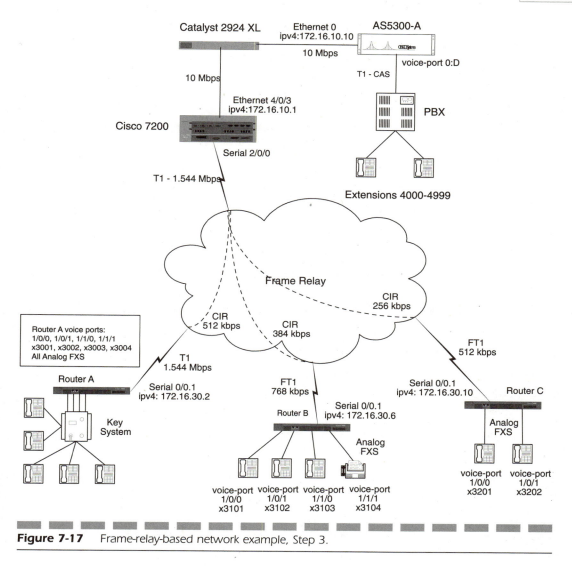

Figure 7-17   Frame-relay-based network example, Step 3.

and area codes, or dialing 911 for emergencies. Other standards may not be as well known, for example, corporate dial plans, central office codes, and carrier access codes. When constructing a dial plan all of these external influences must be considered.

North American Numbering Plan

Americans are familiar with basic structure of this plan where phone numbers are defined by 10-digit number sequences. Numbers are written in the following basic format: (xxx) yyy-zzzz. The first 3 digits, (xxx), represent an area code and need not be dialed when calling within the same area code. The next 7 digits are grouped together and are commonly referred to as the local phone number. However, the middle three digits (yyy from the above example) are actually a central office code. The remaining four digits (zzzz) represent the station id.

Both area and central office codes now conform to the same set of rules for numbering. That is the first digit can be any number from 2 to 9, while the second and third digits can be any number from 0 to 9. Before 1995, the second digit of the area code was restricted to either 0 or 1. Much like the IP world where address classes were based on binary bit configurations, these restrictions were put in place to simplify dialed number processing and expedite call processing. In both cases, growth and demand for address space have necessitated that these restrictions be lifted.

Reserved Addresses

In IP networks, certain addresses are reserved for specific functions, diagnostics, and private use. For instance, the IETF's RFC 1918 defines network addresses that are reserved for private use. Voice networks also reserve sets of addresses for specific functions. Some of the reserved codes used in the PSTN are presented in Table 7-5 along with their functions.

NOTE:

- *Not all of these services are supported in all areas.*
- *The 959 code is particularly handy when trying to identify the phone number associated with a POTS line.*
- *Carrier access codes are used to gain access to a specific long distance carrier and must be preceded with a 10.*
- *Newer access codes attainable using a 10-10 prefix are being rolled out to support additional growth in the competitive long distance arena. Some of these carriers use voice-over-IP transport for their long distance voice offerings.*

The Consultative Committee for International Telecommunications

TABLE 7-5

Special and
Reserved Phone
Codes

Special Action Codes		Central Office Codes		Carrier Access Codes	
Code	Function	Code	Function	Code	Carrier
211	Reserved	555	Toll Directory Assistance	031	ALC/Allnet
311	Reserved	844	Time Service	222	MCI
411	Directory Assistance	936	Weather Service	223	Cable & Wireless
511	Reserved	950	IXC Access	234	ACC
611	Repair Service	958	Plant Test	288	AT&T
711	Reserved	959	Plant Test	333	Sprint
811	Business Office	976	Info. Delivery Service	432	LCI
911	Emergency			464, 555	WilTel
				488	Metromedia

TABLE 7-6

Partial Country
Code List

Country/Region	Country Code	Country/Region	Country Code
United States	1	China	86
United Kingdom	44	Mexico	52
Japan	81	Germany	49
Hong Kong	852	Turkey	90
Korea	82	France	33

(CCITT) (now the ITU) defined country codes to address telephony devices throughout the world. The plan assigns each country or region a country code. This country code precedes the phone numbers allocated within each region in much the way that area codes are placed in front of basic phone numbers in the United States. A few country codes are listed in Table 7-6.

Fitting In

Voice over IP networks that interoperate with the public network must play by the same rules as the PSTN. This means not using the reserved addresses and conforming to the local dialing plan. In the United States this means simply using 10-digit destination patterns for voice ports and conforming to the area and central office codes for the region. Previously, most of the examples assigned simple 4-digit extensions to each voice port. The full number, complete with area code, should be assigned to the individual dial peers to ease integration issues. Also, the number assigned should be in conformance with the actual number block which has been allocated to the corporation.

Revisiting the second example from the dial plan mapping section, the 4-digit extensions should be replaced with full numbers, including CO and area codes. Table 7-7 shows the area and CO codes associated with each site.

Table 7-8 shows the updated dial-peer configuration table that includes the new destination patterns. The patterns are based upon the original extensions and the area and central office code assignments from Table 7-7.

The information from Table 7-8 is then used to update the router configurations from the frame-relay-based network example. Figure 7-18 contains these updated configurations.

AS5300-A

```
!
dial-peer voice 4000 pots
 destination-pattern +12122904...
 port 0:D
!
dial-peer voice 3000 VoIP
 destination-pattern +161726130..
 ip precedence 5
 session target ipv4:172.16.30.2
!
dial-peer voice 3100 VoIP
 destination-pattern +197325731..
 ip precedence 5
 session target ipv4:172.16.30.6
!
dial-peer voice 3200 VoIP
 destination-pattern +170344032..
 ip precedence 5
 session target ipv4:172.16.30.10
!
voice-port 0:D
!
```

TABLE 7-7

Area and CO Codes for Frame-Relay-Based Network Example

Router	Area Code	CO Code
AS5300-A	212	290
Router A	617	261
Router B	973	257
Router C	703	440

TABLE 7-8

Dial-Peer
Configuration
Table with
Complete Phone
Numbers

Dial-Peer Tag	Ext.	Destination Pattern	Type	Voice Port	Session Target	CODEC	QoS
				AS5300-A			
4000		4...	POTS	0:D			
4000		12122904...	POTS	0:D			
3000		161726130..	VoIP		172.16.30.2	G.729	FRTS w/priority queuing (on 7200)
3100		197325731..	VoIP		172.16.30.6	G.729	FRTS w/priority queuing (on 7200)
3200		170344032..	VoIP		172.16.30.10	G.729	FRTS w/priority queuing (on 7200)
				Router A			
1		16172613001	POTS	1/0/0			
2		16172613002	POTS	1/0/1			
3		16172613003	POTS	1/1/0			
4		16172613004	POTS	1/1/1			
4000		12122904...	VoIP		172.16.10.10	G.729	FRTS w/priority queuing
				Router B			
1		19732573101	POTS	1/0/0			
2		19732573102	POTS	1/0/1			
3		19732573103	POTS	1/1/0			
4		19732573104	POTS	1/1/1			
4000		12122904...	VoIP		172.16.10.10	G.729	FRTS w/priority queuing
				Router C			
1		17034403201	POTS	1/0/0			
2		17034403202	POTS	1/0/1			
4000		12122904...	VoIP		172.16.10.10	G.729	FRTS w/priority queuing

Router A

```
!
voice-port 1/0/0
 output attenuation 3
!
voice-port 1/0/1
 output attenuation 3
!
voice-port 1/1/0
 output attenuation 3
!
voice-port 1/1/1
 output attenuation 3
!
...
!
dial-peer voice 1 pots
 destination-pattern +16172613001
 port 1/0/0
!
dial-peer voice 2 pots
 destination-pattern +16172613002
 port 1/0/1
!
dial-peer voice 3 pots
 destination-pattern +16172613003
 port 1/1/0
!
dial-peer voice 4 pots
 destination-pattern +16172613004
 port 1/1/1
!
dial-peer voice 4000 VoIP
 destination-pattern +12122904...
 ip precedence 5
 session target ipv4:172.16.10.10
!
```

Router B

```
!
voice-port 1/0/0
 output attenuation 3
!
voice-port 1/0/1
 output attenuation 3
!
voice-port 1/1/0
 output attenuation 3
!
voice-port 1/1/1
 output attenuation 3
!
...
!
dial-peer voice 1 pots
```

```
    destination-pattern +19732573101
    port 1/0/0
  !
dial-peer voice 2 pots
    destination-pattern +19732573102
    port 1/0/1
  !
dial-peer voice 3 pots
    destination-pattern +19732573103
    port 1/1/0
  !
dial-peer voice 4 pots
    destination-pattern +19732573104
    port 1/1/1
  !
dial-peer voice 4000 VoIP
    destination-pattern +12122904...
    ip precedence 5
    session target ipv4:172.16.10.10
  !
```

Router C

```
  !
voice-port 1/0/0
  output attenuation 3
  !
voice-port 1/0/1
  output attenuation 3
  !
...
  !
dial-peer voice 1 pots
    destination-pattern +17034403201
    port 1/0/0
  !
dial-peer voice 2 pots
    destination-pattern +17034403202
    port 1/0/1
  !
    dial-peer voice 4000 VoIP
    destination-pattern +12122904...
    ip precedence 5
    session target ipv4:172.16.10.10
  !
```

Corporate Networks

In corporate environments where voice over IP networks are being introduced, addressing must also comply with the dial plan in use by the existing phone system. Identifying the details of that plan can be an exhaustive process, but must be done to avoid conflicting or overlapping with preassigned extension numbers. It is recommended that the number of interfaces between the existing system be limited and well controlled to avoid routing loops. Also, the use of wildcards must be carefully controlled to avoid overlapping with preassigned phone numbers.

Addressing Tools

Number Expansions

One way of easing the complexity associated with using full 10-digit phone numbers is to use a number expansion table. Number expansions translate abbreviated dial strings to longer dial strings. This effectively emulates the extension-based dialing that users are used to. It also allows administrators to hide the details of a call from the user while providing them a smaller-length extension to dial. Number expansions can pass wildcard numbers, as well as fully qualified numbers. In the multiple city example above, the routers could be configured to use the same 4-digit extension-based dialing while maintaining compatibility with the PSTN. Tables 7-9 through 7-12 are the number expansion tables for each router.

NOTE: *The wildcards are left intact and the number receives a prefix containing the area and CO code.*

To create number expansions, the num-exp command is used. It is a global configuration command that accepts two parameters: the extension and the expanded number. The syntax is as follows:

```
num-exp extension expanded-number
```

where

extension = the abbreviated extension number expressed in digits

expanded-number = the fully qualified number which the extension must be expanded to

Applying this command to the table created for example 2 results in the configurations presented as follows:

TABLE 7-9

Number Expansion
Table for AS5300-A

Extension	Actual Number*
4...	12122904...
30..	161726130..
31..	197325731..
32..	170344032..

*Destination pattern.

TABLE 7-10

Number Expansion
Table for Router A

Extension	Actual Number*
3001	16172613001
3002	16172613002
3003	16172613003
4...	12122904...

*Destination pattern.

TABLE 7-11

Number Expansion
Table for Router B

Extension	Actual Number*
3101	19732573101
3102	19732573102
3103	19732573103
4...	12122904...

*Destination pattern.

TABLE 7-12

Number Expansion
Table for Router C

Extension	Actual Number*
3201	17034403201
3202	17034403202
4...	12122904...

*Destination pattern.

AS5300-A

```
!
num-exp 4... 121294...
num-exp 30.. 161726130..
num-exp 31.. 197325731..
num-exp 32.. 170344032..
!
```

Router A

```
!
num-exp 3001 16172613001
num-exp 3002 16172613002
num-exp 3003 16172613003
num-exp 3004 16172613004
num-exp 4... 121294...
!
```

Router A

```
!
num-exp 3101 19732573101
num-exp 3102 19732573102
num-exp 3103 19732573103
num-exp 3104 19732573104
num-exp 4... 121294...
!
```

Router C

```
!
num-exp 3201 17034403201
num-exp 3202 17034403202
num-exp 4... 121294...
!
```

Hunt Groups

It's often convenient to bundle multiple phone lines using a single phone number. While each line has a unique phone number, external users can dial a single number and the system will automatically connect them to the first available phone line. This concept offers the following benefits.

- A single number is easier for users to remember
- Users do not have to manually try each phone line until they find an available line
- It allows administrators to take individual lines in and out service without the user community being aware

■ A single number can service more than one phone line and is not dedicated to a single analog port or DS-0

Cisco's implementation of hunt groups within the IOS is simple and straightforward. A hunt group is created when multiple POTS dial-peer statements reference the same phone number (destination pattern), but different voice ports. To control the order in which the software searches through the hunt group, a preference command is added. Dial peers with a higher preference (lower value) are tried first. The syntax for the preference command follows:

```
preference value
```

where `value` can be an integer from 0 through 10 and the default is 0.

A quick example of a basic hunt group is shown in Figure 7-18. A small office uses a key system and is connected to a 3640 router for voice con-

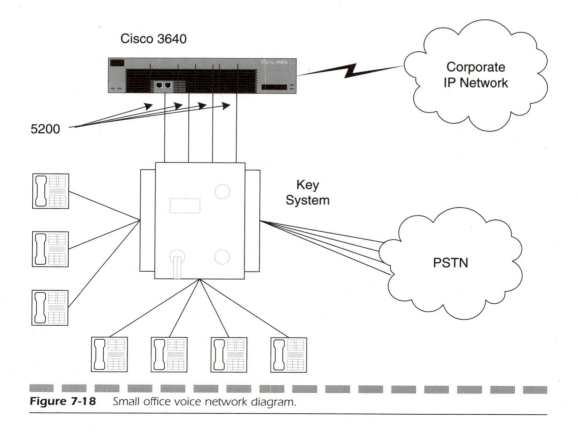

Figure 7-18 *Small office voice network diagram.*

Figure 7-19
Hunt group configu-
ration excerpt.

```
!
voice-port 3/0/0
  input gain 7
!
voice-port 3/0/1
  input gain 7
!
voice-port 3/1/1
  input gain 7
!
voice-port 3/1/1
  input gain 7
!
...
!
dial-peer voice 10 pots
  destination-pattern 5200
  port 3/0/0
  preference 1
!
dial-peer voice 20 pots
  destination-pattern 5200
  port 3/0/1
  preference 4
!
dial-peer voice 30 pots
  destination-pattern 5200
  port 3/1/0
  preference 2
!
dial-peer voice 40 pots
  destination-pattern 5200
  port 3/1/1
  preference 3
!
```

nectivity to headquarters. The four phone lines are configured in a hunt
group so that they can all be reached by dialing 5200 from the main site.
Figure 7-19 is a configuration excerpt providing the relevant configuration statements.

Figure 7-19 provides a simple hunt group function over ports 3/0/0
through 3/1/1. Note that the hunt sequence is 3/0/0, 3/1/0, 3/1/1, 3/0/1
because of the assignment of preferences.

*NOTE: The destination-pattern need not be exact for each dial peer.
However, hunt sequencing is performed by longest pattern match followed by preference. For example, Figure 7-20 shows a variant of the
previous configuration which would make the hunt sequence for 5200 be
3/1/0, 3/1/1, 3/0/0, 3/0/1.*

Figure 7-20
Longest match example.

```
!
dial-peer voice 10 pots
  destination-pattern 52..
  port 3/0/0
  preference 1
!
dial-peer voice 20 pots
  destination-pattern 52..
  port 3/0/1
  preference 4
!
dial-peer voice 30 pots
  destination-pattern 5200
  port 3/1/0
  preference 2
!
dial-peer voice 40 pots
  destination-pattern 5200
  port 3/1/1
  preference 3
!
```

■ *Without the specification of preferences, all dial peers default to a preference of 0.*

■ *When two dial peers have an equal pattern match and preference, the dial peer that is higher in the configuration file is used.*

Wildcards

The use of wildcards helps reduce the complexity and size of dial plans. Quite often, numbers may be summarized alleviating the need for explicit dial-peer statements for every number. The following pointers are helpful when using wildcards.

■ A period (.) is used as a wildcard to match any single valid digit. For multiple consecutive wildcard digits, multiple periods must be used. Wildcards cards can only be used to match the trailing digits of a number. So a destination pattern of 3...is valid, while a destination pattern of 3.11 is not.

■ The longest match for any number is always selected first. If a dialed number were 2122905299, the dial peer with a destination pattern of 21229052.. will be selected over a dial peer with a destination pattern of 2122905...regardless of its location within the configuration.

SUMMARY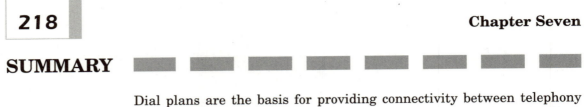

Dial plans are the basis for providing connectivity between telephony devices. When effectively planned and implemented they can provide an efficient and scalable system capable of interconnecting with the PSTN and private telephony networks. Tools like number expansions help ease the administration of dial plans within the voice-enabled router network.

Chapter **8**

Integrating
It All

Introduction

This chapter will cover the following:

- Requirements analysis
- Information gathering
- QoS determination
- QoS configuration guidelines
- Dial plan creation
- Generating the configuration
- Voice connectivity
- Network integration

The previous chapters have all dealt with different aspects of voice networking from basic telephony concepts and quality of service issues, through Cisco-specific implementation details. This chapter integrates these concepts and details to develop sample voice networks from the ground up. The process begins with a preliminary requirements analysis and continues with equipment selection, network design, and finishes with the creation of complete configurations for the voice-enabled routers.

Requirements Analysis

Before building anything, it is appropriate to figure out just what needs to be built and what tasks it must perform. The concepts applied in voice networking are similar to those applied in data-networking design. The only thing that has changed is the type of equipment that the network is interfacing with. In fact, an argument could be made that voice networking is somewhat simpler since the interfaces and protocols are fewer and better defined. Also, the characteristics of the application and its network requirements are well defined and understood, which is in stark contrast to data networking where all too often a lot of guess work is performed because application characteristics are poorly documented.

The first step is to figure out the physical logistics associated with the project. Divide the project into sites and within each site identify the number and types of systems which must be connected. Then, per device, identify specific requirements. The following templates provide a starting point for this process.

Information Gathering

Site Listing

Administrative information should be collected for each site and/or department that the network is divided into. Figure 8-1 provides a sample template that can be used.

Identification of Telephony Equipment

Once the individual sites are organized, the next step is to gather information on the telephony equipment that will be connecting to the voice-enabled router at each site. First identify all phone systems which will connect to the router. Often this is a single PBX or key system. Figure 8-2 provides a sample template that will aid in this process.

Based upon the type of connection to the voice-enabled router, fill out the appropriate worksheet (Figure 8-3 or 8-4).

Existing Data Networking Environment

Once the telephony equipment is identified, the next step is to identify the data-networking environment at each site. The goal of this step is to establish what type of network traffic the voice traffic will be mixed with.

Figure 8-1
Site administrative
information

Site/Department				
Name:		Address:		
City/State:		Approximate Number of Phones:		
Location of Phone Closet:			Site Code:	
Contact Information	Office	Pager	Email	Other
Administrative				
Telecom				
Datacom				
Additional Information:				

Figure 8-2
Telephony
equipment
summary.

Type of System: PBX / Key System / Analog phone / FAX machine

Vendor: Model:

Location in Building: Approx. # of Station Ports:

Connection to PSTN: Analog / T1-CAS / T1-PRI

Type of connection to voice-enabled router: Analog / T1-CAS / T1-PRI

Number of connections to voice-enabled router:

Additional Information:

Figure 8-3
Analog port
information.

Connection Type: Trunk / Tie-Line / PLAR

Signaling Type: FXS / FXO / E&M

E&M-Specific   Type: I / II / III / V   E&M implementation: 2-wire / 4-wire

Off-hook Signaling: Loop Start / Ground Start / Immediate / Delay-dial / Wink

Additional Information:

Figure 8-4
Digital port
information.

Type of Interface: T1 / E1   Line Coding: AMI / B8ZS

Framing: SF(D4) / ESF   Number of Channels:

Clocking Source: Internal / External   Companding: u-law / a-law

Type of Signaling: CAS / PRI

CAS specific   Signaling type: E&M Feature Group B / E&M Feature Group D /

                                   FXS-Loop Start / FXS-Ground Start

PRI specific   Switch-type: 5ESS / 4ESS / DMS100 / NI1

Figure 8-5
Router summary.

Relevant Routers (hostnames):

Vendor: Model: Software Version:

Relevant Interfaces:

Protocols Configured on Router:

Protocols Running on Relevant Interfaces:

Console Password: Enable Password:

TELNET Password: Out of Band Password:

Main IP Address:

Additional Information:

Only information relative to voice traffic flow is important. To quantify this, think of the path that the voice over IP traffic will take from the site to its destination. Figure 8-5 is a template for a router configuration summary and should be filled out for the relevant router(s). For each relevant WAN interface, a template like Figure 8-6 should be filled out.

Voice-Traffic Flow Analysis

After the tedious component information gathering process, the next step is to profile the desired voice-traffic flow. This can be done in many ways, ranging from a thorough analysis to a best guess. There are four steps to performing a traffic analysis:

1. Gather traffic data
2. Profile traffic
3. Determine trunking requirements
4. Match network trunk links with bandwidth requirements

Gathering the Data

If the existing systems communicate with each other through the public network, then traffic can be profiled using the call-detail reports from

| Interface Name: | Queuing: FIFO / WFQ / WRED / Custom / Priority |

WAN Technology: 56 kbps / T1 / T3 / Packet over SONET

| Fractional T1 rate: | Fractional T3 rate: |

| Frame Relay-specific | Port Speed: | LMI-type: ANSI / Cisco / Other |

Per-PVC	DLCI:	CIR:	Protocols Enabled:
	DLCI:	CIR:	Protocols Enabled:
	DLCI:	CIR:	Protocols Enabled:
	DLCI:	CIR:	Protocols Enabled

ATM: T1 / T3 / OC-3c

Per-PVC	VPI/VCI:	QoS Type: CBR / rt-VBR / nrt-VBR / UBR / ABR
	Traffic Rate:	Protocols Enabled
	VPI/VCI:	QoS Type: CBR / rt-VBR / nrt-VBR / UBR / ABR
	Traffic Rate:	Protocols Enabled
	VPI/VCI:	QoS Type: CBR / rt-VBR / nrt-VBR / UBR / ABR
	Traffic Rate:	Protocols Enabled

Additional Information:

the phone systems and/or telco bills. If the existing systems communicate with each other through leased line circuits, then the call-detail reports are probably the only source of traffic information. The pertinent variables to be gathered are time of day, date, length of call, and destination. If the systems do not currently communicate, or, for that matter, don't exist, then some educated guesses will be required.

Processing the Data

The call-detail reports and/or telco bills should be analyzed and broken down into hour-long increments, ideally over one or more months' time.

The information should then be placed into a spreadsheet identifying the 1-h interval in which the call was made, the destination of the call, and its duration in minutes. The spreadsheet should then be manipulated to provide totals for each destination in terms of number of calls per hour/day/month, average call length per hour/day/month, total number of call minutes per hour/day/month.

Profiling the Data

The pertinent information should then be used to determine the network's peak traffic flow. Call-flow rates are determined by multiplying the number of calls per hour by the average call duration during that time. This information is used to identify the busy hour for the voice network. There are several complex methods for busy-hour calculation that involve statistical analysis, probability theory, and extensive computation. Luckily, there is also a simple method which yields reasonable results. The simple method is the following:

1. Use the traffic data to compute the call-flow rate for each 1-h interval ($A = C \times T$; where A = call flow rate, C = number of calls initiated during the time interval, and T = the average call duration during the interval).

2. Sum the call-flow rates from each hour interval across all days in the analysis. That is, add the call-flow rate for day 1, 9 am to 10 am to the call-flow rate from day 2, 9 am to 10 am, etc.

3. Identify time interval with the largest aggregate call-flow rate.

4. Determine the average flow rate during the sample period (divide the sum by the number of days data were collected for).

Determining Trunking Requirements

Using the output from the spreadsheet, the trunking requirements for each site and between each site can be determined. The call-flow rate for the busy hour can be translated to approximate data-network bandwidth requirements. In order to determine the trunking requirements, the busy hour call flow must be converted to a traffic measurement called an *erlang*. An erlang is equivalent to the amount of traffic that can be handled by a single trunk in one hour. To convert the busy hour calculation to erlangs, divide the 1-h call-flow rate by 60 min and multiply by 15 percent. The 15 percent is added to compensate for call setup and teardown overhead. This is depicted in the following equation.

$$\text{Busy hour} = (A/60 \text{ min}) * 1.15 = \text{erlangs}$$

This will leave a dimensionless quantity for the busy hour. The final step is to determine what is called the grade of service or GoS. GoS is essentially an estimate of the number of calls that will be blocked. Typical design goals fall between 0.01 and 0.05, which translates to between 1 out of 100 and 5 out of 100 calls being dropped. Luckily the telecommunications industry has provided guidelines for trunk selection, which are based on busy-hour traffic and grade of service. These charts are derived using complex statistical analyses of call distributions and arrival rates. Table 8-1 provides a guideline for trunk selection. It is usually helpful to document the trunk requirements in a simple chart such as Table 8-2.

TABLE 8-1

Trunking Requirements Based upon Busy Hour and Grade of Service

| Number of Trunks | Grade of Service | | | | | |
	.01	.02	.03	.05	.07	.10
1	0.01	0.02	0.03	0.05	0.07	0.11
2	0.15	0.21	0.27	0.35	0.43	0.53
3	0.44	0.56	0.66	0.82	0.94	1.10
4	0.82	1.01	1.15	1.36	1.53	1.74
5	1.28	1.53	1.71	1.97	2.18	2.43
6	1.79	2.09	2.30	2.61	2.86	3.14
7	2.33	2.68	2.92	3.28	3.56	3.89
8	2.92	3.31	3.58	3.97	4.28	4.67
9	3.50	3.94	4.25	4.69	5.03	5.44
10	4.14	4.61	4.94	5.42	5.78	6.22
11	4.78	5.31	5.67	6.17	6.56	7.03
12	5.42	6.00	6.39	6.92	7.33	7.83
13	6.11	6.69	7.11	7.69	8.11	8.64
14	6.78	7.42	7.86	8.47	8.92	9.47
15	7.47	8.14	8.61	9.25	9.72	10.31
16	8.19	8.89	9.36	10.03	10.53	11.14
17	8.89	9.64	10.14	10.83	11.36	11.97

TABLE 8-2

Voice Trunking Requirements

Source	Destination	No. of Trunks
Site A	Site B	2
Site A	Site C	3
Site A	Site D	1
Site B	Site C	1
Site C	Site D	1

NOTES:

- *The number of trunks required should always be rounded up to the larger integer.*
- *This number needs to be calculated for each remote destination the site will be communicating with.*

Determining Network Bandwidth Requirements

Once the trunking requirements are determined, the final step is to convert the number of trunks to bandwidth requirements for intersite links. This is straightforward and requires the trunking information and the bandwidth per voice call. The formula is

$$\text{Bandwidth} = \text{no. of trunks} \times \text{CODEC bandwidth}$$

For G.729 traffic using CRTP, the formula becomes

$$\text{Bandwidth} = \text{no. of trunks} \times 11.2 \text{ kbps}$$

The bandwidth requirements are then used to assist in the data-network design and QoS selection.

QoS Determinations

One of the more difficult tasks in setting up voice over IP networks is determining what type of QoS mechanism should be used and where it should be applied. This determination requires that a lot of information be gathered from multiple sources. Some of the key determining factors are listed below:

- Path for voice calls
- Voice-encoding algorithm
- Router models deployed in the network
- Relative processor utilization on routers
- Packet-switching mode employed on the routers
- Layer 2 WAN transports
- Additional protocol support
- Existing QoS and queuing models
- Router software versions

Each of these factors and their effect on the decision process is described in the following subsections.

Path for Voice Calls

Determining the path through the data network that the packetized voice calls will take is important because it identifies the individual routers and links that are required to complete the call. Once identified, the individual routers and links are then further analyzed to determine which QoS techniques should be applied. This process serves to identify the critical components that will be supporting voice traffic. Also, if the entire path is not under control of the administrator because it is the Internet, an outsourced WAN, an IP-VPN, or under control of another department, these conditions must be identified so appropriate measures can be taken. Policy-based routing and/or other techniques may be used to direct traffic over the desired links.

The process of evaluating the individual routers and links is described in forthcoming sections.

Voice-Encoding Algorithm

The voice-encoding algorithm in use determines the bandwidth, variability, and latency requirements for the voice calls. These are all important factors when determining the appropriate QoS technique to apply. Tables 8-3 and 8-4 show the characteristics of each voice-encoding algorithm.

This information, along with the voice traffic profiling, helps to deter-

TABLE 8-3

Bandwidth
Characteristics of
Voice-Encoding
Algorithms

Algorithm	Bandwidth (voice stream in kbs)	Bandwidth (packetized in kbs)	Bandwidth (w/CRTP in kbs)
PCM - G.711	64	82	67
CS-ACELP - G.729	8	26	11.2
MP-MLQ - G.723.1	6.3	20	10

TABLE 8-4

Delay
Characteristic of
Voice-Encoding
Algorithms

Algorithm	Algorithm Delay, ms	Playout Buffer Delay, ms	VAD Delay, ms	Packet Size (best), bytes
PCM - G.711	.75	5	5	168
CS-ACELP - G.729	10	5	5	28
MP-MLQ - G.723.1	30	5	5	38

mine the amount of bandwidth required to support the voice traffic. Bandwidth requirements are determined by multiplying the expected number of concurrent calls by the bandwidth consumed by each call. This influences decisions over whether or not to use CRTP, as well as rate limiting QoS features such as frame-relay traffic shaping, generic traffic shaping, RSVP, and committed access rate. Delay characteristics influence prioritization and link-efficiency mechanisms such as multilink PPP with link fragmentation and interleaving or FRF.12 frame-relay fragmentation. Table 8-5 provides rudimentary guidelines for applying CODEC information to QoS techniques.

Router Models

The specific router model number determines a number of factors including processing power, feature availability, interface functionality, switching modes supported, ability to offload processing, and memory availability/performance. It is important to understand which routers the voice traffic will pass through and what capabilities they support. A summary of Cisco router designs is provided below:

Router Design

Shared memory.

Router Models: Cisco 800, 1400, 1600, 1720, 2500, 3800, 4x00, AS5x00.

TABLE 8-5   LFI and FRF.12 Segmentation Suggestions

Link Speed or CIR	Efficiency Mechanism	Bandwidth Reservation/Maximum Recommended Fragment Size/Maximum No. of Calls		
		G.711	G.729/G.729a	G.723.1
32 kbps	LFI	Insufficient bandwidth	12 kbps/15 ms/1	11 kbps/15 ms/1
	FRF.12	Insufficient bandwidth	12 kbps/60 bytes/1	12 kbps/60 bytes/1
56 kbps	LFI	Insufficient bandwidth	24 kbps/20 ms/2	33 kbps/20 ms/3
	FRF.12	Insufficient bandwidth	24 kbps/140 bytes/2	33 kbps/140 bytes/3
128 kbps	LFI	70 kbps/20 ms/1	60 kbps/20 ms/5	66 kbps/20 ms/6
	FRF.12	70 kbps/320 bytes/1	60 kbps/320 bytes/5	66 kbps/320 bytes/6
256 kbps	LFI	140 kbps/20 ms/2	156 kbps/20 ms/13	154 kbps/20 ms/14
	FRF.12	140 kbps/640 bytes/2	156 kbps/640 bytes/13	154 kbps/640 bytes/14
512 kbps	LFI	280 kbps/20 ms/4	264 kbps/20 ms/22	264 kbps/20 ms/24
	FRF.12	280 kbps/1280 bytes/4	264 kbps/1280 bytes/22	264 kbps/1280 bytes/24
768 kbps	LFI	384 kbps/20 ms/6	384 kbps/20 ms/32	385 kbps/20 ms/35
	FRF.12	384 kbps/1600 bytes/6	384 kbps/1600 bytes/32	385 kbps/1600 bytes/32
1.544 Mbps	LFI	Not required	Not required	Not required
	FRF.12	Not required	Not required	Not required

Description: Shared-memory-based routers use a shared memory pool for processing of packets. The CPU is responsible for most packet-processing and memory-transfer functions. Packet and system memory are partitioned either through software or through physically distinct memory banks.

Notes:
- Interface ASICs may be utilized to offload low-level packet processing functions.
- CPU is required to process, queue, classify, and forward all packets.
- CPU is responsible for all system functions, as well as packet functions.
- Router performance is usually CPU bound, but can be memory bound.
- Forwarding capability is bound by CPU and memory transfer rates.
- 4500/4700/AS5300 support significantly higher data rates for process intensive tasks.

QoS Implications:

- QoS functions will directly affect system performance.
- CPU performance limits QoS support.
- Heavy QoS functions are limited to lower-speed interfaces.
- Not all QoS functions are supported.

Router Design

VIP architecture w/PCI interface bus.

Router Models: Cisco 2600 and 3600 series

Description: System architecture is based on the Versatile Interface Processor design used in the 7500 series. The PCI interface for network modules provides sufficient bandwidth for interface rates up to OC-3.

Notes:

- Benefits from VIP-derived enhanced data flow, processing, and memory access
- More processing power than base-shared memory routers
- Flexible interfaces (9.6-kbps async through OC-3c ATM, voice, hard disk, compression, and encryption)
- VIP-based features more easily ported

QoS Implications:

- More processing power enables QoS functions to run at higher rates on more interfaces.
- Optimized data paths provide improved QoS performance.

Router Design

Distributed forwarding/processing.

Router Models: 7200 (processing only), 7500

Description: Routing tables are computed by the main processor and distributed to line cards. Line cards make forwarding decisions independent of the main processor. Distributed processing can offload CPU intensive tasks from the main processor.

Notes:

- Capable of offloading QoS functions to line modules (WRED, WFQ, IP/ATM CoS, RSVP to ATM interworking, CAR, FRTS, GTS)
- Capable of offloading packet forwarding from RSVP

QoS Implications:

- Most scalable QoS implementation
- 7500 series support Cisco's full suite of QoS techniques
- Requires careful selection of features

Router Design

ASIC-based forwarding.

Router Models: Cisco 70x0, Catalyst 8500 CSR, Catalyst 6500 w/MSM, Catalyst 5x00w/RSM and NFFC

Description: Routers with ASIC based forwarding mechanisms rely upon main CPU for routing protocol operation, route computation, table maintenance, console access, and other system functions. Packet forwarding is performed by customized ASICs that are optimized for that function.

Notes:

- The 70x0 and Catalyst 5x00 with RSM and NFFC implement cache based forwarding mechanisms. Initial packets, sometimes called candidate packets, are forwarded through the central routing function. The central route processor then develops a cache entry and updates the ASIC-based caching mechanism that performs subsequent packet forwarding.
- The 8500 and 6500 with MSM perform cacheless forwarding and require that the central route processor develop a complete forwarding table for access by the forwarding ASICs.
- Enhanced functions such as security, queuing, or statistics are often lacking and, if possible, require significant development to implement within the ASICs.
- Extremely high forwarding rates are achieved, but enhanced services often suffer.

QoS Implications:

- The 70x0 is now obsolete and has minimal support for QoS.
- The 5x00, with RSM and NFFC, provides some flow-based QoS using the RSM, but not the NetFlow ASICs, thereby limiting performance.
- The 8500 and 6500 MSM implement a limited QoS set which includes per-flow queuing (PFQ) and weighted round robin (WRR) scheduling based on IP precedence.
- The 8500 and 6500 do not offer FRTS, GTS, RSVP, WFQ, WRED, or CAR today.
- Daughter cards may offer the ability to classify traffic using the Access Lists.

Processor Utilization

Most QoS functions require a significant amount of router processing power to implement. For this reason, it is important to quantify the relative processor utilization both before and after implementing a QoS function. Routers which consistently run at high utilization (over 80 percent) are subject to reduced packet-forwarding rates, as well as lost packets and other anomalies. If processor utilization rates are relatively high (greater than 50 percent), an extremely lightweight QoS mechanism, like IP-precedence tagging at the source and WFQ or WRED, should be chosen.

Packet-Switching Mode

Cisco routers forward packets using a number of different mechanisms and/or algorithms. It is important to identify which forwarding mechanism is in place before implementing any QoS technique. Certain QoS techniques require one form of switching or another. The impact of changing the switching mode in conjunction with a QoS technique should be evaluated before implementing any changes. Tables 8-6 and 8-7 summarize the different packet-switching modes and the implications of QoS functions on them.

Layer 2 WAN Transports

Identifying the pertinent layer 2 WAN transport facilities and their access rates is important as it directly affects the type of QoS mechanism

TABLE 8-6

Router Packet Switching Modes

Switching Mode	Description	Platforms
Process switching	Traditional routing, the CPU processes all layers	All, except GSR, 8500, 6500 MSM
Fast switching	Cache-based forwarding, runs at interrupt level resulting in better performance and greater efficiency	All, except GSR, 8500, 6500 MSM
NetFlow switching	Similar to fast switching; creates cache entries based upon flows, expedites statistics collection	4500, 4700, 7200, 7500, RSM/NFFC
Optimum switching	Uses optimized cache and lookup algorithm for fastest possible cache-based switching	7200, 7500
Cisco Express Forwarding (CEF)	Cacheless routing using expedited route lookup mechanism	All
Distributed switching	Independent VIP2-based packet forwarding; may use fast or optimum switching, as well as CEF	7500, 8500, 12000

TABLE 8-7   QoS Functions and Packet-Switching Modes

	CAR	RSVP	PQ/CQ	WFQ	Policy	WRED	FRTS	GTS	MLPPP	CRTP
Process switching		X	X	X	X	X	X	X	X	X
Fast switching		X	X	X	X	X				
NetFlow switching		X		X	X	X				
Optimum switching				X	X	X				
Cisco express forwarding (CEF)	X		X			X				
Distributed switching	X	X	X	X^{1,2,3,4}	X	X^{1,2,3,4}	X	X		

1. All non-IP traffic is placed into a single queue.
2. Not supported on subinterfaces.
3. Not supported on Fast EtherChannel or Tunnel interfaces.
4. Incompatible with RSP-based priority queuing, custom queuing, or weighted fair queuing.

TABLE 8-8

QoS Challenges for Point-to-Point Circuits

	Interface Speed	
Challenge	**Low Speed**	**High Speed**
Bandwidth Access	CRTP, VAD, RSVP	VAD. (GTS, CAR, RSVP—only if required)
Voice-packet rate variability	MLPPP w/LFI, WFQ—IP precedence	N/A—given proper prioritization
Serialization delay	MLPPP w/LFI	N/A
Prioritization of voice traffic	WFQ—IP Precedence, WRED, RSVP, PQ, CQ	WFQ—IP precedence, WRED, RSVP

to be deployed. Point-to-point and point-to-multipoint links face similar challenges. A generic approach to these challenges is presented below.

Point-to-Point

Point-to-point links have predictable bandwidth characteristics and place the routers in a good position to control transmission rates and variability. The main challenges for point-to-point links and some of their resolutions are presented in Table 8-8.

TABLE 8-9

QoS Challenges for
Point-to-Multipoint
Circuits

Challenge	Interface Speed	
	Low Speed	**High Speed**
Bandwidth access	CRTP, VAD	VAD
Voice-packet rate variability	Reduced MTU size, FRF.12 fragmentation	N/A—given proper prioritization
Serialization delay	FRF.12	N/A
Prioritization of voice traffic	WFQ—IP precedence, PQ, CQ, DE-lists	WFQ—IP precedence, RSVP (ATM only), IP/ATM CoS, policy routing/tag switching, RSVP-ATM interworking
Network queuing delays	FRTS, GTS	FRTS
Central site—remote site speed mismatch	FRTS, GTS, FRF.12	FRTS, GTS, FRF.12
PVC isolation	FRTS, GTS	FRTS, GTS, IP/ATM CoS
Packet loss within the carrier network	FRTS, GTS—each with no bursting	FRTS, GTS—each with no bursting

Point-to-Multipoint Circuits

Point-to-multipoint links face similar challenges, but their operation is complicated by the multiple-access nature of the facility and network queuing delays. Also, it is common for multiaccess networks to be implemented with a central or hub site running at significantly faster data rates than each of the remote or spoke sites. This provides a challenge in that the hub site is capable of overwhelming one or more of the remote sites with traffic. Another unique challenge for point-to-multipoint circuits is isolating the voice-carrying PVC from the ill effects of another PVC on the same physical port. Table 8-9 lists the QoS challenges for this type of circuit.

NOTE: *The techniques described above should be applied to the WAN links that will be supporting voice traffic. Table 8-9 will help in determining the appropriate low- or high-speed technique depending upon the router involved and the interface rate.*

Outsourced WAN

In the event that all or part of the intermediary network is not under one administering control, additional considerations must be made to ensure acceptable voice quality. These concerns include prioritization through the external WAN, control over network latency, and network goodput. Several techniques can be applied and are discussed below.

PRIORITIZATION Given Cisco's dominance in the ISP and backbone-routing environments, there is a good chance that Cisco routers are used in part or all of the transit network. Setting the precedence bits capitalizes on the fact that Cisco's weighted fair queuing implementation automatically considers the precedence bits when prioritizing flows. In many cases you may be able to gain preferential transport through the network without the provider even being aware and therefore not charging you for preferential service. Also, some providers may implement random early detection on their core routers to manage congestion, but may not actively inspect or modify precedence bits. As with WFQ, Cisco's implementation of random early detection automatically prioritizes traffic based upon precedence bits, so preferential access can be achieved. This does not guarantee that all network providers will support this, nor does it guarantee that an ISP will not reset these bits, but it does provide a better probability than simple best effort traffic.

LATENCY Network latency is hard to control when an external party controls the intermediary network. Not knowing or being able to control the traffic and links with which your traffic will be intermixed renders most packet-based latency controls ineffective. The best options are to limit the amount of high-latency effects caused by your own traffic. This can be done by lowering the IP MTU for links connecting to an IP VPN, or by using FRF.12 if the intermediary network offers a frame-relay connection.

NETWORK GOODPUT Many network providers and even ISPs are offering SLAs that promise throughput levels through their own network. In order to maximize goodput, traffic offered to the outsourced network should not exceed the guaranteed throughput levels. This can be performed using traffic shaping tools at the network edge.

IP PRECEDENCE Setting the precedence level within the appropriate dial-peer statements provides the flexibility of configuring priority for only the appropriate sessions and/or offering preferential service on a per-session basis. In environments where nonvoice traffic may be using precedence bits or where all voice-enabled routers cannot be modified to set the precedence bits, it may be appropriate to use policy-based routing or committed access rate at the network edge to control which packets

TABLE 8-10

QoS Options for Externally Controlled WANs

	Outsourced WAN	WAN Group	IP-VPN	Internet
Prioritization	IP precedence	IP precedence	IP precedence	IP precedence
Latency	Latency SLA IP precedence FRF.12 if frame relay	IP precedence	Latency SLA Reduced IP mtu IP precedence	Latency SLA within ISP network IP precedence
Goodput	Throughput SLA and GTS or CAR		Throughput SLA and GTS or CAR	Throughput SLA and GTS or CAR

are prioritized. Policy-based routing is recommended unless committed access rate is already in use.

OTHERS All the other techniques discussed should be applied at the network edge interfacing with the external network. FRF.12 is only applicable when an outsourced WAN is nothing more than a frame-relay network where the nodes will be communicating with each other over predefined PVCs. If the intermediary network terminates any of the PVCs along the way, FRF.12 will not work unless the intermediary router agrees to run FRF.12 as well.

Table 8-10 summarizes the types of QoS which may be applied for each type of outsourced WAN.

Additional Protocols

In many environments, IP is not the only protocol running over the corporate WAN. Protocols like IPX and SNA will also vie for network resources. Table 8-11 identifies some of the requirements for IPX and SNA.

Novell IPX

IPX brings several challenges to integrated voice/data networks. Among them are controlling routing advertisement, service advertisements, and packet burst (pburst) streams.

ROUTING UPDATES By default, IPX-based NetWare servers use a version of RIP to advertise network reachability information. The update interval is 60 s and the maximum packet size is close to 500 bytes. To advertise a large number of networks, multiple packets are required.

TABLE 8-11

IPX and SNA
Network
Characteristics and
Requirements

Traffic Characteristic	IPX	SNA	Voice
Bandwidth	Variable and flexible, PBURST improves performance over slow links	Moderate: requires consistent bandwidth availability	Consistent: with low requirements per call
Jitter	Flexible to varying levels of jitter	Moderate: requires relatively consistent packet arrival rates	High: requires extremely low variation in packet arrival rates
Prioritization	Not required	Moderate: required to ensure timely responses	High: required to meet jitter and latency requirements
Latency	Adaptable to latency conditions	Moderate: limited tolerance for latency	High: extremely stringent latency requirements
Support for network layer fragmentation	No	Limited, requiring DLSw or RSRB	Yes
Traffic flow rates	Variable, and bursty	Consistent and predictable	Predictable

These form trains of packets that can disrupt voice traffic when transmitted over low-speed links. This can be prevented in one of two ways. The first is to use a link-fragmentation technique like LFI or FRF.12, and the second is to increase the time between successive RIP updates. The second can be performed globally for all interfaces in the routers with the global command

```
ipx default-output-rip-delay time
```

or on specific interfaces using the interface command

```
ipx output-rip-delay time
```

where *time* is the desired interval specified in milliseconds and the default is 55 ms.

SAP Updates

A similar phenomenon occurs with Novell Service Advertisement Protocol (SAP) updates. SAP updates are also transmitted every 60 s and have a maximum size of approximately 500 bytes. As with RIP, trains of packets can disrupt voice traffic running over a common link. The options available to combat this are link fragmenting and/or controlled interpacket spacing. Interpacket spacing can be adjusted globally for all IPX interfaces using the command

```
ipx default-output-sap-delay time
```

or on specific interfaces using the interface command

```
ipx output-sap-delay time
```

where *time* is the desired interval specified in milliseconds and the default is 55 ms.

Another helpful technique for controlling interference from SAP updates is to reduce the number of SAP packets that must be sent. Often, many services do not need to be advertised to all locations. Judicious application of SAP filtering can reduce the amount of bandwidth consumed by the SAP process. To configure an SAP filter, the filter must first be built using a 1000 series access list and then applied to the appropriate interface. The command for building an IPX SAP filter access list is the following:

```
access-list access-list-number {deny | permit} network[.node]
  [network-mask.node-mask] [service-type [server-name]]
```

where *access-list-number* is a number between 1000 and 1099 identifying the access list

deny specifies that packets which match this line should be blocked

permit specifies that packets which match this line should be accepted

network specifies the network number for the filter

.node specifies the node address from the filter and is optional

network-mask specifies a bit mask for matching network numbers and is optional

.node-mask specifies a bit mask for matching node numbers and is optional

service-type specifies the SAP code for service to be matched and is optional

server-name specifies the name of the service to be matched and is optional

The SAP filter can then be applied to a specific interface using the following interface command:

```
ipx output-sap-filter access-list-number
```

where `access-list-number` corresponds to the appropriate 1000 series access list.

PBURST   After the release of NetWare 3.11, Novell introduced an enhancement to the NetWare Core Protocol (NCP) called PBURST, which allowed for the acknowledgment of multiple packets with a single packet. Prior to PBURST, an acknowledgment was required for every packet transmitted. PBURST emulates most of the functionality of TCP and, accordingly, exhibits the same behaviors. Large file transfers can create trains of packets that disrupt voice traffic streams. In order to prevent this from occurring, the router must queue these flows separately and schedule their transmission effectively. Since most QoS mechanisms only apply to IP traffic, weighted fair queuing emerges as the appropriate technique. WFQ's ability to individually queue and prioritize multiple IPX and IP flows enables it to more effectively handle PBURST flows and allocate bandwidth more fairly. Table 8-12 summarizes the different challenges and workarounds encountered by voice traffic when transporting IPX traffic over lower-speed WAN links.

NOTE: *The techniques in Table 8-12 should be applied on the routers connected to the low-speed WAN links in the network. They are effective on links running below 768 kbps and on multiaccess links where one or more PVC supports Novell IPX traffic.*

TABLE 8-12	Issue	Appropriate Technique
Novell QoS Issues and Workarounds	RIP update "blasts"	Increase interpacket delay
		MLPPP with LFI or FRF.12
	SAP update "blasts"	Increase interpacket delay
		Filter SAPs
		MLPPP with LFI or FRF.12
	PBURST streams	WFQ
	Lack of support for network-layer fragmentation	Data-link-layer fragmentation—MLPPP with LFI or FRF.12

SNA

IBM SNA traffic requires consistent response times and bandwidth availability from the network. Integrating SNA traffic into IP networks presented one of the first QoS challenges for IP networks. The issues were originally addressed through application and network layer prioritization schemes. For instance, priority and custom queuing provided adequate prioritization and bandwidth access for SNA/IP networks. This model works well when SNA is the only high-priority traffic stream.

The introduction of voice traffic into such an environment stresses that model. In essence, voice traffic requires higher priority access than SNA. In reworking the networkwide QoS implementation, care must be taken to ensure that SNA's requirements are still met. The following recommendations are made for integrating voice into an existing SNA/IP environment.

1. Evaluate WAN bandwidth requirements versus current levels—upgrade where necessary.

2. Replace older queuing models with weighted fair queuing.

3. Provide prioritization through IP precedence and allow WFQ to control link access (i.e., Voice = 5, SNA = 3).

4. On point-to-point links lower than 768 kbps look to implement MLPPP with LFI.

5. On frame-relay links implement traffic shaping, CRTP, and TCP header compression.

Existing QoS and Queuing Models

While many data networks do not currently support QoS, some may have already implemented QoS techniques within the routed network. At a minimum, most networks implement weighted fair queuing, as it is the default on all interfaces running at less than 2 Mbps. Before designing and implementing a QoS strategy for voice networking, it is important to identify any and all existing QoS implementations. This can be done by scanning the existing router configurations for each of the QoS techniques and documenting their location. Each implementation must be analyzed to determine the effect that voice traffic will have on it, as well as the implications of switching to a different QoS technique. Important questions to ask are

▪ Why is this technique being applied?

TABLE 8-13

QoS Feature and
Router-Model
Support Matrix

| QoS Class | Classification and Prioritization | | | | | | Traffic Shaping | |
	CAR (H)	RSVP (H)	PQ/CQ (M)	WFQ (L)	Policy Routing (L)	WRED (L)	FRTS (H)	GTS (H)
1600	No	11.2P	11.2P	11.2P	11.2P	11.2P	11.2P	11.2P
2500	No	11.2	9.14	11.2	11.0	11.2	11.2	11.2
2600	12.0	12.0	12.0	12.0	12.0	12.0	12.0	12.0
3600	12.0	11.2	11.3	11.2	11.2	11.2	11.2	11.2
3810	No	11.3	11.3	11.3	11.3	11.3	11.3	11.3
4500	12.0	11.2	11.2	11.2	11.0	11.2	11.2	11.2
4700	12.0	11.2	11.2	11.2	11.0	11.2	11.2	11.2
AS5300	No	11.2P	11.2P	11.2P	11.2P	11.3	No	11.2P
7200	11.1 CC	11.2	11.1	11.2	11.0	11.2	11.2	11.2
7500	11.1 CC	11.2	11.1	11.2	11.0	11.2	11.2	11.2
RSM	12.0	11.2	11.2	11.2	11.2	No	11.2	11.2
8500	No	No	No	No/WRR	12.0	No/WRR	No	No
6500 MSM	No	No	No	No/WRR	12.0	No/WRR	No	No

H = heavy, M = medium, and L = light weighting; CAR = committed access rate; PQ/CQ = priority queuing and custom queuing; WFQ = weighted fair queuing; WRED = weighted random early detection; FRTS = frame-relay traffic shaping; GTS = generic traffic shaping; MLPPP with LFI = multilink PPP with link fragment interleaving; CRTP = compressed real-time protocol; WRR = weighted round robin scheduling.

- What traffic does it support? Neglect?
- What systems and/or applications does it affect?
- How do the newer QoS techniques interact with it?
- What are the effects of making voice traffic a higher priority within the existing scheme?
- If a different technique is required, how can the new technique emulate the service provided by the older one?
- If WFQ is enabled, will transmitting voice at a higher priority (IP precedence = 5) significantly affect existing traffic?

The answers to the questions above should provide some direction toward resolving any conflicts with the existing QoS configurations. As with any network configuration change, time and resources must be dedicated to planning and testing the change before putting it into production.

Link Efficiency		Enhanced Integration		QoS Policy	
MLPPP with LFI (M)	CRTP (M)	RSVP-ATM Interworking (H)	IP to ATM CoS (H)	Propagation via BGP (H)	Tag Switching/ MPLS (H)
11.3	11.3	No	No	No	No
11.3	11.3	No	No	No	No
12.0	12.0	No	No	No	No
11.3	11.3	No	No	No	No
11.3	11.3	No	No	No	No
11.3	11.3	No	No	No	No
11.3	11.3	No	No	No	No
11.3	11.3	No	No	No	No
11.3	11.3	12.0	12.0	11.1 CC	12.0
11.3	11.3	12.0	11.1 CC	11.1 CC	12.0
No	No	No	No	No	No
No	No	No	No	No	12.0
No	No	No	No	No	Planned

Router Software Versions

The voice-enabled routers will most likely be running up-to-date software due to the currency of the voice hardware and software; however, the existing network environment may not be running the latest software. In order to implement many of the QoS techniques mandated by voice over IP, IOS versions 11.3 and 12.0 are required. The software versions for all routers that will be involved in transporting voice traffic must be gathered and reviewed. At times, these routers may not able to be upgraded due to hardware support, interface compatibility, DRAM and FLASH memory sizes, corporate policy, or other political and/or business requirements. These issues must be considered when developing a networkwide QoS policy.

QoS Configuration Guidelines

Tables 8-13 and 8-14 provide relative guidelines for implementing the QoS techniques discussed. They serve as a reference for planning and should not be used as absolute metrics.

TABLE 8-14

Subjective Platform
Configuration
Limits

QoS Rating/ Router Class	Light	Medium	Heavy
1600/2500/3810	2 × T1	1 × T1	256 kbps (1600)/ 512 kbps (2500/3810)
2600/3600	4 × T1/6 × T1	2 × T1/4 × T1	1 × T1/2 × T1
4500/4700/AS5300	10 × T1	6 × T1	4 × T1
7200	12 × T1	6 × T1	4 × T1
7500—RSP4	10 × T1	5 × T1	
7500—VIP2	Limited by VIP2 port density	155 Mbps per VIP2-50 45 Mbps per VIP2-40	155 Mbps per VIP2-50 45 Mbps per VIP2-40

WARNING: *These figures are only a guideline! Actual implementation results may vary greatly depending upon several factors including but not limited to protocol mix, interface traffic rates, traffic mix, router software versions, configuration and implementation issues, network design and topology, and additional processes running on the router. Proper planning and testing should be conducted before implementing QoS techniques or any network configuration change.*

Dial Plan Creation

After the initial information has been gathered and a direction has been set for QoS application, the next step is to develop the dial plan. This process is described in detail in Chapter 7 and won't be repeated here. The output from that process should be a dial-peer configuration table and network diagrams.

Generating the Configuration

Generating configurations for the voice-enabled routers is an iterative process that draws from all of the information gathered up to this point. The configuration process can be broken into four steps: base configuration, voice configuration, IP integration, and QoS. These steps are described in more detail below.

Base Configuration

This entails all of the mundane configuration details that should be present in each router configuration to provide consistency and base functionality.

Hostname: The hostname should be a simple functional name that is part of the corporate naming scheme. It is a good practice to represent the site or building location, router type, function, and a unique router identifier in the hostname. The complexity of the network will usually determine the complexity of the name. For instance, a company with a single site and router per city could name a router: newyork3640voice1. Whereas, a company with 18 buildings within a city may use a more complex scheme involving building numbers, department codes, etc.

The following global command sets the router's hostname.

```
hostname hostname
```

Timestamping: When reviewing log entries and tracing through debug statements it is always helpful to know the time and date of the event. This is done by enabling the timestamps service for logging and debugging. The following global configuration statements are recommended:

```
service timestamps log datetime msec
service timestamps debug datetime msec
```

NOTE: *The router's time should be set using an NTP server or by using the* `clock set` *command.*

Testing service: Cisco routers implement the basic test facilities for the TCP stack which help test connectivity throughout the network. Echo and character generator facilities are available by Telneting to the router's IP address on ports 7 and 19, respectively. The echo function establishes a TCP connection and simply echoes back every character typed. The character-generator function establishes a TCP connection and then transmits a continuous stream of ASCII characters.

```
service tcp-small-servers
```

WARNING: *Enabling TCP-small-servers is a potential security risk as it opens the router up to denial-of-service attacks from malicious host(s). It should not be enabled on publicly accessible routers or routers in an insecure environment.*

Telnet and Console Passwords

Passwords should be assigned to the console port for security and the virtual terminals (Telnet) to enable access. This is done with the following sequence of commands:

```
Router(config)#line con 0
Router(config-line)#password password
Router(config-line)#line vty 0 4
Router(config-line)#password password
```

If the AUX port will be in use for out-of-band access, it should be configured appropriately with passwords and any necessary physical-layer attributes.

```
Router(config-line)#line aux 0
Router(config-line)#speed 9600
Router(config-line)#stopbits 1
Router(config-line)#flowcontrol hardware
Router(config-line)#modem dialin
Router(config-line)#login
Router(config-line)#password password
```

Enable Password

The enable password restricts privileged access to the router. It is set with the following global command:

To use a more secure, one-way-encrypted enable password, the following command is used:

```
enable secret password
```

Password Encryption

Encrypting passwords is always a good idea. The basic encryption invoked for console and Telnet access can be broken using a decryption program, but it does prevent the casual observer from gaining your password by looking over your shoulder. Password encryption is enabled with the following global command:

```
service password-encryption
```

NOTE: *The enable secret password uses a stronger one-way-encryption algorithm.*

Interface Descriptions

It is often helpful to include descriptions under each network and voice interface. In general the description should identify what the router is connecting to and any details associated with the connection. Examples are

```
!
voice-port 1/0/0
 description PBX port 1
!
or
!
interface Serial0/0
 description Carrier FR - 512k circuit ID: 555010101
 encapsulation frame-relay
 frame-relay lmi-type ansi
!
interface Serial0/0.1 point-to-point
 description DLCI: 240 to NY3640V1
 ip address 192.168.100.5 255.255.255.252
 no ip directed-broadcast
 frame-relay interface-dlci 240
!
```

Enable DNS

To enable the router use DNS to resolve hostnames for ping, Telnet, traceroutes, dial peers, and other functions, a DNS server must be configured as well as a default domain name. This is accomplished with the following commands:

```
ip domain-name domain_name
ip name-server IPaddress
```

where *domain_name* specifies the domain for the site
Ipaddress specifies the IP address of the DNS server.

An example DNS configuration follows:

```
ip domain-name realtech.com
ip name-server 10.4.1.2
```

Enable SNMP

The routers should be configured for SNMP access to enable CiscoWorks or other network management packages to manage them. At a minimum, SNMP read-access should be provided. Access to the SNMP process can be restricted using a standard IP access list in addition to the standard community strings. The command for enabling SNMP is the following:

```
snmp-server community communitystring [ RO | RW ] {acl-number}
```

where *communitystring* is the desired SNMP community string or password for access

RO specifies that the community string is for read-only access

RW specifies that the community string is for read-write access

acl-number specifies the number from 1 to 99 of the standard IP access list used to restrict access to the SNMP process

The access-list feature is recommended in insecure environments, especially when the default community strings are in use (public for read-only and private for read-write).

IDENTIFICATION It is also helpful to set location, contact information, and chassis id so that the management station can readily retrieve this information. The following example demonstrates how this is performed:

```
snmp-server location Springfield
snmp-server contact Homer Simpson
snmp-server chassis-id SHN031400NJ
```

SNMP Traps

The router can send unsolicited messages, called traps, to alert the management stations of network events. When enabling traps, several commands are helpful. Traps must be enabled using the following global command:

```
snmp-server enable traps
```

The types of traps sent can be limited by qualifying the above command with a specific trap set, such as voice. The list of available traps varies slightly depending upon the router hardware and software version. For managing voice networks, the following trap sets are recommended:

```
snmp-server enable traps voice poor-qov
snmp-server enable traps config
snmp-server enable traps envmon                 - if applicable
snmp-server enable traps rsvp                   - if applicable
snmp-server enable traps frame-relay            - if applicable
```

Enabling the traps is only helpful if they are given a place to go. To define the host or hosts that are to receive traps use the following command:

```
snmp-server host host community {trap-list}
```

> where *host* specifies the IP address or DNS name of the destination management station
>
> *community* specifies the community string for trap reception on the host (this almost always set to `public`)
>
> *trap-list* is an optional list of trap type to be sent to a specific host. If configured, the list created with the `snmp-server enable traps` command is ignored for that particular host.

Lastly, it is a good habit to specify a single source address to be used in sending traps. By default, the router uses the IP address of the interface closest to the management station when sending traps. However, it is helpful to use a consistent address, so that only a single address needs to be stored in the management station's host table or DNS server. This can be accomplished using the command

```
snmp-server trap-source interface
```

> where *interface* is the name of any valid interface in the router. Usually this is set to an Ethernet or loopback interface. For example:

```
snmp-server trap-source Ethernet0/0
```

SNMP SUMMARY The following configuration is an example of an SNMP configuration for a voice router.

```
!
snmp-server community public RO 10
snmp-server trap-source Ethernet0/0
snmp-server location Springfield
snmp-server contact Homer Simpson
snmp-server chassis-id SHN031400NJ
snmp-server enable traps hsrp
snmp-server enable traps config
snmp-server enable traps envmon
```

```
snmp-server enable traps rsvp
snmp-server enable traps frame-relay
snmp-server enable traps voice poor-qov
snmp-server host 10.1.2.199 public
!
access-list 10 permit 10.1.2.199
!
```

Enable Logging and Syslog

The router generates informational messages as events occur. This information can be critical when attempting to resolve network issues. Messages can be stored in the router's internal memory log as well as on an external syslog server. Cisco also provides control over the severity of messages that are transmitted, allowing managers to filter out unnecessary information. The steps for enabling internal and external logging follow.

1. Enable internal logging:

```
logging buffered log-size {info-level}
```

where `buffered` indicates that the messages should be sent to the internal log

`log-size` specifies the size, in bytes, of the internal log. The log implements a FIFO queue, so old messages are flushed when the log fills. Unless memory is scarce, a size of 8 to 16 kB is usually appropriate.

`info-level` controls the severity of messages sent. Available options, in order of severity are: debugging, informational, notifications, warnings, errors, critical, alerts, and emergencies. When set, messages of the specified level and higher are logged.

2. Enable external syslog logging:

```
logging hostname
logging trap info-level
```

where `hostname` is the IP address or DNS name of the destination server

`info-level` controls the severity of messages sent. Available options, in order of severity are: debugging, informational, notifications, warnings, errors, critical, alerts, and emergencies. When set, messages of the specified level and higher are transmitted.

3. Set the source address

As with SNMP traps, it is useful to have all syslog messages from a particular host be transmitted from a consistent IP address. This is accomplished with the following command:

```
logging source interface
```

where *interface* is the name of the interface in the router.

Logging Summary

The following configuration is an example of the logging commands that should be enabled.

```
logging buffered 16384 debugging
logging trap debugging
logging source-interface Ethernet0/0
logging 10.1.1.100
```

Base Configuration Summary

Figure 8-7 is an example configuration that implements all of the suggestions discussed in the base configuration section.

Voice Connectivity

Configuring voice connectivity is surprisingly simple once the external issues like addressing and QoS are dealt with. Most of the trouble with voice connectivity comes from external interfacing issues that require tweaking of gain and attenuation levels. The basic steps are the following:

1. Configure voice ports
2. Configure local dial peers (POTS)
3. Configure remote dial peers (VoIP)
4. Configure enhanced services

Voice Ports

Voice ports are the router's connection to telephony devices. They control physical-layer connectivity. Configuration work for voice ports involves describing the port to ease administration and adjusting input and output gain and attenuation levels.

Most of the information for configuring voice ports is obtained during the initial survey of the telephony equipment. The type signaling is the most important. For E&M interfaces the type and 2-wire/4-wire operation are important as well. The following short checklists are provided.

Figure 8-7
Base configuration
example.

```
!
version 12.0
service timestamps debug datetime msec
service timestamps log datetime msec
service password-encryption
service tcp-small-servers
!
hostname RTSNY1-2613-V1
!
logging buffered 16384 debugging
enable password 7 030752180500
!
ip subnet-zero
ip domain-name realtech.com
ip name-server 10.4.1.2
!
!
!
!
voice-port 1/0/0
 timeouts call-disconnect 0
 description PBX analog slot 5 port 1
!
voice-port 1/0/1
 timeouts call-disconnect 0
 description PBX analog slot 5 port 2
!
voice-port 1/1/0
 timeouts call-disconnect 0
 description PBX analog slot 5 port 3
!
voice-port 1/1/1
 timeouts call-disconnect 0
 description analog test phone - server room
!
!
interface Ethernet0/0
 description connects to SWC5501 port 5/1
 ip address 10.1.99.108 255.255.0.0
 no ip directed-broadcast
!
interface Serial0/0
 description FR 512k circuit ID: 555010101
 no ip address
 no ip directed-broadcast
 encapsulation frame-relay
 no ip mroute-cache
 no fair-queue
!
interface Serial0/0.1 point-to-point
 description DLCI: 240 to RTSBOS-2621-V1
 ip address 192.168.100.5 255.255.255.252
 no ip directed-broadcast
 frame-relay interface-dlci 240
```

Figure 8-7
Base configuration
example. (*Continued*)

```
!
interface TokenRing0/0
 description Tok0/0: not in use
 no ip address
 no ip directed-broadcast
 shutdown
 ring-speed 16
!
interface BRI0/0
 description BRI0/0: not in use
 no ip address
 no ip directed-broadcast
 shutdown
!
interface Serial0/1
 description S0/1: not in use
 no ip address
 no ip directed-broadcast
 shutdown
!
ip classless
ip http server
!
logging trap debugging
logging source-interface Ethernet0/0
logging 10.1.1.100
access-list 10 permit 10.1.2.199
!
snmp-server engineID local 00000009020000D058220400
snmp-server community public RO 10
snmp-server trap-source Ethernet0/0
snmp-server location Springfield
snmp-server contact Homer Simpson
snmp-server chassis-id SHN031400NJ
snmp-server enable traps hsrp
snmp-server enable traps config
snmp-server enable traps envmon
snmp-server enable traps rsvp
snmp-server enable traps frame-relay
snmp-server enable traps voice poor-qov
snmp-server host 10.1.2.199 public
!
line con 0
 password 7 104D000A0618
 transport input none
line aux 0
 password 7 060506324F41
 login
 modem Dialin
 flowcontrol hardware
line vty 0 4
 password 7 060506324F41
 login
!
no scheduler allocate
                    end
```

Analog Voice Port Checklists

FXS/FXO ports

1. Signaling—loop or ground start
2. Description
3. Set dial type, if pulse (FXO only)
4. Set comfort noise if VAD will be used

E&M ports

1. Description
2. Signaling—immediate, wink, or delay
3. Set E&M type—I, II, III, or V
4. Operation mode—2- or 4-wire
5. Impedance—600c, 600r, 900c
6. Dial type, if pulse

DIGITAL VOICE PORT CHECKLIST   Most of the configuration is on the controller interface

1. Switch-type—primary-5ess, primary-4ess, primary-dms100, primary-ni
2. Configure framing to ESF
3. Configure line coding to B8ZS
4. Configure all 24 PRI timeslots

Fine Tuning

For analog voice ports, fine tuning input and output gain and attenuation on a per-port basis may be required. When connecting to a PBX, it is best to leave the router's settings as is and adjust the gain on the PBX. Table 8-15 presents the goals for gain and loss levels on the router.

To accurately adjust the router to achieve these goals, a tone generator capable of generating tone at reference dB level is required. If one is

TABLE 8-15

Input/Output Gain and Attenuation Goals

Interface Type	Input Gain	Output Attenuation
FXS	0	−6
FXO	−2	−3
E & M	0	0

available, it should be used to place calls among the routers and generate tone. The command `show call active voice` should then be used to check input signal levels. With a goal of introducing −2 dB of loss on each switched leg, the levels should be adjusted on each voice port using the input gain and output attenuation commands.

Configure Local Dial Peers

Local dial peers or POTS dial peers assign phone numbers to the physical ports. The same number may be assigned multiple physical ports, which is convenient when interfacing with a PBX or key system. POTS dial peers require only a destination pattern and a port number to become functional.

DIRECT-INWARD DIALING Support for direct-inward dialing, or DID, allows the router to automatically route POTS voice calls based upon the number dialed. Use of DID enables external users to dial internal phone sets directly without requiring an operator to forward the call to the final destination. DID only works seamlessly with digital interfaces where DNIS (called number) and/or ANI (caller id) is provided. For analog ports this can't be achieved because there is no way for the telephone switch to pass this information to the router. Configuring DID on an AS5300 requires the command `direct-inward-dial` to be placed on the POTS dial peer. As long as the router has a dial peer with a destination pattern that matches the received number, it will route the call appropriately. The following example demonstrates the syntax.

```
!
dial-peer voice 9 pots
 destination-pattern +9.......
 direct-inward-dial
 port 0:D
!
```

The example shows a POTS dial peer bound to port 0 on an AS5300. Users can dial 9 plus a 7-digit number to gain an outside line. Also, inbound calls are compared with the existing dial peers and routed appropriately.

PRIVATE LINE AUTOMATIC RINGDOWN Private line automatic ringdown (PLAR) dial peers are used to emulate dedicated circuit connections between phones. When a phone connected to a POTS dial peer configured for PLAR is taken off hook, the dial peer immediately establishes a con-

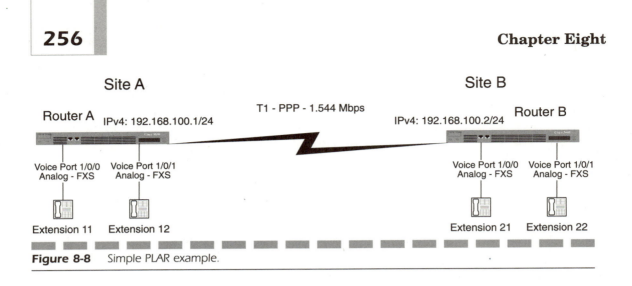

Figure 8-8   Simple PLAR example.

nection to the destination specified by the PLAR statement. This can be helpful for PBX trunking or for dedicated phone mappings. The benefit of voice over IP PLAR connections is that no bandwidth is consumed while the phone is on hook. To configure a PLAR connection, determine the two endpoint voice ports and the destination port's phone number. Then use the command `connection plar` on the source port and point it toward the destination port's phone number. Figure 8-8 demonstrates this.

In the network depicted in Figure 8-8, the goal is to have Extension 21 ring every time Extension 11's phone is taken off hook. The relevant configuration segments follow:

Router A

```
voice-port 1/0/0
description connect to Site A phone 1
connection plar 21
!
voice-port 1/0/1
 description connect to Site A phone 2
!
dial-peer voice 1 pots
 destination-pattern 11
 port 1/0/0
!
dial-peer voice 2 pots
 destination-pattern 12
 port 1/0/1
!
dial-peer voice 3 voip
 destination-pattern 2.
 ip precedence 5
 no vad
 session target ipv4:192.168.100.2
!
```

Router B

```
voice-port 1/0/0
 description connect to Site B phone 1
!
voice-port 1/0/1
 description connect to Site B phone 2
!
dial-peer voice 1 pots
 destination-pattern 21
 port 1/0/0
!
dial-peer voice 2 pots
 destination-pattern 22
 port 1/0/1
!
dial-peer voice 3 voip
 destination-pattern 1.
 ip precedence 5
 no vad
 session target ipv4:192.168.100.1
!
```

This configuration is essentially similar to the basic configuration for interoffice voice connectivity with the only additional being `connection plar 21` under Router A's voice port 1/0/0. As soon as the voice port detects an off-hook condition, the dial string 21 is immediately looked up, matched to the VoIP dial peer, the connection is established, and extension 21 rings.

Configure VoIP Dial Peers

Voice over IP dial peers define the call legs which traverse the IP network. On a basic level they require only a destination pattern and a destination-IP address (session target). Additional parameters can be set to adapt to faxes, adjust the voice-encoding algorithm, and facilitate hunt groups.

FAXING The voice modules' DSPs can detect fax transmissions. Once detected, the DSP intercepts the call and assumes the roll of the far-end fax machine during the negotiation stage. This allows the DSP to control the rate at which the fax machine transmits, which is useful when interfacing with the packet network. RSVP reservations are made based upon the voice-encoding algorithm for the interface, so if G.729 is configured, the reservation will be for 8 kbps voice plus IP overhead. If a 14,400 bps fax is sent using that reservation, it will quickly exceed the bandwidth reserved and be at risk for signal degradation due to lost or delayed packets within the IP network. In order to avoid this scenario, the fax-rate command can be used to either statically configure the fax-rate or to set it to the maximum voice rate. The syntax for the fax-rate command is

```
fax-rate rate
```

where `rate` can be 2400, 4800, 7200, 9600, 14400, or voice.

Setting the fax rate to voice automatically configures it to run at the maximum voice rate. This is the recommended setting since it avoids potential QoS issues.

VOICE ENCODING By default, the voice-enabled routers use the voice-encoding algorithm specified by G.729. This can be changed to G.729a or G.711, if desired. G.711 is helpful for interacting with external systems and software, which may not support G.729. To change the voice encoding on per-dial-peer basis, use the dial-peer command `codec`. The syntax for codec follows:

```
codec { g711alaw | g711ulaw | g729r8 }
```

Other environments where G.711 encoding is advantageous are configurations with multiple encoding-decoding cycles or bandwidth-rich environments where high quality is chosen over network efficiency.

HUNT GROUPS Hunt groups are helpful in simplifying dial plans and providing single number access to a facility. Hunt groups are configured by assigning the same destination pattern to multiple dial peers, each mapping to a different voice port. To control the order in which voice ports are selected, the preference command is used.

Network Integration

This section discusses some of the issues associated with integrating voice over IP into an existing IP network. It is not intended to provide detailed configuration information for building the IP network from scratch, but rather information to help augment the IP network to better support voice over IP traffic.

Security Filters

Packet filters are often used to control traffic in IP networks. Cisco's access-list structure offers the ability to deny, permit, or log traffic based upon a wide range of criteria. When modifying an access list to permit voice traffic, a few parameters must be considered. They are

1. Destination IP address of all VoIP dial peers
2. Number of voice channels in each voice-enabled router

3. Source address used to reach all dial peers

Extracting the session targets from all of the VoIP dial peers in the configuration easily identifies the first parameter.

The number of voice channels supported by the router is also easy to identify and its value determines the range of UDP ports that will be used for voice calls. The UDP ports allocated begin with port 16384 and end with $16384 + (4 * N)$, where N is the number of voice channels in the router. For example, an AS5300 supporting 24 voice channels would use a UDP port range of 16384 through 16480.

The third parameter may seem strange, but must be given consideration. When a router initiates a call, the source IP address for the call is that of the interface used as the exit path toward the destination. If Serial 0/0 is the output interface, then Serial 0/0's IP address is used. This can be confusing if the remote routers' dial peers point to the Ethernet interface's IP address instead of the serial interface's and may cause problems if packets are filtered by both source and destination IP address.

A voice over IP call includes both RTP/RTCP traffic and H.225 session initiation traffic. RTP/RTCP uses the UDP ports as determined in step 2 above, while H.225 uses TCP port 1720. The access list must include both of these items for calls to be completed. Sample access-list lines to achieve this are

```
access-list 101 permit tcp host 172.16.1.1 host 172.16.1.2 eq 1720
access-list 101 permit udp host 172.16.1.1 host 172.16.1.2 range
16384 16480
```

Remember, when adding lines to an existing access list that the router processes access lists sequentially and exits after the first match. Therefore, it is important to verify that target traffic is not denied earlier in the access list.

Other firewalling systems using proxy servers present additional challenges. Their configuration is beyond the scope of this book.

Rerouting

Many IP networks are designed to provide enhanced fault tolerance through the use of multiple routers and links. Routing protocols are then used to establish loop-free paths through the network. It is important to be cognizant of the traffic flows and paths during failure conditions. This will affect dial-peer session target assignments, security filters, and interface-bound QoS functions.

In fault-tolerant WAN environments, avoid using serial-port IP addresses as the session target for VoIP dial peers. Serial port IP addresses become unavailable when the WAN link they are connected to goes down. This leads to the undesirable effect of not being able to route voice calls to a remote router, even though connectivity to the router is available through a backup or secondary WAN link. A possible workaround for this is to use IP-unnumbered for WAN links, in which case, the same IP address will be assigned to all WAN links and therefore will be reachable in most rerouting scenarios.

Security filters and QoS functions that are applied to specific interfaces must also be considered. More to the point, the application of these same functions must be applied to the backup paths as well as the primary paths.

Network Address Translation

Network Address Translation (NAT) is increasingly being used within corporate networks to overcome address space limitations and increase security and networking issues created due to corporate mergers. Port-address translation offers the ability to translate multiple IP addresses to a single external IP address by multiplexing TCP or UDP port numbers. Both NAT and PAT present challenges for voice over IP networking. NAT's use of dynamic address pools is incompatible with voice over IP's need to map sessions to a consistent IP address. Port Address Translation's changing of source UDP ports is incompatible with how the voice over IP software establishes sessions and passes session responsibility for H.245 to RTCP. For these reasons, static translations must be used to support voice over IP calls across NAT boundaries.

SUMMARY ▪ ▪ ▪ ▪ ▪ ▪ ▪ ▪ ▪

Implementing voice networks requires thorough planning for both the telephony aspects and their impact on the data network infrastructure. Voice traffic engineering requirements must be mapped to data networking requirements. This process fuels the implementation of quality of service functions within the equipment and influences network design, product selection, and software configuration. Careful evaluation of these criteria provides the basis for building high-performance integrated voice and data networks.

Chapter **9**

Sample
Configurations

Introduction

This chapter covers the following five VoIP scenarios:

- Simple voice over IP network
- Simple voice over IP network with enhancements
- PBX trunking
- Multipoint frame-relay configuration
- Additional phone support and management servers

Chapter 9 provides sample configurations for several common voice networking scenarios. Each configuration attempts to provide insight into how the IOS tools set is applied to specific network challenges.

Several configurations are presented beginning with a simple one and quickly progressing to more complex configurations.

Simple Voice over IP Network

The basic configuration represented in Figure 9-1 has been used several times in this book. For the first time, the entire configuration of both routers will be presented. The details are as follows:

- Each site has a Cisco 2610 router, which is used for intersite connectivity over a T1 and for linking two analog phones at each site. An NM-2V with one VIC-2FXS is installed in each of the 2600's. This pro-

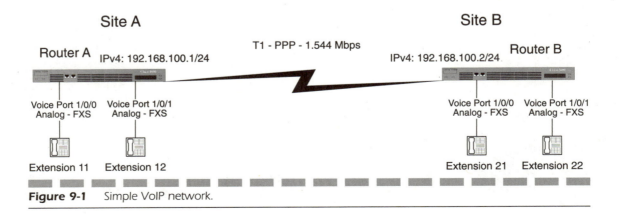

Figure 9-1   Simple VoIP network.

vides connectivity for the two analog phones and leaves room for an additional two-port VIC to be added later.

Network Summary

- Routers:
  Site A: 2610—(1) NM-2V with (1) VIC-2FXS; (1) WIC-2T
  Site B: 2610—(1) NM-2V with (1) VIC-2FXS; (1) WIC-2T
- Protocols: IP with static routing
- WAN Links: site A to site B—dedicated point-to-point T1
- Management Stations:
  SNMP: None
  Syslog: None
- QoS Plan: Weighted Fair Queuing/IP precedence. The T1 provides ample bandwidth to support a maximum of two concurrent calls between sites. Setting the IP precedence to 5 for voice calls ensures that the WFQ scheduler will automatically prioritize voice traffic.

Basic Configurations

The basic configurations for Sites A and B are shown in Figures 9-2 and 9-3, respectively.

Configuration Review

The review of Site A's configuration is broken into 5 separate sections based on common functionality (Figures 9-4 through 9-8.)

Section 1 is depicted in Figure 9-4. It enables timestamping for log and debug commands, gives the router a hostname, configures internal logging of all events (debug level), and sets the enable password.

Section 2, depicted in Figure 9-5, enables the use of IP subnet zero, disables DNS lookups, and configures the hostname to IP address mappings for easy PINGing and TELNETing to Site B.

Figure 4-6 contains Section 3, which provides the meat of the voice connectivity. The voice ports simply identify the device they're connected to. Dial peers 1 and 2 assign phone numbers to the physical voice ports. Dial peer 3 defines the VoIP call to Site B and associates the pattern 2. with Site B's router. The IP precedence bits are set to 5 which will give the voice call priority in the weighted-fair-queuing scheduler running on

```
!
version 12.0
service timestamps debug datetime msec
service timestamps log datetime msec
service password-encryption
service tcp-small-servers
!
hostname SiteA2610
!
logging buffered 16384 debugging
enable password xxxx
!
ip subnet-zero
no ip domain-lookup
ip host SiteB2600 192.168.100.2
ip host SB 192.168.100.2
!
!
!
voice-port 1/0/0
 description connect to Site A phone 1
!
voice-port 1/0/1
 description connect to Site A phone 2
!
dial-peer voice 1 pots
 destination-pattern 11
 port 1/0/0
!
dial-peer voice 2 pots
 destination-pattern 12
 port 1/0/1
!
dial-peer voice 3 voip
 destination-pattern 2.
 ip precedence 5
 no vad
session target ipv4:192.168.100.2
!
!
interface Ethernet0/0
description connection to LAN - SWA port 1/1
 ip address 192.168.1.1 255.255.255.0
 no ip directed-broadcast
!
interface Serial0/0
 description T1 to Site B circuit ID:11104040
 ip address 192.168.100.1 255.255.255.0
 no ip directed-broadcast
 encapsulation ppp
 no ip mroute-cache
!
interface Serial0/1
 description S0/1: not in use
 no ip address
 no ip directed-broadcast
 shutdown
```

Figure 9-2
Site A—router config-
uration. (*Continued*)

```
!
ip classless
ip route 192.168.2.0 255.255.255.0 192.168.100.2
no ip http server
!
!
!
line con 0
 password 7 104D000A0618
 transport input none
line aux 0
 password 7 060506324F41
 login
 modem Dialin
 flowcontrol hardware
line vty 0 4
 password 7 060506324F41
 login
!
no scheduler allocate
end
```

the serial port. Also, because of the abundant bandwidth, voice-activity detection is disabled.

Section 4, depicted in Figure 9-7, configures the network ports on the router. Serial 0/0 is connected to the T1 and labeled as such. Also PPP is configured with weighted fair queuing. WFQ is the default, so it does not appear in the configuration. Serial 0/1 is not in use.

Figure 9-3
Site B—router config-
uration.

```
!
version 12.0
service timestamps debug datetime msec
service timestamps log datetime msec
service password-encryption
service tcp-small-servers
!
hostname SiteB2610
!
logging buffered 16384 debugging
enable password xxxx
!
ip subnet-zero
no ip domain-lookup
ip host SiteA2600 192.168.100.1
ip host SA 192.168.100.1
!
!
!
voice-port 1/0/0
 description connect to Site B phone 1
!
```

Figure 9-3
Site B—router config-
uration. (*Continued*)

```
voice-port 1/0/1
 description connect to Site B phone 2
!
dial-peer voice 1 pots
 destination-pattern 21
 port 1/0/0
!
dial-peer voice 2 pots
 destination-pattern 22
 port 1/0/1
!
dial-peer voice 3 voip
 destination-pattern 1.
 ip precedence 5
no vad
session target ipv4:192.168.100.1
!
!
interface Ethernet0/0
description connection to LAN - SWB port 1/1
 ip address 192.168.2.1 255.255.255.0
 no ip directed-broadcast
!
interface Serial0/0
 description T1 to Site A circuit ID:11104040
 ip address 192.168.100.2 255.255.255.0
 no ip directed-broadcast
 encapsulation ppp
 no ip mroute-cache
!
interface Serial0/1
 description S0/1: not in use
 no ip address
 no ip directed-broadcast
 shutdown
!
ip classless
ip route 192.168.1.0 255.255.255.0
192.168.100.1
no ip http server
!
!
!
line con 0
 password 7 104D000A0618
 transport input none
line aux 0
 password 7 060506324F41
 login
 modem Dialin
 flowcontrol hardware
line vty 0 4
 password 7 060506324F41
 login
!
no scheduler allocate
end
```

Figure 9-4
Section 1 of Site A's
configuration.

```
service timestamps debug datetime msec
service timestamps log datetime msec
service password-encryption
service tcp-small-servers
!
hostname SiteA2610
!
logging buffered 16384 debugging
enable password xxxx
```

Figure 9-5
Section 2 of Site A's
configuration.

```
ip subnet-zero
no ip domain-lookup
ip host SiteB2600 192.168.100.2
ip host SB 192.168.100.2
```

Figure 9-6
Section 3 of Site A's
configuration.

```
voice-port 1/0/0
 description connect to Site A phone 1
!
voice-port 1/0/1
 description connect to Site A phone 2
!
dial-peer voice 1 pots
 destination-pattern 11
 port 1/0/0
!
dial-peer voice 2 pots
 destination-pattern 12
 port 1/0/1
!
dial-peer voice 3 voip
 destination-pattern 2.
 ip precedence 5
 no vad
 session target ipv4:192.168.100.2
```

Figure 9-7
Section 4 of Site A's
configuration.

```
interface Ethernet0/0
description connection to LAN - SWA port 1/1
 ip address 192.168.1.1 255.255.255.0
 no ip directed-broadcast
!
interface Serial0/0
 description T1 to Site B circuit ID:11104040
 ip address 192.168.100.1 255.255.255.0
 no ip directed-broadcast
 encapsulation ppp
 no ip mroute-cache
!
interface Serial0/1
 description S0/1: not in use
 no ip address
 no ip directed-broadcast
 shutdown
```

Figure 9-8
Section 5 of Site A's
configuration.

```
ip classless
ip route 192.168.2.0 255.255.255.0 192.168.100.2
no ip http server
!
!
!
line con 0
 password 7 104D000A0618
 transport input none
line aux 0
 password 7 060506324F41
 login
 modem Dialin
 flowcontrol hardware
line vty 0 4
 password 7 060506324F41
 login
!
no scheduler allocate
end
```

Section 5, shown in Figure 9-8, completes the configuration by assigning passwords and disabling the router's internal web server. The IP classless command enables the router to forward IP datagrams based upon supernets. The single IP route is for Site B's network (192.168.2.0/24). In this simple scenario, an IP routing protocol is not required.

Simple VoIP Network with Enhancements

Tough times have fallen on the mythical company and the boss doesn't want to pay for the full T1 line charge any more. Not only that, the boss was appalled to find out that there was no backup for the leased line. The solution was to scale the T1 down to a 128-kbps fractional T1 and to implement ISDN-based dial backup. Figure 9-9 shows the new network configuration.

Design Changes

- Hardware additions:
  Site A: (1) WIC-1B-U - 1 Port ISDN WIC with integrated NT1
  Site B: (1) WIC-1B-U - 1 Port ISDN WIC with integrated NT1
- WAN Links:
  Site A to Site B: dedicated point-to-point Fractional T1 - 128 kbps
  Site A to Site B: basic rate ISDN dial backup

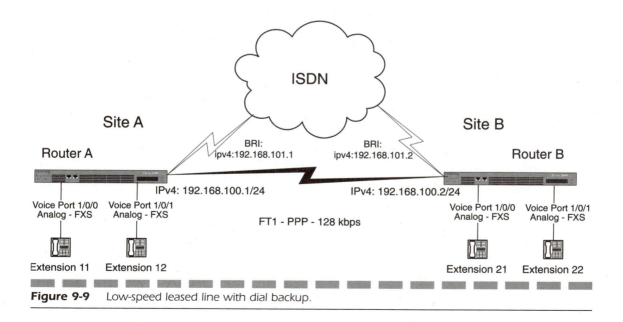

Figure 9-9 Low-speed leased line with dial backup.

- Protocols: IP with EIGRP and floating-static routing
- QoS Plan: CRTP, Multilink PPP with LFI, VAD

Configuration Changes

The following configuration changes must be made:

1. Configure BRI interface for intersite connectivity
2. Configure to dial backup over the ISDN link
3. Configure QoS and link-efficiency techniques for 128-kbps link
4. Configure QoS and link-efficiency techniques for dial-backup link
5. Rework VoIP dial peers to work over primary or backup line

The first change is to add the BRI interfaces to the routers and configure connectivity over them.

Basic ISDN Configuration

Once the BRI interfaces are added, a section will be added into the configuration which looks like:

```
interface BRI0/0
 no ip address
 no ip directed-broadcast
 shutdown
```

The basic ISDN configuration is then performed and dialer profiles are used because they are more flexible than legacy backup interface constructs. The resulting configuration for Site A is depicted in Figure 9-10.

Dial Backup Configuration

To configure dial backup, floating static routes will be used along with EIGRP. While this may be overkill for the small scenario, it is helpful for larger more complex configurations. The plan is to remove the static route for the far site's Ethernet network, and allow the router to learn the route using EIGRP. A new static route for the remote site's Ethernet will be added with a higher administrative distance than that of EIGRP. This route will point to the remote site's dialer interface. In the event of a link failure, the EIGRP-learned route will be removed from the table and the floating static route will be installed causing traffic to be routed through the dialer interface.

Figure 9-10
Router to router
ISDN connectivity.

```
!
username SiteB2610 password xxxxx
!
isdn switch-type basic-dms100
!
interface BRI0/0
 description ISDN port: 5554444, 5554445
 no ip address
 no ip mroute-cache
 encapsulation ppp
 bandwidth 128
 isdn spid1 21255544440101 5554444
 isdn spid2 21255544450101 5554445
 dialer pool-member 1
 no cdp enable
!
!
interface Dialer1
 description Dialer-interface to Site B
 ip address 192.168.102.1 255.255.255.0
 no ip mroute-cache
 encapsulation ppp
 dialer remote-name SiteB2610
 dialer idle-timeout 300
 dialer string 5557777
 dialer load-threshold 5 either
 dialer pool 1
 dialer-group 1
 no cdp enable
 ppp authentication chap
 ppp multilink
!
access-list 101 permit ip any any
!
dialer-list 1 protocol ip list 101
!
```

To implement this plan, the following modifications to router A's configuration are required:

```
!
no ip route 192.168.2.0 255.255.255.0 192.168.100.2
router eigrp 1
 network 192.168.1.0
 network 192.168.100.0
!
!
ip route 192.168.2.0 255.255.255.0 192.168.101.2 200
!
```

Note the administrative distance of 200 assigned to the static route for Site B's Ethernet network.

Configure QoS and Link Efficiency for 128-kbps Link

The reduction in WAN bandwidth requires that measures be taken to ensure that voice quality does not suffer. To accomplish this, several techniques are applied.

First, the amount of bandwidth required for each call is reduced using compressed RTP. CRTP reduces the bandwidth requirements from 24 kbps per call to 11.2 kbps per call.

Second, latency is reduced by implementing multilink PPP with link fragment interleaving. This feature performs layer 2 fragmentation of packets and provides a mechanism for interleaving priority frames in between fragments of a larger frame. The 20-ms fragment delay causes the router to fragment all frames larger than 320 bytes while the RTP reserve queue ensures that RTP voice frames are interleaved between fragmented packets. This requires that a virtual template be created and used for communication over the serial link.

Third, to further reduce the amount of voice traffic, voice-activity detection is enabled on each VoIP dial peer. With VAD, data are not transmitted when the user is not speaking. VAD can save up to 50 percent of the bandwidth normally consumed.

To implement these changes, the following commands are removed from Serial 0/0 in the router configuration:

```
!
interface Serial0/0
 description T1 to Site B circuit ID:11104040
 ip address 192.168.100.1 255.255.255.0
!
```

To enable MLPPP with LFI, the following commands are added:

```
!
multilink virtual-template 1
!
!
interface Serial0/0
 description FT1 to Site B (128kbps) Circuit ID: 3413413
 bandwidth 128
 no fair-queue
 ppp multilink
!
!
interface Virtual-Template1
 ip address 192.168.100.1 255.255.255.0
 no ip directed-broadcast
 ip rtp reserve 16384 20
 fair-queue 64 256 1
 ppp multilink
```

```
  ppp multilink fragment-delay 20
  ppp multilink interleave
 !
```

To enable CRTP, the following commands are added to the router:

```
 !
interface Serial0/0
 ip rtp header-compression iphc-format
 ip tcp header-compression iphc-format
 !
 !
interface Virtual-Template1
 ip rtp header-compression iphc-format
 ip tcp header-compression iphc-format
 !
 !
```

To enable VAD, the following commands are added to the router:

```
dial-peer voice 3 voip
 vad
```

Note that `vad` will not appear in the configuration as its default setting is on.

Configure QoS and Link Efficiency for Dial-Backup Link

For voice calls to receive the same quality of service when the ISDN link is active, the same QoS techniques must be applied. To achieve this, the same commands need to be added to the dialer interface. The necessary additions are presented below:

```
interface Dialer1
 ip rtp reserve 16384 20
 encapsulation ppp
 ip rtp header-compression iphc-format
 ip tcp header-compression iphc-format
 ppp multilink fragment-delay 20
 ppp multilink interleave
 !
```

Rework Dial Peers

The initial configuration had the VoIP dial peers pointing to the IP address of the remote router's serial port. While this worked well in the limited environment, it will not work when the primary link goes down because the IP address will no longer be reachable. For this reason, it is a good idea to configure dial peers to connect to the IP address of the remote router's Ethernet interface, or, if it has one, its loopback interface. The configuration is modified to point the dial peers to the IP address of the remote router's Ethernet interface using the following commands:

```
!
dial-peer voice 3 voip
 session target ipv4:192.168.2.1
 !
```

Complete Configurations

The complete configurations for both routers are presented below.

Site A

```
!
version 12.0
service timestamps debug datetime msec
service timestamps log datetime msec
service password-encryption
service tcp-small-servers
!
hostname SiteA2610
!
logging buffered 16384 debugging
enable password xxxx
!
username SiteB2610 password xxxx
ip subnet-zero
no ip domain-lookup
ip host SiteB2600 192.168.100.2
ip host SB 192.168.100.2
!
multilink virtual-template 1
isdn switch-type basic-dms100
!
!
voice-port 1/0/0
 description connect to Site A phone 1
 !
voice-port 1/0/1
 description connect to Site A phone 2
 !
dial-peer voice 1 pots
 destination-pattern 11
 port 1/0/0
 !
dial-peer voice 2 pots
 destination-pattern 12
 port 1/0/1
 !
dial-peer voice 3 voip
```

```
 destination-pattern 2.
 ip precedence 5
 session target ipv4:192.168.2.1
!
!
interface Ethernet0/0
description connection to LAN - SWA port 1/1
 ip address 192.168.1.1 255.255.255.0
 no ip directed-broadcast
!
interface Serial0/0
 description FT1 to Site B (128kbps) Circuit ID: 3413413
 bandwidth 128
 no ip address
 no ip directed-broadcast
 encapsulation ppp
 ip rtp header-compression iphc-format
 ip tcp header-compression iphc-format
 no ip mroute-cache
 no fair-queue
 ppp multilink
!
interface BRI0/0
 description ISDN port: 5554444, 5554445
 no ip address
 no ip mroute-cache
 encapsulation ppp
 bandwidth 128
 isdn spid1 21255544440101 5554444
 isdn spid2 21255544450101 5554445
 dialer pool-member 1
 no cdp enable
!
interface Serial0/1
 description S0/1: not in use
 no ip address
 no ip directed-broadcast
 shutdown
!
interface Virtual-Template1
 ip address 192.168.100.1 255.255.255.0
 no ip directed-broadcast
 ip rtp reserve 16384 20
 ip rtp header-compression iphc-format
 ip tcp header-compression iphc-format
 fair-queue 64 256 1
 ppp multilink
 ppp multilink fragment-delay 20
 ppp multilink interleave
!
interface Dialer1
 ip address 192.168.101.1 255.255.255.0
 no ip directed-broadcast
 ip rtp reserve 16384 20
 encapsulation ppp
 ip rtp header-compression iphc-format
 ip tcp header-compression iphc-format
 no ip mroute-cache
 dialer remote-name SiteB2610
```

```
    dialer idle-timeout 300
    dialer string 5551212
    dialer load-threshold 5 either
    dialer pool 1
    dialer-group 1
    fair-queue 64 256 1
   no cdp enable
   ppp authentication chap
   ppp multilink
   ppp multilink fragment-delay 20
   ppp multilink interleave
!
router eigrp 1
 network 192.168.1.0
 network 192.168.100.0
!
ip classless
ip route 192.168.2.0 255.255.255.0 192.168.101.2 200
no ip http server
!
!
access-list 101 permit ip any any
dialer-list 1 protocol ip list 101
!
line con 0
 password xxxx
 transport input none
line aux 0
 password xxxx
 login
 modem Dialin
 flowcontrol hardware
line vty 0 4
 password xxxx
 login
!
no scheduler allocate
end
```

Site B

```
!
version 12.0
service timestamps debug datetime msec
service timestamps log datetime msec
service password-encryption
service tcp-small-servers
!
hostname SiteB2610
!
logging buffered 16384 debugging
enable password xxxx
!
username SiteA2610 password xxxx
ip subnet-zero
no ip domain-lookup
ip host SiteA2600 192.168.1.1
ip host SB 192.168.1.1
```

```
!
multilink virtual-template 1
isdn switch-type basic-dms100
!
!
voice-port 1/0/0
 description connect to Site A phone 1
!
voice-port 1/0/1
 description connect to Site A phone 2
!
dial-peer voice 1 pots
 destination-pattern 11
port 1/0/0
!
dial-peer voice 2 pots
 destination-pattern 12
 port 1/0/1
!
dial-peer voice 3 voip
 destination-pattern 2.
 ip precedence 5
 session target ipv4:192.168.1.1
!
!
interface Ethernet0/0
description connection to LAN - SWB port 1/1
 ip address 192.168.2.1 255.255.255.0
 no ip directed-broadcast
!
interface Serial0/0
 description FT1 to Site A (128kbps) Circuit ID: 3413413
 bandwidth 128
 no ip address
 no ip directed-broadcast
 encapsulation ppp
 ip rtp header-compression iphc-format
 ip tcp header-compression iphc-format
 no ip mroute-cache
 no fair-queue
 ppp multilink
!
interface BRI0/0
 description ISDN port: 5557777, 5557778
 no ip address
 no ip mroute-cache
 encapsulation ppp
 bandwidth 128
 isdn spid1 21255577770101 5557777
 isdn spid2 21255577780101 5557778
 dialer pool-member 1
 no cdp enable
!
interface Serial0/1
 description S0/1: not in use
 no ip address
 no ip directed-broadcast
 shutdown
```

```
!
interface Virtual-Template1
 ip address 192.168.100.2 255.255.255.0
 no ip directed-broadcast
 ip rtp reserve 16384 20
 ip rtp header-compression iphc-format
 ip tcp header-compression iphc-format
 fair-queue 64 256 1
 ppp multilink
 ppp multilink fragment-delay 20
 ppp multilink interleave
!
interface Dialer1
 ip address 192.168.101.2 255.255.255.0
 no ip directed-broadcast
 ip rtp reserve 16384 20
 encapsulation ppp
 ip rtp header-compression iphc-format
 ip tcp header-compression iphc-format
 no ip mroute-cache
 dialer remote-name SiteA2610
 dialer idle-timeout 300
 dialer string 5551212
 dialer load-threshold 5 either
 dialer pool 1
 dialer-group 1
 fair-queue 64 256 1
 no cdp enable
 ppp authentication chap
 ppp multilink
 ppp multilink fragment-delay 20
 ppp multilink interleave
!
router eigrp 1
 network 192.168.2.0
 network 192.168.100.0
!
ip classless
ip route 192.168.1.0 255.255.255.0 192.168.101.1 200
no ip http server
!
!
access-list 101 permit ip any any
dialer-list 1 protocol ip list 101
!
line con 0
 password 7 104D000A0618
 transport input none
line aux 0
 password 7 060506324F41
 login modem Dialin
 flowcontrol hardware
line vty 0 4
 password 7 060506324F41
 login
!
no scheduler allocate
end
```

PBX Trunking

Proud of your success with a simple VoIP network with enhancements, your boss bragged about it in a meeting and left the meeting with a promise to link the company's newly purchased PBX systems at each site. Four analog E&M trunks are required, so the FXS ports are removed and four E&M ports (2 VIC-2E/Ms) are added to the NM-2V at each site. The new design is depicted in Figure 9-11.

Design Changes

- Hardware additions:
  Site A: Remove VIC-2FXS and add (2) VIC-2E/M
  Site B: Remove VIC-2FXS and add (2) VIC-2E/M
- WAN Links: Same as previous
- Protocols: Same as previous
- QoS Plan: Same as previous

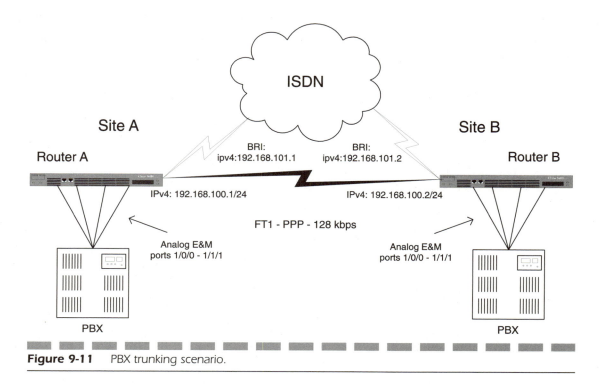

Figure 9-11   PBX trunking scenario.

Configuration Changes

1. Configure physical layer parameters.
2. Create virtual trunk between voice ports.

Configure Physical-Layer Parameters

The PBX system's ports are 2-wire E&M type I with wink start. The router commands to support this configuration are as follows:

```
!
voice-port 1/0/0
 description connect to PBX trunk 1
 signal wink-start
 operation 2-wire
 type 1
!
voice-port 1/0/1
 description connect to PBX trunk 2
 signal wink-start
 operation 2-wire
 type 1
!
voice-port 1/1/0
 description connect to PBX trunk 3
 signal wink-start
 operation 2-wire
 type 1
!
voice-port 1/1/1
 description connect to PBX trunk 4
 signal wink-start
 operation 2-wire
 type 1
!
```

The commands for SiteA2610 and SiteB2610 are exactly the same and therefore only one set of commands is shown.

Create Virtual Trunk between Routers

The first step is to assign destination patterns to the voice ports using dial peers as would normally be done. The following commands achieve this:

Router SiteA2610

```
!
dial-peer voice 1 pots
 destination-pattern 2903001
 port 1/0/0
```

```
!
dial-peer voice 2 pots
 destination-pattern 2903002
 port 1/0/1
!
dial-peer voice 3 pots
 destination-pattern 2903003
 port 1/1/0
!
dial-peer voice 4 pots
 destination-pattern 2903004
 port 1/1/1
!
dial-peer voice 11 voip
 destination-pattern 5561001
 ip precedence 5
 session target ipv4:192.168.2.1
!
dial-peer voice 12 voip
 destination-pattern 5561002
 ip precedence 5
 session target ipv4:192.168.2.1
!
dial-peer voice 13 voip
 destination-pattern 5561003
 ip precedence 5
 session target ipv4:192.168.2.1
!
dial-peer voice 14 voip
 destination-pattern 5561004
 ip precedence 5
 session target ipv4:192.168.2.1
!
```

Router SiteB2610

```
!
dial-peer voice 1 pots
 destination-pattern 5561001
 port 1/0/0
!
dial-peer voice 2 pots
 destination-pattern 5561002
 port 1/0/1
!
dial-peer voice 3 pots
 destination-pattern 5561003
 port 1/1/0
!
dial-peer voice 4 pots
 destination-pattern 5561004
 port 1/1/1
!
dial-peer voice 11 voip
 destination-pattern 2903001
 ip precedence 5
 session target ipv4:192.168.1.1
!
```

```
dial-peer voice 12 voip
 destination-pattern 2903002
 ip precedence 5
 session target ipv4:192.168.1.1
!
dial-peer voice 13 voip
 destination-pattern 2903003
 ip precedence 5
 session target ipv4:192.168.1.1
!
dial-peer voice 14 voip
 destination-pattern 2903004
 ip precedence 5
 session target ipv4:192.168.1.1
!
```

The next step is to configure the virtual trunk between the ports. This is done by applying the connection trunk command to each voice port. The updated voice-port configurations are as follows.

Router SiteA2610

```
voice-port 1/0/0
 description connect to PBX trunk 1
 connection trunk 5561001
 signal wink-start
 operation 2-wire
 type 1
!
voice-port 1/0/1
 description connect to PBX trunk 2
 connection trunk 5561002
 signal wink-start
 operation 2-wire
 type 1
!
voice-port 1/1/0
 description connect to PBX trunk 3
 connection trunk 5561003
 signal wink-start
 operation 2-wire
 type 1
!
voice-port 1/1/1
 description connect to PBX trunk 4
 connection trunk 5561004
 signal wink-start
 operation 2-wire
 type 1
!
```

Router SiteA2610

```
voice-port 1/0/0
 description connect to PBX trunk 1
 connection trunk 2903001
```

```
    signal wink-start
    operation 2-wire
    type 1
!
voice-port 1/0/1
    description connect to PBX trunk 2
    connection trunk 2903002
    signal wink-start
    operation 2-wire
    type 1
!
voice-port 1/1/0
    description connect to PBX trunk 3
    connection trunk 2903003
    signal wink-start
    operation 2-wire
    type 1
!
voice-port 1/1/1
    description connect to PBX trunk 4
    connection trunk 2903004
    signal wink-start
    operation 2-wire
    type 1
!
```

 # Multipoint Frame-Relay Configuration

This scenario (see Figure 9-12) addresses the challenges of supporting voice connectivity over a multipoint network. A single AS5300 connects to a PBX at the main site, while smaller remote sites use 3620 routers configured with FXS analog ports. WAN connectivity at the central site is facilitated by a single 7206 router which also supports several local Ethernet segments.

Network Summary

- Routers:
  AS5300-A: AS5300: (1) 4-port T1 controller card; (2) 24-port voice/fax modules
  Router A: 3620: (1) NM-2V with (2) VIC-2FXS; 1 2E2W module with (1) WIC-2T installed
  Router B: 3620: (1) NM-2V with (2) VIC-2FXS; 1 2E2W module with (1) WIC-2T installed

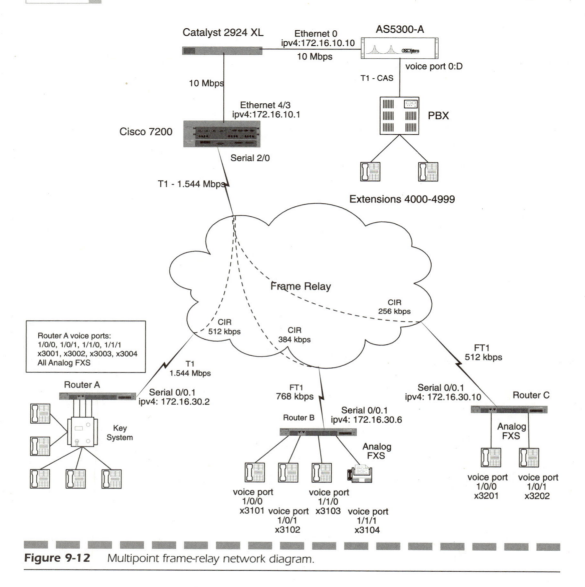

Figure 9-12 Multipoint frame-relay network diagram.

Router C: 2610: (1) NM-2V with (1) VIC-2FXS

Cisco 7200: 7200: (1) NPE-200 with 64-MB DRAM, 20 MB Flash; (1) PA-4E; (1) PA-4T+

■ Protocols: IP with static routing to remote sites

■ WAN links:

> 7200 to Router A: frame-relay link: 512-kbps CIR
> 7200 to Router B: frame-relay link: 384-kbps CIR
> 7200 to Router C: frame-relay link: 256-kbps CIR

- Management stations:

  SNMP: None

  Syslog: None

- QoS Plan:

  Frame-relay traffic shaping for bandwidth control

  Reduced mtu for frame-relay interfaces

  CRTP

  VAD

The dial-peer configuration table is illustrated in Table 9-1.

Router Configurations

The router configurations for the multipoint network are as follows.

AS5300-A

```
!
service timestamps debug datetime msec
service timestamps log datetime msec
service password-encryption
service tcp-small-servers
!
hostname AS5300-A
!
logging buffered 16384 debugging
enable password xxxx
!
ip subnet-zero
no ip domain-lookup
ip host c7200 172.16.10.1
ip host routera 172.16.30.2
ip host routerb 172.16.30.6
ip host routerc 172.16.30.10
!
!
isdn switch-type primary-5ess
!
!
controller T1 0
 description link to PBX slot 2 port1
 framing esf
 clock source internal
 linecode b8zs
 pri-group timeslots 1-24
!
controller T1 1
 framing esf
```

TABLE 9-1 Initial Dial-Peer Configuration Table

Dial-Peer Tag	Ext.	Destination Pattern	Type	Voice Port	Session Target	CODEC	QoS
				AS5300-A			
4000		12122904...	POTS	0:D			
3000		161726130..	VoIP		172.16.30.2	G.729	FRTS w/priority queuing (on 7200)
3100		197325731..	VoIP		172.16.30.6	G.729	FRTS w/priority queuing (on 7200)
3200		170344032..	VoIP		172.16.30.10	G.729	FRTS w/priority queuing (on 7200)
				Router A			
1		16172613001	POTS	1/0/0			
2		16172613002	POTS	1/0/1			
3		16172613003	POTS	1/1/0			
4		16172613004	POTS	1/1/1			
4000		12122904...	VoIP		172.16.10.10	G.729	FRTS w/priority queuing
				Router B			
1		19732573101	POTS	1/0/0			
2		19732573102	POTS	1/0/1			
3		19732573103	POTS	1/1/0			
4		19732573104	POTS	1/1/1			
4000		12122904...	VoIP		172.16.10.10	G.729	FRTS w/priority queuing
				Router C			
1		17034403201	POTS	1/0/0			
2		17034403202	POTS	1/0/1			
4000		12122904...	VoIP		172.16.10.10	G.729	FRTS w/priority queuing

```
   clock source internal
   linecode b8zs
!
controller T1 2
 framing esf
 clock source internal
 linecode b8zs
!
controller T1 3
 framing esf
 clock source internal
 linecode b8zs
!
dial-peer voice 3000 voip
 destination-pattern 161726130..
 ip precedence 5
 session target ipv4:172.16.30.2
!
dial-peer voice 3100 voip
 destination-pattern 197325731..
 fax-rate 9600
 ip precedence 5
 session target ipv4:172.16.30.6
 !
dial-peer voice 3200 voip
 destination-pattern 170344032..
 ip precedence 5
 session target ipv4:172.16.30.10
 !
dial-peer voice 4000 pots
 destination-pattern 12122904...
 direct-inward-dial
 port 0:D
!
num-exp 4... 12122904...
num-exp 30.. 161726130..
num-exp 31.. 197325731..
num-exp 32.. 170344032..
 !
voice-port 0:D
!
voice-port 1:D
!
voice-port 2:D
 !
interface Ethernet0
 description NY LAN dedicated port to C2924A port 0/10
 ip address 172.16.10.10 255.255.255.0
 no ip directed-brodcast
!
interface Serial0:23
 no ip address
 no ip mroute-cache
 isdn incoming-voice voice
 no cdp enable
 !
```

```
interface Serial1:23
 no ip address
 no ip mroute-cache
 isdn incoming-voice modem
 no cdp enable
!
interface Serial2:23
 no ip address
 no ip mroute-cache
 isdn incoming-voice modem
 no cdp enable
!
interface FastEthernet0
 no ip address
 shutdown
 duplex full
!
!
no ip classless
ip route 0.0.0.0 0.0.0.0 172.16.10.1
!
line con 0
 password xxxx
 transport input none
!
line aux 0
!
line vty 0 4
 password xxxx
 login
!
scheduler interval 1000
end
```

Cisco 7200

```
!
service timestamps debug datetime msec
service timestamps log datetime msec
service password-encryption
service tcp-small-servers
!
hostname 7200
!
logging buffered 16384 debugging
!
boot system flash slot1:c7200-ds-mz_113-8.bin
enable password xxxx
!
ip subnet-zero
no ip domain-lookup
ip host AS5300A 172.16.10.10
ip host routera 172.16.30.2
ip host routerb 172.16.30.6
ip host routerc 172.16.30.10
!
!
interface Serial 2/0
```

```
 description FR link to remotes, circuit ID: 5043031
 mtu 640
 no ip address
 no ip directed-broadcast
 encapsulation frame-relay
 no ip mroute-cache
 shutdown
 no fair-queue
 frame-relay traffic-shaping
 frame-relay lmi-type ansi
!
interface Serial2/0.1 point-to-point
 description FR link to routerA - DLCI: 100
 mtu 640
 ip address 172.16.30.1 255.255.255.252
 no ip directed-broadcast
 no ip mroute-cache
 frame-relay interface-dlci 100
  class rtra
 frame-relay ip rtp header-compression
!
interface Serial2/0.2 point-to-point
 description FR link to routerB - DLCI: 101
 mtu 640
 ip address 172.16.30.5 255.255.255.252
 no ip directed-broadcast
 no ip mroute-cache
 frame-relay interface-dlci 101
  class rtrb
 frame-relay ip rtp header-compression
!
interface Serial2/0.3 point-to-point
 description FR link to routerC - DLCI: 102
 mtu 640
 ip address 172.16.30.9 255.255.255.252
 no ip directed-broadcast
 no ip mroute-cache
 frame-relay interface-dlci 102
  class rtrc
 frame-relay ip rtp header-compression
!
!
interface Ethernet4/0
 description Enet connection to Engineering LAN
 ip address 172.16.1.1 255.255.255.0
 no ip directed-broadcast
 no ip mroute-cache
!
interface Ethernet4/1
 description Enet connection to Sales LAN
 ip address 172.16.2.1 255.255.255.0
 no ip directed-broadcast
 no ip mroute-cache
!
interface Ethernet4/2
 description Enet connection to Admin LAN
 ip address 172.16.3.1 255.255.255.0
 no ip directed-broadcast
 no ip mroute-cache
```

```
!
interface Ethernet4/3
 description Enet connection to AS5300 voice gateway LAN
 ip address 172.16.10.1 255.255.255.0
 no ip directed-broadcast
no ip mroute-cache
!
!
ip classless
ip route 172.16.50.0 255.255.255.0 172.16.30.2
ip route 172.16.60.0 255.255.255.0 172.16.30.6
ip route 172.16.70.0 255.255.255.0 172.16.30.10
!
!
map-class frame-relay rtra
 frame-relay cir 512000
 frame-relay bc 32000
 frame-relay be 0
 frame-relay mincir 512000
 no frame-relay adaptive-shaping
 frame-relay fair-queue
!
map-class frame-relay rtrb
 frame-relay cir 384000
 frame-relay bc 24000
 frame-relay be 0
 frame-relay mincir 384000
 no frame-relay adaptive-shaping
 frame-relay fair-queue
!
map-class frame-relay rtrc
 frame-relay cir 256000
 frame-relay bc 16000
 frame-relay be 0
 frame-relay mincir 256000
 no frame-relay adaptive-shaping
 frame-relay fair-queue
!
!
!
line con 0
 password xxxx
 transport input none
line aux 0
 password xxxx
 login
 modem Dialin
 flowcontrol hardware
line vty 0 4
 password xxxx
 login
!
end
```

Router A

```
!
version 12.0
```

```
service timestamps debug datetime msec
service timestamps log datetime msec
service password-encryption
service tcp-small-servers
!
hostname RouterA
!
logging buffered 16384 debugging
enable password xxxx
!
ip subnet-zero
no ip domain-lookup
ip host AS5300A 172.16.10.10
ip host 7200 172.16.10.1
ip host routerb 172.16.30.6
ip host routerc 172.16.30.10
!
!
!
voice-port 1/0/0
 description Key system port 4
!
voice-port 1/0/1
 description Key system port 5
!
voice-port 1/1/0
 description Key system port 6
!
voice-port 1/1/1
 description Key system port 7
!
dial-peer voice 1 pots
 destination-pattern 16172613001
 port 1/0/0
!
dial-peer voice 2 pots
 destination-pattern 16172613002
 port 1/0/1
!
dial-peer voice 3 pots
 destination-pattern 16172613003
 port 1/1/0
!
dial-peer voice 4 pots
 destination-pattern 16172613004
 port 1/1/1
!
dial-peer voice 4000 voip
 destination-pattern 12122904...
 ip precedence 5
 session target ipv4:172.16.10.10
!
num-exp 3001 16172613001
num-exp 3002 16172613002
num-exp 3003 16172613003
num-exp 3004 16172613004
num-exp 4... 12122904...
!
interface Ethernet0/0
```

```
 description sales and admin LAN
 ip address 172.16.50.1 255.255.255.0
 no ip directed-broadcast
!
interface Ethernet0/1
 no ip address
 no ip directed-broadcast
 shutdown
!
interface Serial0/0
 description FR link 1.544 Mbps circuit id: 3048053
 mtu 640
 no ip address
 no ip directed-broadcast
 encapsulation frame-relay
 no ip mroute-cache
 no fair-queue
 frame-relay traffic-shaping
 frame-relay lmi-type ansi
!
interface Serial0/0.1 point-to-point
 description PVC to 7200 DLCI 50
 mtu 640
 ip address 172.16.30.2 255.255.255.252
 no ip directed-broadcast
 no ip mroute-cache
 frame-relay interface-dlci 50
  class rtra
 frame-relay ip rtp header-compression
!
interface Serial0/1
 no ip address
 no ip directed-broadcast
 shutdown
!
!
ip classless
ip route 0.0.0.0 0.0.0.0 172.16.30.1
no ip http server
!
!
map-class frame-relay rtra
 frame-relay cir 512000
 frame-relay bc 64000
 frame-relay be 0
 frame-relay mincir 512000
 no frame-relay adaptive-shaping
 frame-relay fair-queue
!
!
line con 0
 password xxxx
 transport input none
line aux 0
line vty 0 4
 password xxxx
 login
!
```

```
no scheduler allocate
end
```

Router B

```
!
version 12.0
service timestamps debug datetime msec
service timestamps log datetime msec
service password-encryption
service tcp-small-servers
!
hostname RouterB
!
logging buffered 16384 debugging
enable password xxxx
!
ip subnet-zero
no ip domain-lookup
ip host AS5300A 172.16.10.10
ip host 7200 172.16.10.1
ip host routera 172.16.30.2
ip host routerc 172.16.30.10
!
!
!
voice-port 1/0/0
 description phone 1
!
voice-port 1/0/1
 description phone 2
!
voice-port 1/1/0
 description phone 3
!
voice-port 1/1/1
 description fax
!
dial-peer voice 1 pots
 destination-pattern 19732573101
 port 1/0/0
!
dial-peer voice 2 pots
 destination-pattern 19732573102
 port 1/0/1
!
dial-peer voice 3 pots
 destination-pattern 19732573103
 port 1/1/0
!
dial-peer voice 4 pots
 destination-pattern 19732573104
 port 1/1/1
!
dial-peer voice 4000 voip
 destination-pattern 12122904...
 ip precedence 5
```

```
     session target ipv4:172.16.10.10
 !
num-exp 3101 19732573101
num-exp 3102 19732573102
num-exp 3103 19732573103
num-exp 3104 19732573104
num-exp 4... 12122904...
 !
interface Ethernet0/0
 description sales and admin LAN
 ip address 172.16.60.1 255.255.255.0
 no ip directed-broadcast
 !
interface Ethernet0/1
 no ip address
 no ip directed-broadcast
 shutdown
 !
interface Serial0/0
 description FR link 768 kbps circuit id: 1539349
 mtu 640
 no ip address
 no ip directed-broadcast
 encapsulation frame-relay
 no ip mroute-cache
 no fair-queue
 frame-relay traffic-shaping
 frame-relay lmi-type ansi
 !
interface Serial0/0.1 point-to-point
 description PVC to 7200 DLCI 50
 mtu 640
 ip address 172.16.30.6 255.255.255.252
 no ip directed-broadcast
 no ip mroute-cache
 frame-relay interface-dlci 50
  class rtrb
 frame-relay ip rtp header-compression
 !
interface Serial0/1
 no ip address
 no ip directed-broadcast
 shutdown
 !
 !
ip classless
ip route 0.0.0.0 0.0.0.0 172.16.30.5
no ip http server
 !
 !
map-class frame-relay rtrb
 frame-relay cir 384000
 frame-relay bc 24000
 frame-relay be 0
 frame-relay mincir 384000
 no frame-relay adaptive-shaping
 frame-relay fair-queue
 !
 !
```

```
line con 0
 password xxxx
 transport input none
line aux 0
line vty 0 4
 password xxxx
 login
!
no scheduler allocate
end
```

Router C

```
!
version 12.0
service timestamps debug datetime msec
service timestamps log datetime msec
service password-encryption
service tcp-small-servers
!
hostname RouterC
!
logging buffered 16384 debugging
enable password xxxx
!
ip subnet-zero
no ip domain-lookup
ip host AS5300A 172.16.10.10
ip host 7200 172.16.10.1
ip host routera 172.16.30.2
ip host routerb 172.16.30.6
!
!
!
voice-port 1/0/0
 description phone 1
!
voice-port 1/0/1
 description phone 2
!
dial-peer voice 1 pots
 destination-pattern 17034403201
 port 1/0/0
!
dial-peer voice 2 pots
 destination-pattern 17034403202
 port 1/0/1
!
!
dial-peer voice 4000 voip
 destination-pattern 12122904...
 ip precedence 5
 session target ipv4:172.16.10.10
!
num-exp 3201 17034403201
num-exp 3202 17034403202
num-exp 4... 12122904...
!
```

```
interface Ethernet0/0
 description sales and admin LAN
 ip address 172.16.70.1 255.255.255.0
 no ip directed-broadcast
!
interface Ethernet0/1
 no ip address
 no ip directed-broadcast
 shutdown
!
interface Serial0/0
 description FR link 512 kbps circuit id: 1539349
 mtu 640
 no ip address
 no ip directed-broadcast
 encapsulation frame-relay
 no ip mroute-cache
 no fair-queue
 frame-relay traffic-shaping
 frame-relay lmi-type ansi
!
interface Serial0/0.1 point-to-point
 description PVC to 7200 DLCI 50
 mtu 640
 ip address 172.16.30.10 255.255.255.252
 no ip directed-broadcast
 no ip mroute-cache
 frame-relay interface-dlci 50
  class rtrb
 frame-relay ip rtp header-compression
!
interface Serial0/1
 no ip address
 no ip directed-broadcast
 shutdown
!
!
ip classless
ip route 0.0.0.0 0.0.0.0 172.16.30.9
no ip http server
!
!
map-class frame-relay rtrc
 frame-relay cir 256000
 frame-relay bc 16000
 frame-relay be 0
 frame-relay mincir 256000
 no frame-relay adaptive-shaping
 frame-relay fair-queue
!
!
line con 0
 password xxxx
 transport input none
line aux 0
line vty 0 4
 password xxxx
 login
!
```

```
no scheduler allocate
end
```

Notes on the Multipoint Frame-Relay Configuration

AS5300-A

The AS5300 is configured to speak with all remote sites and the locally connected PBX. All VoIP sessions are set to use IP precedence 5 for added priority. A single default route is configured to forward all traffic to the 7200.

7200

The 7200 is responsible for LAN and WAN routing. Frame-relay traffic shaping is configured to control transmission into the frame-relay network. A Be of 0 is configured and adaptive shaping is disabled to prevent bursting above CIR. This is done to ensure that all transmitted packets reach their destination. Bursting can be configured, but should be applied carefully as it incurs the potential for lost traffic. Compressed RTP is also configured to reduce the amount of frame-relay bandwidth consumed by voice traffic. The mtu for the frame-relay interface is lowered to 640 bytes to accommodate latency requirements for the lowest-speed link. The same mtu must be used for all subinterfaces on a frame-relay interface. Static routes are configured for all of the remote LANs.

Routers A–C

Each of these routers are configured for frame-relay traffic shaping and compressed RTP to both control traffic rates and reduce the amount of WAN bandwidth consumed by voice traffic. An mtu of 640 bytes is configured to control latency due to serialization delay over the WAN link.

Additional Phone Support and Management Servers

Given the success of the initial voice-over-IP network, a new site has been added in Chicago. It is connected over a T1 link and supports two Ethernet LAN segments, eight analog phones, and four analog links to the PSTN. In addition to the new site, a management station and DNS server have been installed at the main site. The routers should be configured to make use of them as well. Figure 9-13 depicts the new configuration.

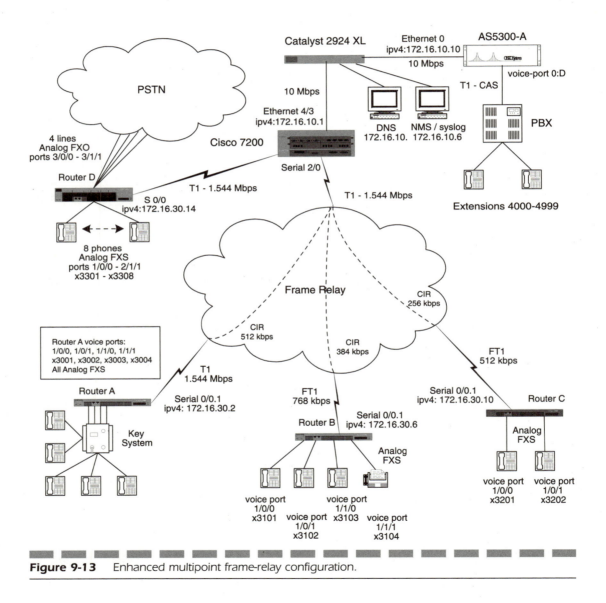

Figure 9-13   Enhanced multipoint frame-relay configuration.

Design Changes

- Hardware additions:
  Router D: 3640—2 NM-2Vs each with (2) VIC-2FXS; (1) NM-2V with (2) VIC-2FXO; 1 2E2W module with (1) WIC-2T installed; DNS Server: IP address 10.1.10.5; NMS/syslog Server: IP address 10.1.10.6
- WAN links: 7200 to Router D: Full T1, 1.544 Mbps
- Protocols: DNS, SNMP, and syslog must be enabled on all of the routers
- QoS plan: RSVP for the new link

Configuration Changes

1. Configure the new link on both the 7200 and Router D
2. Enabled RSVP on the T1 link between Router D and the 7200
3. Configure FXS and FXO ports on Router D
4. Configure the AS5300 and Router D to use RSVP when calling the Chicago link
5. Configure DNS, SNMP, and syslog on all routers

Configure New Link

To support the new link, the 7200 must allocate another port and both the 7200 and Router D must be configured with the appropriate IP subnet information. The following commands should be applied to the 7200:

```
!
interface Serial2/1
 description T1 to Chicago-Router D-1.536 Mbps
 bandwidth 1536
 ip address 172.16.30.13 255.255.255.252
 no ip directed-broadcast
 encapsulation ppp
!
```

Similarly, the 3640 is configured to communicate with the 7200 using the following commands:

```
!
interface Serial0/0
 description T1 to NY-7200-1.536 Mbps
 bandwidth 1536
 ip address 172.16.30.14 255.255.255.252
 no ip directed-broadcast
 encapsulation ppp
!
```

Enable RSVP over the T1 Link

Assuming all 12 phones were active and using the T1 link from Router D to the 7200, 288 kbps of bandwidth would be required to support the connections. To accommodate this requirement plus that of any other RSVP applications, an upper limit of 640 kbps reservable bandwidth is set. The upper limit is set to prevent voice and other RSVP applications from taking too much bandwidth from the bandwidth-hungry non-RSVP applications. To enable RSVP over the T1 link, the following interface command should be added to both routers' serial interfaces:

```
ip rsvp bandwidth 640 192
```

As a result of adding this command, the fair-queuing scheduler for the interface will be updated to reserve queue for the RSVP traffic and the following command will appear under the serial interface in each router:

```
fair-queue 64 256 20
```

Configure FXS and FXO Ports on Router D

Router D needs to be configured for telephony operation. The same basic techniques are applied to the FXS ports that were applied to the FXS ports in routers A, B, and C.

The following configuration statements are added to Router D to enable local calling amongst the FXS ports.

```
!
voice-port 1/0/0
 description phone 1
!
voice-port 1/0/1
 description phone 2
!
voice-port 1/1/0
 description phone 3
!
voice-port 1/1/1
 description phone 4
!
```

```
voice-port 2/0/0
 description phone 5
!
voice-port 2/0/1
 description phone 6
!
voice-port 2/1/0
 description phone 7
!
voice-port 2/1/1
 description phone 8
!
dial-peer voice 1 pots
 destination-pattern 18473183301
 port 1/0/0
!
dial-peer voice 2 pots
 destination-pattern 18473183302
 port 1/0/1
!
dial-peer voice 3 pots
 destination-pattern 18473183303
 port 1/1/0
!
dial-peer voice 4 pots
 destination-pattern 18473183304
 port 1/1/1
!
dial-peer voice 5 pots
 destination-pattern 18473183305
 port 2/0/0
!
dial-peer voice 6 pots
 destination-pattern 18473183306
 port 2/0/1
!
dial-peer voice 7 pots
 destination-pattern 18473183307
 port 2/1/0
!
 dial-peer voice 8 pots
 destination-pattern 18473183308
 port 2/1/1
!
```

The FXO ports present a new challenge. They are used to send calls to the public-switched telephone network. The telephone company has provisioned the links for ground start. To access the PSTN, local users must dial 8 and then they will draw dialtone from the PSTN. The following configuration statements achieve this.

```
!
voice-port 3/0/0
 description PSTN link 1
 signal groundStart
!
```

```
voice-port 3/0/1
 description PSTN link 2
 signal groundStart
!
voice-port 3/1/0
 description PSTN link 3
 signal groundStart
!
voice-port 3/1/1
 description PSTN link 4
 signal groundStart
!
dial-peer voice 800 pots
 destination-pattern 8
 port 3/0/0
!
dial-peer voice 801 pots
 destination-pattern 8
 port 3/0/1
!
dial-peer voice 802 pots
 destination-pattern 8
 port 3/1/0
!
dial-peer voice 804 pots
 destination-pattern 8
 port 3/1/1
!
!
num-exp 33.. 184731833..
!
```

Router D then needs to be configured to communicate with the main site using voice over IP. As with the other routers, a VoIP dial peer is created referencing the AS5300. The configuration commands are as follows:

```
!
dial-peer voice 804 voip
 destination-pattern 12122904...
 ip precedence 5
 session target 172.16.10.10
!
!
num-exp 4... 12122904...
!
```

Enable RSVP for Calls over the T1

The serial interface configurations prepared the routers to support RSVP requests from voice and other applications. In order for voice calls to make use of RSVP, they must request reservations on a per-call basis. This function is handled within the IOS by VoIP dial peers. The following configuration changes are made to Router D to enable RSVP for its calls over the T1 link.

```
!
dial-peer voice 804 voip
  destination-pattern 12122904...
  ip precedence 5
  req-qos controlled-load
  session target 172.16.10.10
!
```

The following configuration additions for the AS5300 enable intersite calling to phone extensions in Chicago, the ability to draw dialtone from the Chicago PSTN, and the use of RSVP for these calls.

```
!
dial-peer voice 800 voip
  destination-pattern 184731833..
  ip precedence 5
  req-qos controlled-load
  session target 172.16.30.14
!
dial-peer voice 804 voip
  destination-pattern 8
  ip precedence 5
  req-qos controlled-load
  session target 172.16.20.14
!
!
num-exp 33.. 184731833..
!
```

Configure DNS, SNMP, and Syslog on all Routers

To gain the functionality of the newly installed servers, support must be enabled on the routers. Most of the configuration information is the same for all of the routers and will only be presented once. Exceptions are noted at the end.

```
!
logging buffered 16384 debugging
!
ip domain-name company.com
ip name-server 172.16.10.5
!
!
logging trap debugging
logging source-interface Ethernet0/0
logging 172.16.10.6
access-list 10 permit 172.16.10.6
!
!
```

```
snmp-server community public RO 10
snmp-server trap-source Ethernet0/0
snmp-server location NewYork
snmp-server contact network support: 555-1234
snmp-server chassis-id SHN031400NJ
snmp-server enable traps hsrp
snmp-server enable traps config
snmp-server enable traps envmon
snmp-server enable traps rsvp
snmp-server enable traps frame-relay
snmp-server enable traps voice poor-qov
snmp-server host 172.16.10.6 public
!
```

The exceptions are

1. The contact and location fields should be adjusted to fit each site.

2. The `trap-source` and `logging-source` should be changed on the 7200 to Ethernet 4/3 and on the AS5300 to Ethernet0.

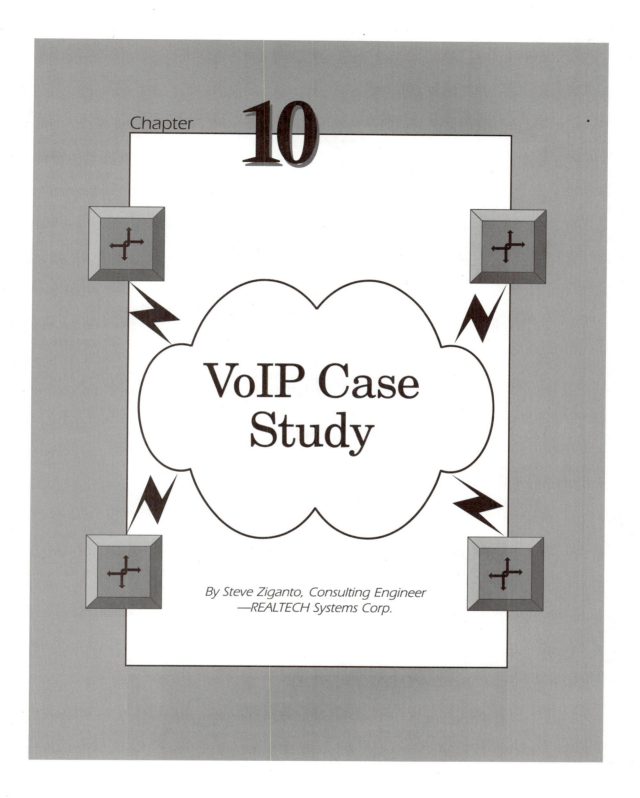

Chapter **10**

VoIP Case Study

By Steve Ziganto, Consulting Engineer
—REALTECH Systems Corp.

Overview

The application to be discussed is a power monitoring system. The system uses a single master station to support several client stations. The master-station computer collects performance statistics from the client stations. The system uses integrated modems to provide dial-up connectivity between the master-station computer and the client computers. The data exchange occurs at regular intervals and supports on-demand collection. The amount of data exchange is typically 1–2 MB contained in several files. Both the master station and the client station are built on heavy-duty PC platforms and run a modified version of DOS.

A new contract for the customer required that the system be deployed into remote Middle Eastern geography. The proposed locations did not have any public phone service. In fact, the sites lacked any terrestrial communication facilities. As part of the deployment the customer planned to have single-mode fiber-optic cable installed between the sites. This fiber was to be used to satisfy the data exchange between the master and client computers. Figure 10-1 is a diagram of the system layout.

Connectivity Requirements

The connectivity requirements were broken into two phases.

Phase I: Dial-up connectivity was required between the master station and client stations 1, 2, 3, and 9.

Phase II: IP over Ethernet connectivity between all devices was required.

This study will only concentrate on the requirements for phase I.

Network Design

Several products for running voice over fiber-optic cable were reviewed; however none was able to provide voice switching at the same price point as the Cisco VoIP technology. In order to maintain the current dial-up

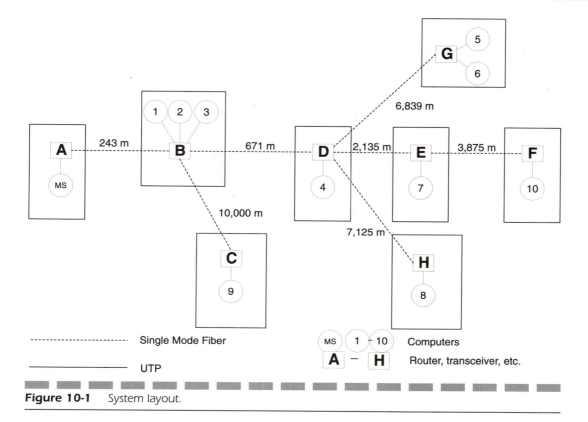

Figure 10-1 *System layout.*

configuration of the system, voice switching was required in order to allow the master-station site to call multiple clients. The VoIP solution also had the advantage of providing the data network infrastructure for the second phase of the project. Based upon phase II's requirements and the low price point of the Cisco 2600 series routers, a VoIP solution using a switched Ethernet network was selected.

The first most critical portion of the design was to ensure that the fiber-optic equipment selected would meet the anticipated power budget of the fiber runs. The fiber cable plant was designed in a hub-and-spoke architecture. The master-station site is the hub of the network. Each remote site has two strands of fiber optics home run to the master station site. In this configuration, the maximum cable run was approximately 10 km. There are several vendors who supply single-mode Ethernet components that will support the 10-km plus runs. In order to reduce costs, media converters and transceivers were used to eliminate the requirement for native fiber-optic ports on the LAN switching hardware. This selection significantly reduced the Ethernet switch price, since the Ethernet switches required only a single AUI port (transceiver support) and some additional UTP ports. The fiber-optic products selected were from Digi International. A rack-mount media conversion system was used at the master station site, while single-mode transceivers were used at all other locations.

The Cisco 1912 Ethernet switch was selected for its low price and inclusion of a single AUI port. The Cisco 2610 was selected as the VoIP platform. Below is a list of the material that was used in this project. Figure 10-2 is a high-level view of connectivity over the network.

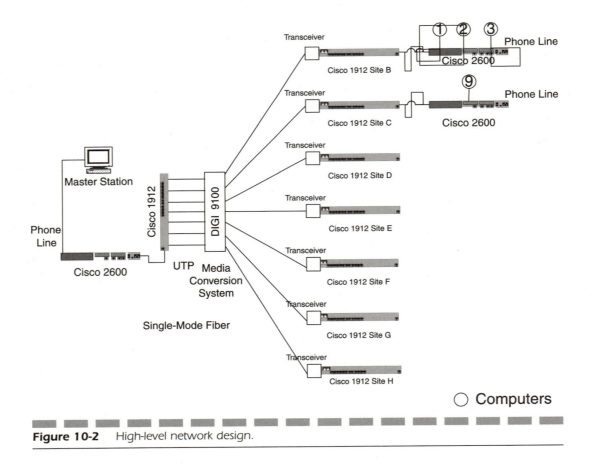

Figure 10-2   High-level network design.

Materials List

Site A

Cisco 2610 router (1 each)

IP feature set for the 2600 (1 each)

CINM2V, Two-slot voice fax network module (1 each)

CIVIV2FXS, Two-port voice interface card—FXS (1 each)

Cisco 1912, 12-port 10-MB switch (1 each)

Digi 9100x media-conversion system (1 each)

DGMIL9000PSAC, redundant power supply for 9100x (1 each)

Digi 170TRM modules, 9100x 10baseT to ST converter, 15km (8 each)

Site B

Cisco 2610 router (1 each)

IP feature set for the 2600 (1 each)

CINM2V, Two-slot voice fax network module (1 each)

CIVIV2FXS, Two-port voice interface card—FXS (2 each)

Cisco 1912, 12-port 10-MB switch (1 each)

Digi AUI to ST transceiver, 15 km (1 each)

Site C

Cisco 2610 router (1 each)

IP feature set for the 2600 (1 each)

CINM2V, Two-slot voice fax network module (1 each)

CIVIV2FXS, Two-port voice interface card—FXS (1 each)

Cisco 1912, 12-port 10-MB switch (1 each)

Digi AUI to ST transceiver, 15 km (1 each)

Site D

Cisco 1912, 12-port 10-MB switch (1 each)

Digi AUI to ST transceiver, 15 km (1 each)

Site E

Cisco 1912, 12-port 10-MB switch (1 each)

Digi AUI to ST transceiver, 15 km (1 each)

Site F

Cisco 1912, 12-port 10-MB switch (1 each)

Digi AUI to ST transceiver, 15 km (1 each)

Site G

Cisco 1912, 12-port 10-MB switch (1 each)

Digi AUI to ST transceiver, 15 km (1 each)

Site H

Cisco 1912, 12-port 10-MB switch (1 each)

Digi AUI to ST transceiver, 15 km (1 each)

Network Configuration/Tuning Parameters/Performance

The IP configuration on the network used a single subnet from the private class A address space. Since the entire network was switched, no subnetting/routing was required. The 10.1.1.x/24 network was used for management of the routers/switches and for the VoIP connectivity. The dial plan used abbreviated 4-digit phone numbers. Below is a list of the phone numbers and the associated computers. Hierarchical addressing was used to allow for future growth and scalability. In this small deployment the hierarchical addressing was not a strong requirement, but did save time in the configuration of the dial peers.

Master station	1111
Computer 1	2221
Computer 2	2222
Computer 3	2223
Computer 9	3331

Figure 10-3 depicts the voice/modem connectivity. Additional tuning was required to achieve acceptable performance of the modem connections. The voice compression methods available on the Cisco 2600 (at the time of this deployment) were only G.729 and G.729a. These algorithms compress a voice call to 8 kbps. Both of these algorithms are predictive algorithms and are optimized for human speech. The predictive nature and the voice optimization make these algorithms unsuitable for modem

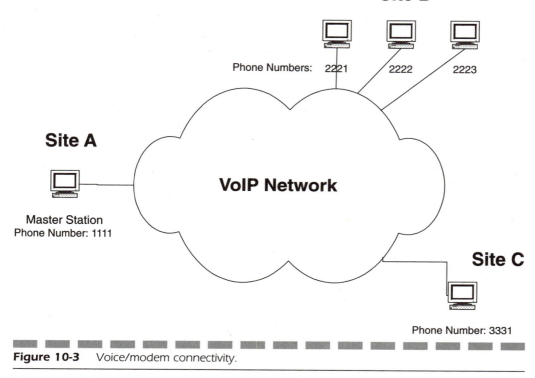

Figure 10-3   Voice/modem connectivity.

data connections. As a result, standard PCM (G.711) voice compression was used throughout the network. At first testing, modem connections failed approximately 25 percent of the time and performance was very poor. Additional tuning was performed to improve the reliability and performance. The voice-activity detection (VAD) feature of the voice codecs was disabled for the data calls. The disabling of VAD made the modem connections extremely reliable and improved performance considerably. The system met the customer's expectations with this configuration. A final adjustment was made by disabling the echo cancellation on the voice codecs. The disabling of the echo cancellors improved the modem throughput approximately 0.3 kbps. The modem throughput over the VoIP network was approximately 5 kbps. Below are the associated router configurations from the network.

Router Configurations

Site A. Router Configuration

```
SiteA2610#sh conf
Using 1347 out of 29688 bytes
!
! Last configuration change at 08:23:30 UTC Fri Mar 12 1999
! NVRAM config last updated at 08:39:02 UTC Fri Mar 12 1999
!
version 12.0
service timestamps debug uptime
service timestamps log uptime
service password-encryption
!
hostname SiteA2610
!
logging buffered 4096 debugging
enable secret xxxx
enable password xxxx
!
ip subnet-zero
no ip domain-lookup
ip host siteD2610 10.1.1.3
ip host SiteB2610 10.1.1.2
ip host SiteA1912 10.1.1.10
ip host Siteb1912 10.1.1.11
ip host Sitec1912 10.1.1.12
ip host Sited1912 10.1.1.13
ip host SiteE1912 10.1.1.14
ip host SiteF1912 10.1.1.15
ip host SiteG1912 10.1.1.16
ip host SiteH1912 10.1.1.17
!
!
voice-port 1/0/0
 no echo-cancel enable
!
voice-port 1/0/1
 no echo-cancel enable
!
dial-peer voice 1 pots
 destination-pattern 1111
 port 1/0/1
!
dial-peer voice 2 voip
destination-pattern 2...
 codec g711ulaw
 no vad
 session target ipv4:10.1.1.2
!
 dial-peer voice 3 voip
 destination-pattern 3...
 codec g711ulaw
 no vad
 session target ipv4:10.1.1.3
!
dial-peer voice 4 pots
 destination-pattern 1112
```

```
   port 1/0/0
!
!
!
!
interface Ethernet0/0
 ip address 10.1.1.1 255.255.255.0
 no ip directed-broadcast
!
ip classless
no ip http server
!
!
line con 0
 transport input none
 password xxxx
 line aux 0
line vty 0 4
 password xxxx
 login
!
no scheduler allocate
end
```

Site A: Router Version Information

```
SiteA2610#sh ver
Cisco Internetwork Operating System Software
IOS (tm) C2600 Software (C2600-IS-M), Version 12.0(2)XC2, EARLY
DEPLOYMENT RELEASE SOFTWARE (fc1)
TAC:Home:SW:IOS:Specials for info
Copyright (c) 1986-1999 by cisco Systems, Inc.
Compiled Wed 20-Jan-99 19:39 by rnapier
Image text-base: 0x80008088, data-base: 0x8096A6F4
ROM: System Bootstrap, Version 11.3(2)XA3, PLATFORM SPECIFIC
RELEASE SOFTWARE (fc1)
ROM: C2600 Software (C2600-IS-M), Version 12.0(2)XC2, EARLY
 DEPLOYMENT RELEASE SOFTWARE (fc1)

SiteA2610 uptime is 1 week, 1 day, 2 hours, 48 minutes
System restarted by power-on at 05:52:07 UTC Thu Mar 4 1999
System image file is "flash:c2600-is-mz.120-2.XC2"

cisco 2610 (MPC860) processor (revision 0x202) with 18432K/6144K
bytes of memory
 .
Processor board ID JAB030705N7 (4038711036)
M860 processor: part number 0, mask 49
Bridging software.
X.25 software, Version 3.0.0.
1 Ethernet/IEEE 802.3 interface(s)
2 Voice FXS interface(s)
32K bytes of non-volatile configuration memory.
8192K bytes of processor board System flash (Read/Write)

Configuration register is 0x2102

SiteA2610#
```

Site B: Router Configuration

```
SiteB2610#sh conf
Using 1317 out of 29688 bytes
!
version 12.0
service timestamps debug uptime
service timestamps log uptime
service password-encryption
!
hostname SiteB2610
!
logging buffered 4096 debugging
enable secret xxxx
enable password xxxx
!
username realtech password xxxx
ip subnet-zero
!
!
voice-port 1/0/0
 no echo-cancel enable
!
 voice-port 1/1/0
no echo-cancel enable
!
voice-port 1/0/1
 no echo-cancel enable
!
voice-port 1/1/1
 no echo-cancel enable
!
dial-peer voice 1 pots
 destination-pattern 2221
 port 1/1/1
!
dial-peer voice 2 pots
 destination-pattern 2222
 port 1/1/0
!
dial-peer voice 3 pots
 destination-pattern 2223
 port 1/0/1
!
dial-peer voice 4 voip
 destination-pattern 1...
 codec g711ulaw
 no vad
 session target ipv4:10.1.1.1
!
dial-peer voice 5 voip
 destination-pattern 3...
 codec g711ulaw
 no vad
 session target ipv4:10.1.1.3
!
dial-peer voice 6 pots
 destination-pattern 2224
 port 1/0/0
```

```
!
!
!
!
interface Ethernet0/0
 ip address 10.1.1.2 255.255.255.0
 no ip directed-broadcast
!
ip classless
no ip http server
!
!
line con 0
 transport input none
line aux 0
 login local
 modem InOut
 modem autoconfigure type usr_courier
 transport input all
 stopbits 1
 speed 38400
 flowcontrol hardware
line vty 0 4
 password xxxx
 login
!
no scheduler allocate
end
```

Site B: Router Version Information

```
SiteB2610#sh ver
Cisco Internetwork Operating System Software
IOS (tm) C2600 Software (C2600-IS-M), Version 12.0(2)XC2, EARLY
EPLOYMENT RELEASE SOFTWARE (fc1)
TAC:Home:SW:IOS:Specials for info
Copyright (c) 1986-1999 by cisco Systems, Inc.
Compiled Wed 20-Jan-99 19:39 by rnapier
Image text-base: 0x80008088, data-base: 0x8096A6F4

ROM: System Bootstrap, Version 11.3(2)XA3, PLATFORM SPECIFIC
RELEASE SOFTWARE (fc1)
ROM: C2600 Software (C2600-IS-M), Version 12.0(2)XC2, EARLY
 DEPLOYMENT RELEASE SOFTWARE (fc1)

SiteB2610 uptime is 9 minutes
System restarted by power-on
System image file is "flash:c2600-is-mz.120-2.XC2"
cisco 2610 (MPC860) processor (revision 0x202) with 18432K/6144K
bytes of memory
.
Processor board ID JAB030705JB (3019060078)
M860 processor: part number 0, mask 49
Bridging software.
X.25 software, Version 3.0.0.
1 Ethernet/IEEE 802.3 interface(s)
4 Voice FXS interface(s)
32K bytes of non-volatile configuration memory.
```

```
8192K bytes of processor board System flash (Read/Write)

Configuration register is 0x2102

SiteB2610#exit
```

Site D: Router Configuration

```
SiteD2610#sh conf
Using 905 out of 29688 bytes
!
version 12.0
service timestamps debug uptime
service timestamps log uptime
service password-encryption
!
hostname SiteD2610
!
logging buffered 4096 debugging
enable secret xxxx
enable password xxxx
!
ip subnet-zero
!
!
voice-port 1/0/0
 no echo-cancel enable
!
voice-port 1/0/1
 no echo-cancel enable
!
dial-peer voice 1 pots
 destination-pattern 3331
 port 1/0/1
!
dial-peer voice 2 voip
 destination-pattern 1...
 codec g711ulaw
 no vad
 session target ipv4:10.1.1.1
!
dial-peer voice 3 voip
 destination-pattern 2...
 codec g711ulaw
 no vad
 session target ipv4:10.1.1.2
!
dial-peer voice 4 pots
 destination-pattern 3332
 port 1/0/0
!
!
!
!
interface Ethernet0/0
 ip address 10.1.1.3 255.255.255.0
 no ip directed-broadcast
!
```

```
ip classless
no ip http server
!
!
line con 0
 transport input none
line aux 0
line vty 0 4
 password xxxx
 login
!
end
```

Site D: Router Version Information

```
SiteD2610#sh ver
Cisco Internetwork Operating System Software
IOS (tm) C2600 Software (C2600-IS-M), Version 12.0(2)XC2, EARLY
DEPLOYMENT RELEASE SOFTWARE (fc1)
TAC:Home:SW:IOS:Specials for info
Copyright (c) 1986-1999 by cisco Systems, Inc.
Compiled Wed 20-Jan-99 19:39 by rnapier
Image text-base: 0x80008088, data-base: 0x8096A6F4

ROM: System Bootstrap, Version 11.3(2)XA3, PLATFORM SPECIFIC
RELEASE SOFTWARE (fc1)
ROM: C2600 Software (C2600-IS-M), Version 12.0(2)XC2, EARLY
 DEPLOYMENT RELEASE SOFTWARE (fc1)

SiteD2610 uptime is 16 hours, 14 minutes
System restarted by power-on
System image file is "flash:c2600-is-mz.120-2.XC2"

cisco 2610 (MPC860) processor (revision 0x202) with 18432K/6144K
bytes of memory
.
Processor board ID JAB030705K1 (3946299184)
M860 processor: part number 0, mask 49
Bridging software.
X.25 software, Version 3.0.0.
1 Ethernet/IEEE 802.3 interface(s)
2 Voice FXS interface(s)
32K bytes of non-volatile configuration memory.
8192K bytes of processor board System flash (Read/Write)

Configuration register is 0x2102
```

APPENDIX

Webliography

This appendix includes many of the Web links which were referenced during the creation of this book. It is divided into the following categories: Quality of service (QoS), IP services, frame relay, Cisco voice technical references, voice compression algorithms, voice over IP, H.323, AS5300-specific, Cisco 2600/3600-specific, and general.

Quality of Service

Advanced QoS Services for the Intelligent Internet

http://www.cisco.com/warp/public/cc/cisco/mkt/ios/qos/tech/qos_wp.htm

Advanced Services for the Intelligent Internet

http://www.cisco.com/warp/public/732/qos/0792_047.ppt

Cisco—IOS Technologies—Quality—Link Fragmentation and
  Interleaving (LFI)

http://www.netsystech.com/warp/public/732/Tech/link/

Classification Overview

*http://www.cisco.com/univercd/cc/td/doc/product/software/ios120/12cgcr/
  qos_c/qcpart1/qcclass.htm*

Configuring Committed Access Rate

*http://www.cisco.com/univercd/cc/td/doc/product/software/ios120/12cgcr/
  qos_c/qcpart1/qccar.htm*

Configuring Compressed Real-Time Protocol

*http://www.cisco.com/univercd/cc/td/doc/product/software/ios120/12cgcr/
  qos_c/qcpart6/qcrtphc.htm*

Configuring Custom Queueing

*http://www.cisco.com/univercd/cc/td/doc/product/software/ios120/12cgcr/
  qos_c/qcpart2/qccq.htm*

Configuring Frame Relay and Frame-Relay Traffic Shaping

*http://www.cisco.com/univercd/cc/td/doc/product/software/ios120/12cgcr/
  qos_c/qcpart4/qcfrts.htm*

Configuring Generic Traffic Shaping

http://www.cisco.com/univercd/cc/td/doc/product/software/ios120/12cgcr/ qos_c/qcpart4/qcgts.htm

Configuring Link Fragmentation and Interleaving for Multilink PPP

http://www.cisco.com/univercd/cc/td/doc/product/software/ios120/12cgcr/ qos_c/qcpart6/qclfi.htm

Configuring Policy-Based Routing

http://www.cisco.com/univercd/cc/td/doc/product/software/ios120/12cgcr/ qos_c/qcpart1/qcpolicy.htm

Configuring Priority Queuing

http://www.cisco.com/univercd/cc/td/doc/product/software/ios120/12cgcr/ qos_c/qcpart2/qcpq.htm

Configuring RSVP

http://www.cisco.com/univercd/cc/td/doc/product/software/ios120/12cgcr/ qos_c/qcpart5/qcrsvp.htm

Configuring Weighted Fair Queuing

http://www.cisco.com/univercd/cc/td/doc/product/software/ios120/12cgcr/ qos_c/qcpart2/qcwfq.htm

Configuring Weighted Random Early Detection

http://www.cisco.com/univercd/cc/td/doc/product/software/ios120/12cgcr/ qos_c/qcpart3/qcwred.htm

Congestion Avoidance Overview

http://www.cisco.com/univercd/cc/td/doc/product/software/ios120/12cgcr/ qos_c/qcpart3/qcconavd.htm

Congestion Management Overview

http://www.cisco.com/univercd/cc/td/doc/product/software/ios120/12cgcr/ qos_c/qcpart2/qcconman.htm

Differential Services for the Internet

http://diffserv.lcs.mit.edu/

Link Efficiency Mechanisms Overview

http://www.cisco.com/univercd/cc/td/doc/product/software/ios120/12cgcr/ qos_c/qcpart6/qclemech.htm

Policing and Shaping Overview

http://www.cisco.com/univercd/cc/td/doc/product/software/ios120/12cgcr/ qos_c/qcpart4/qcpolts.htm

Quality of Service Commands (a–q)

*http://www.cisco.com/univercd/cc/td/doc/product/software/ios120/12cgcr/
qos_r/qrcmda.htm*

Quality of Service Commands (r–z)

*http://www.cisco.com/univercd/cc/td/doc/product/software/ios120/12cgcr/
qos_r/qrcmdr.htm*

Quality of Service FAQ

http://www.qosforum.com/docs/faq/

Quality of Service for the Cisco 7200/7500

*http://www.cisco.com/warp/partner/synchronicd/cc/cisco/mkt/ios/qos/tech/
qos72_wp.htm*

Quality of Service over IP: References

http://www.netlab.ohio-state.edu/~jain/refs/ipqs_ref.htm

Signaling Overview

*http://www.cisco.com/univercd/cc/td/doc/product/software/ios120/12cgcr/
qos_c/qcpart5/qcsignal.htm*

IP Services

Cisco—IOS Technologies—Quality—Compressed Real-Time Transport
Protocol

http://www.netsystech.com/warp/public/732/Tech/real/

Cisco—IOS Technologies—Quality—RSVP

http://www.netsystech.com/warp/public/732/Tech/rsvp/

CRTP: RFC2508

ftp://ftp.isi.edu/in-notes/rfc2508.txt

Higher-Level Protocols used with IP Multicast

http://www.ipmulticast.com/community/whitepapers/highprot.html

IETF: Audio/Video Transport (avt)

http://www.ietf.org/html.charters/avt-charter.html

IP Switching for Scalable IP Services

http://www.pitt.edu/~bidst/IPNav/sld001.htm

Multimedia over IP: RSVP, RTP, RTCP, RTSP

http://www.cis.ohio-state.edu/~cliu/ipmultimedia/

ReSerVation Protocol

http://www.isi.edu/div7/rsvp/rsvp-home.html

RSVP: RFC2205

ftp://ftp.isi.edu/in-notes/rfc2205.txt

RTCP: RFC1890

ftp://ftp.isi.edu/in-notes/rfc1890.txt

RTP: About RTP and the Audio-Video Transport Working Group

http://www.cs.columbia.edu/~hgs/rtp/

RTP: RFC1889

ftp://ftp.isi.edu/in-notes/rfc1889.txt

Frame Relay

Configuring Frame Relay

http://www.cisco.com/univercd/cc/td/doc/product/software/ios120/12cgcr/ wan_c/wcfrelay.htm#23937

Configuring Frame-Relay Traffic Shaping

http://www.cisco.com/univercd/cc/td/doc/product/software/ios120/12cgcr/ qos_c/qcpart4/qcfrts.htm

The Frame-Relay Service Level Management Sourcebook

http://www.paradyne.com/frame_sourcebook/

Level 1 Frame Relay and Voice Tutorial

http://www.level1.com/product/frtutorial/index.htm

Voice over Frame Relay Gets New Standard

http://www.cisco.com/warp/customer/803/26.html

Cisco Voice Technical References

Dial-Peer Matching

http://www.cisco.com/warp/customer/793/voip/dial_peer_concepts.htm

Financial Institution Enterprise Network with VoIP and SNA

http://www.cisco.com/warp/public/cc/cisco/mkt/access/2600/profiles/ mfien_bc.htm

How to Debug Analog E&M Signaling

http://www.cisco.com/warp/public/788/21.html

Packet Voice Networking

http://www.cisco.com/warp/public/cc/cisco/mkt/access/c3800/prodlit/ pvnet_in.htm

Voice and Multimedia Technologies

http://www.cisco.com/warp/customer/788/index.shtml

Voice Design and Implementation Guide

http://www.cisco.com/warp/customer/788/7.html

Voice Port Commands

http://www.cisco.com/univercd/cc/td/doc/product/software/ios120/12cgcr/ voice_r/vrprt1/vrvpcmds.htm

Voice-Related Commands

http://www.cisco.com/univercd/cc/td/doc/product/software/ios120/12cgcr/ voice_r/vrprt1/vrcmds.htm

Voice Compression Algorithms

[G.711] Recommendation G.711 (11/88): Pulse code modulation (PCM) of voice frequencies

http://www.itu.int//itudoc/itu-t/rec/g/g700-799/g711.html

[G.723.1] Recommendation G.723.1 (03/96): Speech coders: Dual-rate speech coder for multimedia communications transmitting at 5.3 and 6.3 kbps

http://www.itu.int//itudoc/itu-t/rec/g/g700-799/g723-1.html

G.723.1 Tutorial

http://www.comsoc.org.mx/standard/g_7231.htm

[G.726] Recommendation G.726 (12/90): 40, 32, 24, 16-kbps adaptive differential pulse code modulation (ADPCM)

http://www.itu.int//itudoc/itu-t/rec/g/g700-799/g726.html

[G.729] Recommendation G.729 (03/96): Coding of speech at 8 kbps using conjugate-structure algebraic-code-excited linear-prediction (CS-ACELP)

http://www.itu.int//itudoc/itu-t/rec/g/g700-799/g729.html

[G.729 Annex A] Annex A (11/96) to Recommendation G.729: Coding of speech at 8 kbps using conjugate structure algebraic-code-excited linear-prediction (CS-ACELP)—Annex A: Reduced complexity 8 kbps CS-ACELP speech codec

http://www.itu.int//itudoc/itu-t/rec/g/g700-799/g729anxa.html

Summary of ITU-T Speech/Audio Codecs

http://standard.pictel.com/reference/summary_itu_codecs.htm

Voice over IP

Configuring Voice over IP for the Cisco 3600 Series

http://www.cisco.com/univercd/cc/td/doc/product/software/ios120/12cgcr/ voice_c/vcprt1/vcvoip.htm

Internet Telephony—An Overview

http://www.fokus.gmd.de/research/cc/glone/projects/ipt/

MSIN Internet Telephony Project 1998

http://www.ini.cmu.edu/von/

Voice Dial Plan Considerations

http://www.cisco.com/univercd/cc/td/doc/product/access/multicon/3810soft/ swcfg/dplan.htm

Voice over IP Quick Start Guide

http://www.cisco.com/univercd/cc/td/doc/product/access/acs_mod/cis3600/ voice/4936vqsg.htm

Voice over IP: References

http://www.netlab.ohio-state.edu/~jain/refs/ref_voip.htm

Voice over IP Technology Tutorial and First Approach

http://www.comsoc.org.mx/standard/voip.htm

Voice over Packet Tutorial

http://www.webproforum.com/voice_packet/index.html

Voice Technologies for IP and Frame-Relay Networks

http://www.mot.com/MIMS/ISG/mnd/papers/voice_technologies_for_ip_ and_frame_relay_networks.html

H.323

H.323: Multimedia Conferencing for Packet Switched Networks
http://standards.pictel.com/reference/9706_itca_h323/default.htm
A Primer on the H.323 Series Standard
http://gw.databeam.com/h323/h323primer.html

AS5300 Specific

Basic Configuration
*http://www.cisco.com/univercd/cc/td/doc/product/access/acs_serv/5300/
5300swbk/5300bas.htm#xtocid1968913*
Cisco AS5300 Software Configuration Guide
*http://www.cisco.com/univercd/cc/td/doc/product/access/acs_serv/5300/
53swcf2/index.htm*
Configuring T1 CAS for VoIP on Cisco Access Platforms
*http://www.cisco.com/univercd/cc/td/doc/product/access/acs_serv/5300/
cfios/0048t1ca.htm*
Configuring the Cisco AS5300 for Voice Service Provider Features
*http://www.cisco.com/univercd/cc/td/doc/product/access/acs_serv/5300/
cfios/sprvvoip.htm*
Voice over IP for the Cisco AS5300
*http://www.cisco.com/univercd/cc/td/doc/product/access/nubuvoip/voip5300/
index.htm*

Cisco 2600/3600 Series

Voice over IP for the Cisco 2600 and Cisco 3600 Series Overview
*http://www.cisco.com/univercd/cc/td/doc/product/access/nubuvoip/voip3600/
voipover.htm*
Voice over IP for the Cisco 2600/3600 Series
*http://www.cisco.com/univercd/cc/td/doc/product/access/nubuvoip/voip3600/
index.htm*

General

Communications Library
http://www.wcom.com/tools-resources/communications_library/index.shtml
IP Convergence: Links
http://www.nwfusion.com/netresources/0810ip11.html
Multimedia Networking References
http://www.netlab.ohio-state.edu/~jain/refs/mul_refs.htm
Nexial Mailing List Archive
http://www.nexial.com/mailinglists/
SIP and Internet Telephony: Papers and Talks
http://www.cs.columbia.edu/~hgs/sip/papers.html
The SS7-ization of the Internet
http://www.nwfusion.com/forum/0119briereheck.html

INDEX

A

a law, 49
Adaptive differential pulse code modulation (ADPCM), 53
Addresses, reserved, 206–207
ADPCM (adaptive differential pulse code modulation), 53
ADSL (Asymmetric DSL), 16
Amplitude, 34
Analog telephony, 32–46
  basic call processing sequence in, 38–40
  cabling/connectors for, 32–33
  interface types with, 42–43
  and key systems, 41
  and PBX, 41–42
  signaling in, 34–38, 43–46
  voice signal in, 34
Analog voice, 46
Analog voice ports, 146–160
  configuring, 148–160
  dialing timers for, 158–159
  echo cancellation with, 157–158
  gain/loss parameters for, 157
  and signaling types, 146–148
  timing parameters for, 158
ANI (automatic number identification), 50
Application-specific integrated circuits (ASICs), 15
Asymmetric DSL (ADSL), 16
ATM networks, 21
Automatic number identification (ANI), 50
Automatic ring down, private-line, 151
Availability of voice networks, 26

B

Backward explicit congestion notification (BECN), 115–117, 119, 122–123, 128, 129, 132
Bandwidth requirements, determining, 227
Base configuration, 245–253
  and DNS configuration, 247
  interface descriptions, 247
  and logging configuration, 250–251
  passwords, 246–247
  and SNMP configuration, 248–250
B_c (see Committed burst size)
B_e (see Excess burst size)
BECN (see Backward explicit congestion notification)
Break time, 36
Business advantages of voice over IP, 8–9

C

Cabling, standard network, 32–33
Call detail recording, 27
Call leg identification, 13
Call legs, 165–166
Call processing sequence (analog telephony), 38–40
Call-progress tones, 37–38, 150, 154
CAR (see Committed access rate)
CAS (see Channel-associated signaling)
Case study, configuration, 306–317
  connectivity requirements for, 306
  design considerations, 306–308
  materials list for, 309–310

ABOUT THE AUTHOR

Robert Caputo, CCIE #13312, is Senior Systems Engineer with REALTECH Systems where he works on LAN and WAN design, consulting, implementation, and support. He actively consults on the deployment and implementation of Cisco-based products and has taught several seminars for Cisco Systems on voice and data convergence.

McGraw-Hill's

Cisco

Technical Expert Series

Unlock the Power

of Cisco

Field tested solutions, guidance & diagnostic tips in McGraw-Hill's Cisco Technical Expert Series

Whether you want to unleash the power of Cisco routers, accelerate your career via Cisco certification, or both, McGraw-Hill's groundbreaking Cisco Technical Expert Series is your one-stop solution. Written by the world's foremost Internetworking experts and leading Cisco-certified trainers, McGraw-Hill's Cisco Technical Expert Series gives you a combination of advantages no other resource can offer.

- **Step-by-step advice on designing and implementing Cisco-routed networks**
- **Troubleshooting methodologies applicable to every situation**
- **Specialized guidance on solving especially tough configuration problems**
- **Vital coverage of internetworking Cisco products with top vendors**
- **Surefire techniques for securing Cisco networks**
- **Preparation for the demanding CCIE exam**

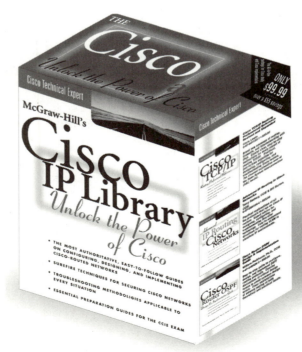

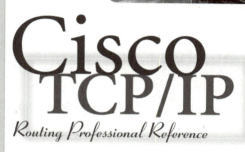

Get today's most authoritative, easy-to-follow guidance on how to configure, design, implement, and troubleshoot Cisco-routed networks! From solving difficult configuration problems to securing Cisco-routed networks, the help you need is here!

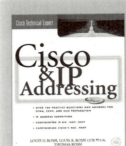

Cisco & IP Addressing

Louis D. Rossi, Louis R. Rossi, CCIE & Thomas Rossi

0-07-134925-1 • $55.00

Written by the professionals at CCprep.com and backed by the CCprep.com Website, *Cisco & IP Addressing* is the first book to clearly and completely explain IP addressing, subnet masking, and IP Routing Protocols. This reference gives you crystal-clear, step-by-step instructions for every aspect of configuring IP on Cisco routers.

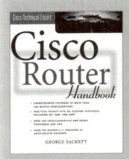

Cisco Multicast Routing &Switching

William Parkhurst, Ph.D.,CCIE

0-07-134647-3 • $55.00

Filled with tips, techniques, and solutions for implementing Cisco's new generation of routers and switches that are designed to handle IP multicasting— this is the one book you'll need to successfully use IP Multicasting.

Cisco Router Handbook

George Sackett

0-07-058098-7 • $70.00

Offers all the practical guidance you'll need on more than 500 possible configurations, including detailed coverage of all routing protocols that can run on a Cisco network. This is an indispensable resource for all technicians and network professionals.

Cisco Catalyst LAN Switching

Louis R. Rossi, CCIE, Louis D. Rossi & Thomas L. Rossi

0-07-134982-0 • $55.00

Here's the first hands-on guide to the Cisco Catalyst Switch— a breakthrough in internetworking technology. It shows how to configure, manage, and troubleshoot the entire Cisco Catalyst 5000 LAN switching family of products and offers insight into the Catalyst 1900, 2900XL, and 4000 series of switches as well as static and dynamic VLANs.